The Key to Chinese Cooking

The Key to
Chinese Cooking

ISABELLE C. CHANG

GALAHAD BOOKS · NEW YORK

Reprinted by Galahad Books by arrangement with Liveright Publishing Corporation. Formerly published as *What's Cooking at Chang's.*

Standard Book Number: 0–88365–021–5

Library of Congress Catalog Card Number: 73–81659

Manufactured in the United States of America

*To the memory of my beloved
parents, Mr. and Mrs. Chin Que Wah*

REFERRING TO HIS FAVORITE COOK, A CHINESE POET NAMED Yan Mei, who wrote a cookbook in 1796, said, "Good cooking does not depend on whether the dish is big or little, costly or inexpensive. If one has the talent, then a piece of vegetable can be cooked into a delightful delicacy; on the other hand if one hasn't the talent, not the finest food in the universe is of any good. . . . So much planning and hard thinking go into the preparing of every dish that one may well say I serve it with my whole soul. . . . Real culinary appreciation comprise as much in detecting faults as in finding merits."

Contents

5

Preface

Why another Chinese cookbook?

HERE ARE MY REASONS, MY TWO DAUGHTERS. THEY WERE ONLY one and four years of age when this idea was conceived, but I like to dream of the days when they will be grown and on their own. I would like to feel that they will be capable of taking good care of themselves and able to create joy and delight for others around them. One way to achieve this goal is to be able to cook. The recipes here need only be springboards to better and different ideas in the culinary art.

A second reason I wrote this book is that I want my three American-born children to have a taste of their ancient heritage.

A third reason is that Cathayan cuisine is reputedly one of the best in the world. China, a land laden with tradition, had many dining customs just to foster gracious living. Thus the variety of foods used and methods of preparation were and are, almost limitless. Precisely because my ignorance has been so great I have set out to rediscover all I could on this subject. Amazingly, I was able to dig up a few facts that passed down the generations through word of mouth. Despite this, I know I have scratched only the surface. However, there seemed no reason why some of these ancient secrets should be reburied. I endeavored to write them down before cookery becomes a lost art in this modern world of "mixes," canned, frozen and radiated foods.

Finally, I want to share the knowledge of how nutritious, low in calories, inexpensive, and simple, Chinese cooking can be! Being an American myself, I couldn't help but modify

9

cooking methods and tone down ingredients to suit most American palates.

I wanted to get in all the festival and seasonable foods in regular order; so I followed the calendars. (Most Chinese used the old Chinese and modern Gregorian calendars side by side.) Seasonable foods were used whenever possible for healthful as well as economical reasons.

Since we often entertain foreign guests with special diets, I have tried to work out a scheme whereby only certain foods are served on a particular day of the week:

Sunday—Poultry day
Monday—Pork day
Tuesday—Beef day
Wednesday—Vegetarian day
Thursday—Lamb day
Friday—Seafood day
Saturday—Egg day
Holidays

The bill of fare need not be at all fixed. For instance if a vegetarian spent a Sunday with us we would serve vegetable, rather than poultry dishes. Or, if festival foods broke into a week, the special food would take precedence. On the other hand, if we were dining alone in an ordinary week, such a scheme might be most convenient in avoiding monotony and excessive planning, besides providing a well-rounded diet.

Leftovers? Warm them up, or make soup with them for lunch the next day.

I have written one recipe for each day according to the old Chinese calendar numbering 383 days in 4654, Year of the Cock. (Whenever there are festival days I have tried to track down the stories behind them and discover why certain foods are eaten. My children appreciate some of the stories so much I have kept them with the recipes so they can be readily located.)

Introduction

IN ITS INFINITE VARIETY, CHINESE COOKERY IS THE MOST SOPHIS-
ticated in the world. It is wider in scope than the French and
more imaginative in its creative techniques and ingredients
than the Italian. This art is within the mastery of American
home cooks—with the help of this cookbook and an under-
standing of a few of the basic terms found on Chinese menus.

"choy" (in the Cantonese dialect) means vegetable
"dun" means egg
"fon" means rice
"gai" means chicken
"har" means shrimp
"mien" means noodle
"moo ghoo" means mushroom
"op" means duck
"pien" means sliced
"suen" means sour
"tiem" means sweet

Unusual dishes calling for tiger lily buds, bean curd, wheat
starch, and seaweed should not keep anyone from enjoying
other mouth-watering meals which do not require such exotic groceries.

An authentic Chinese bill of fare begins with a clear soup.
The clearest of broth may be joined by a leaf of watercress,
a sliver of scallion, or a shave of carrot to beguile the eye.
Next comes firm, flaky rice and a favorite dish. This may be
a mixed vegetable dish, a thrifty plate made with leftover
pork or beef, or an economical vegetable dish combined with

small amounts of shrimp or chicken. Thus delicious, inexpensive, authentic Chinese recipes may be added to your culinary repertoire by simply following the directions in this book and using quite ordinary and easily obtainable ingredients which can be found today in supermarkets, in health food stores, or in Chinese groceries including:

The Yuet Hing Grocery, 23 Mott Street, New York, N.Y.
Tung Hing Lung, Inc., 9 Hudson Street, Boston, Mass.
China Trading Co., 271 Crown Street, New Haven, Conn.

Finally, you should keep the three objectives of all Chinese chefs in mind as you cook: First, *the food must have visual appeal*. The result must be an exquisitely artistic dish. Second, *the food must impart a fragrant aroma*. Contrary to some misconceptions, good Chinese cooking does not produce offensive odors. Third, *the taste is the final test of a well-cooked dish*. No matter how simple the fare, every mealtime should be a "feast."

While these age-old principles are followed by all good cooks everywhere in the world, the secret key to successful Chinese cookery is quick cooking. Most Chinese foods are prepared well in advance. The vegetables are cut, the meats are seasoned, and the dried foods are soaked ahead of time. Thus the final cooking can be done quickly, very often in thirty minutes. This preserves vitamins, the garden-fresh coloring in vegetables, and all the delicate flavors that Chinese cuisine has been famous for throughout history.

Confucius said, "Better than to be king, is to have a wife in the kitchen who sings!" So housewives, if you wish to make your husbands feel better than kings, sing in your kitchens and serve your families gourmet dishes. Try the Chinese approach to cooking!

1970   ISABELLE C. CHANG

The Chinese Calendar

Since this book is based somewhat upon the Chinese calendar, there are recipes listed for 365 days. Recipes from Sunday through Saturday are provided for, *but necessarily the numbered days will vary in some years.* It seems appropriate at this point to give a brief review of Chinese astronomy.

In China the periods of rainfall and drought are so marked that the difference of 1½ weeks can mean success or failure for the year's crop. This practical application spurred the development of the calendar. Another contribution towards astronomy was the consistent recordings of solar-eclipses, sun-spots, comets and Novae, observed without benefit of modern telescopes.

From earliest times, the Chinese were able to divide the year into seasons by observing the movement of the stars. This was done long before the names of the "Fire Stars" (constellation Scorpio) and "Bird Stars" (constellation Hydra) were etched on to the earliest Chinese records known as the inscribed oracle bones of the Shang-Yin Dynasty (17th-12th centuries B.C.)

In the "Shu Ching" the first history edited by Confucius in the 5th century B.C. one may learn that the spring equinox, summer solstice, autumn equinox and winter solstice were marked when the constellations Hydra, Scorpio, Aquarius and Pleiades reached the meridian at dusk.

Many have the misconception that the old Chinese calendar was based completely on the movement of the moon and that the solar calendar was imported from the occident. Although the phases of the moon was a handy measure for

13

marking time the oracle bones (17th-12th centuries B.C.) recorded that 30 centuries ago the Chinese used their knowledge of the movement of the sun as the basis for calculating the year.

Earth takes a little over 365 days to complete a revolution around the sun, whereas the moon takes 29½ days to revolve around the earth (approximately 12½ courses in 365 days). To fit them together was indeed a problem. That they did combine the two into a solar-lunar calendar with a "thirteenth month" year can be checked in the oracle bone (17th-12th centuries B.C.) The history book "Shu Ching" also recorded that the statutes of the Emperor Yao (c.2500 B.C.) set a year of 366 days with the four seasons, regulated by an extra or intercalary moon. The lunar moons are 29-30 days.

Chinese astronomers around 595 B.C. worked out the rule that an intercalary moon (month) inserted into 7 out of 19 lunar years made them equal to 19 solar years.

The solar year was divided into 24 periods based on the sun's position. Dates of the equinoxes and solstices were known by the "Spring and Autumn Annals" (722-481 B.C.) The other 20 periods had been established by the Western Han Dynasty (202 B.C.-A.D. 9). This system became the Chinese farmers' almanac.

Chang Heng (A.D. 78-139) theorized that the universe is infinite in time and space. He invented a celestial globe on which metal rings represented the paths of the sun and other important heavenly bodies. It was the first planetarium. Among his other inventions was a seismoscope for detecting earthquakes. Moreover he was the first Chinese to view the moon as a non-luminous star reflecting the sunlight. He said that eclipses of the moon were caused by the shadow of the earth on it.

It was in the 6th century that Chang Tze-hsin formulated the law of eclipses.

The measurement of the meridian (earth's size) was undertaken by the Buddhist Chang Sui whose monastic name was Yi Hsing (A.D. about 683-727).

Shen Kuo (A.D. 1032-1096) advocated a calendar reform. He urged the dropping of the lunar moons in favor of a 12-month system based on the old 24 solar periods because the four seasons would always be correct. However he was unsuccessful in this attempt.

Kuo Shou-ching (A.D. 1231-1316) calçulated the solar year as 365.2425 days—24 seconds short of its actual length, thus enabling him to predict eclipses of the sun correctly within an hour. He was the first astronomer to formulate the theory of interpolation and utilized it to improve his calendar.

The old Chinese calendar operated until 1911 when the Republic of China came into being. At that time the Gregorian calendar was adopted in keeping with modern trends and the scientific West. However, even now many Chinese still use the old Chinese and Gregorian calendars simultaneously.

The Kitchen God

Now, WHO IS THIS KITCHEN GOD AND WHY IS HIS PICTURE SO prominent in so many Chinese kitchens?

Long ago there lived an old, old man named Chang Kung. Within his huge gates four generations of his large family dwelt in quiet content. Even the hundred dogs within the Chang walls lived in peace.

This peaceful family became famous throughout the land. Even the Emperor of the Dragon Throne heard of them. So on his way home from his annual pilgrimage to the Eastern Mountain the Emperor decided to pay the Chang family a visit.

In a long procession they marched to the Chang gates.

Old Chang Kung greeted his Emperor on bended knees.

"Old and gentle Sir," began the Emperor, "it is said only peace reigns within your household."

"Your Royal Highness," answered Chang, "it is not for my unworthy self to say. Please give great honor to this humble household by judging for yourself, O most Illustrious Grace."

The Emperor and his men went from court to court. They observed and questioned each family member down to the youngest child. Love predominated throughout the clan.

Before the Emperor left he wanted old Chang's secret for keeping peace among so many, many people.

Chang Kung ordered his servant to bring his writing equipment. In his best calligraphy he painted 100 characters on a bamboo tablet. With both hands he presented the tablet to the Emperor.

17

"But," said the bewildered Emperor, "you wrote the same character one hundred times."

"Yes, Most High, that word 'KINDNESS' holds the only secret to peace," replied Chang Kung.

The Emperor was so grateful he wrote high praise of wise Chang Kung on a large tablet. This tablet was mounted on the Chang gates and his fame grew greater than ever.

From everywhere people begged for Chang Kung's portrait They placed his picture on a nook over the stove, which symbolized the family hearth. In their hearts they prayed they might grow to be kind like him so that love and peace might reign in their homes too. That was how the saintly Chang became the famed kitchen god.

Brief History of Chinese Cookery

Long ago stoves were clumsy and crude. Cooking was simple then. Food was broiled over coals or buried in hot ashes. It was but a step for man from baking in hot ashes and broiling meats through a stick to make a simple oven. One of these ovens served an entire community. Fires were lit in the oven. When the fire died down the oven was swept clean and food placed inside to be cooked by the hot heated bricks. Some later styled brick ovens can still be seen in a few ancient farmhouses in China. They had a space underneath for a separate fire. Charcoal was the primitive fuel used in temperate provinces. As time went on Franklin stoves and kitchen wood ranges were imitated for home use. They were a far cry from the gas and electrical appliances of today. This great progress undoubtedly contributed to vast improvements in Chinese cookery.

It is said that long, long ago the Chinese too used knives and forks. As time went on they found that silver sometimes impaired the delicate flavor of foods. Moreover, silver spoons are apt to burn the tongue with hot food, so they changed to chopsticks and china spoons. Chopsticks * were named "Chu"

* To use chopsticks, place the first stick in the hollow of the right hand between thumb and index finger and rest its lower end below the first joint of the third finger. This first stick remains fixed. Hold the second chopstick between the tips of the index and middle fingers, and use the tip of the thumb to keep it in position. To pick up food, move the second stick with index and middle fingers.

19

in the beginning, meaning helper. As it had the same pronunciation as "stop" in Chinese, the people didn't like its sound so the name was changed to "K'uai-Tzu" meaning quick ones. The character "K'uai" has the same pronunciation as the first character in "pleasure." Indeed it is with pleasure one ought to pick up one's food.

Early Chinese Pottery and Porcelain

THROUGH EXCAVATIONS IN 1950 AT CHENGCHOW, HONAN, Chinese archaeologists made new and significant findings about the early Shang period (15th-12th centuries B.C.) Before these discoveries there was a gap in the story of what happened prior to the neolithic age known as Lungshan (20th-15th centuries B.C.) famous for its black pottery and the late Shang period (1300-1027 B.C.) outstanding for its bronze objects.

Modern Chengchow is a flourishing industrial city located south of the Yellow River at the junction of the Peking-Hankow and Lunghai Railways. The path the trains follow have been main routes of central China from times immemorial. This favorable location explains Chengchow's importance.

The Shang period was the second of the "Three Dynasties— Hsia, Shang and Chou" which formulated the beginning of Chinese history. However, Shang is the first dynasty with recorded facts. Around 1300 B.C., Emperor Pan Keng moved his subjects from the south side of the Yellow River and built a new city, Anyang (100 miles north of Chengchow), on the northern side.

Fourteen kilns were unearthed in 1955 on the west side of Chengchow. This was evidently a potters' district. The kilns were vertical with an oval oven chamber approximately four feet wide. Across the bottom of this chamber runs a central wall approximately one and one half feet high supporting a perforated clay shelf on which pots were laid while a fire burned in the space below.

Through the one-half inch perforations escaped hot gases which were deflected back to the shelf by the domed roof.

A hole full of unfired wares was found. These had probably been left there to dry in the sun before being placed in the hot kilns.

Clay stamps used by the potters for pressing designs on pots were found.

People of the early Shang Dynasty made many types of plain and decorated pottery. Though the vertical kilns show the continuity of craftsmanship from the neolithic Yangshao culture (approximately 2000 B.C.) the Yangshao fashion of painting pottery died out. Finds in Chengchow were mostly grey. Some wares had a glossy black surface like the black pottery of the neolithic Lungshan period but lacked the fine egg-shell quality of the Lungshan pottery. Cooking pots sometimes had cord impressions on them while other wares were carved with designs similar to bronze articles.

The "Li" tripod is a cooking pot. Its three bulging legs brought the food into direct contact with the fire. These tripods were first made in the late neolithic period and were still very popular in the Shang Dynasty.

The Hsien, a steamer with a perforated bottom was usually made in one piece with the tripod pot.

Another popular ware of the early Shang period was the tulip beaker, used for cooking.

The Kuei dish, the Tou cup (hollow pedestalled) and the Ting tripod (with solid legs) were used for eating, drinking and cooking. Wine cups were similar to bronze ones of the Shang Dynasty. Some big jars were one and one half feet tall.

White pottery was a favorite ceramic product of the late Shang period. Pieces of glazed earthenware have been reconstructed into pots—the very first glazed pottery found in China.

The use of glaze was an important technical advancement

for that early period because its manufacture and application are intricate processes requiring infinite patience and skill. These glazed wares were forerunners of the proto-porcelain of medieval China.

It is said that the Chinese are the greatest race of potters that the world has ever seen. From their glazed hard-fired pottery there emerged the marvelous white translucent porcelain, a source of wonder to the medieval world.

During the 15th and 16th centuries, Chinese porcelain began to find its way into Europe. The whiteness of its substance and its marvelous translucence excited the attention of the Italian alchemists. This famous porcelain was first imitated by potters in Florence (1575-1585) under the patronage of Francesco de' Medici.

In the Ch'ien Lung reign (1736-1795) specialities were "lace work" porcelain with designs deeply incised and forming semi-transparencies; and "rice-grain" * porcelain in which the designs were actually cut out of the side of the vessel though allowed to fill up with glaze.

During the 18th century there was a very large trade in imported Chinese porcelain. There were also great developments of porcelain manufacture in Europe.

The great porcelain town of Ching-tê Chên near the Poyang Lake in Kiangsi supplied products to the court as early as the 6th century. The staple product of Ching-tê Chên is the fine white porcelain which has made china a household word throughout the world.

* Pieces of rice pattern china may still be available in some Chinese gift shops. Relatives and friends are still sending me pieces to add to my collection.

PART I

Preparation and Serving

Marketing

FOR THE MOST EFFICIENT MARKETING ASK THE STORE MANAGER which day fresh supplies come into your favorite supermarket, then make a habit of shopping once a week early in the day, if possible, so you will get the best choices. Shopping once a week will also get you in the good habit of planning your meals by the week, and this kind of planning cannot help but save money in contrast to the costly hand-to-mouth buying. Shop the week-end bargains. Purchase the largest quantity practicable.

Green, leafy and yellow vegetables are valuable sources of minerals and vitamins. Choose vegetables in season. Not only are they less expensive when plentiful, but they are most nutritious when garden fresh. Other times buy grades B or C canned vegetables to use in cooking. They may not look as good as grade A products but they are just as nutritious and a lot cheaper. Save the vegetable water to add to soups. Carrots are nearly always good bargains and can be used raw as well as cooked. Use the leafy tops of young beets, cauliflower, celery and turnips. They are economical sources of vitamin A as are collard, kale, mustard and spinach. Besides vitamin A they provide other vitamins and iron.

When shopping for citrus fruits, select the heavier fruits. Use fresh, canned, or tomato juice whenever citrus fruits are high in price. Use twice as much tomatoes as orange or grapefruit to get the same amount of vitamin C. Canned or frozen orange and grapefruit juices are usually less expensive than the fresh fruits. Raw cabbage, turnips and lettuce, are good sources of vitamin C, too. Buy sliced peaches rather than halves.

27

Use powdered milk for cooking and baking. No difference can be detected in the cooked product and it is so much cheaper than whole milk. However powdered milk is skim milk. Since the vitamin A is removed from whole milk with the cream, be sure you're getting vitamin A in green and yellow vegetables, liver and butter. Try margarine instead of butter. Cream is expensive. To economize, use top or evaporated milk for cereals, puddings and beverages.

When the budget is slim, select the less expensive cuts of meats. Grades B and C are economical grades of beef. Red beef is fresh without any strong odor, but very fresh meat tends to be tough. Meat may be made more tender by grinding, pounding, marinating in acid, or salting with a meat tenderizer. When purchasing a big roast such as a rib roast of beef, or half a ham, have the butcher saw the roast into three steaks, or cut off two center slices of ham. That way, you can cook three entirely different meals on three different occasions. The meat will cook much quicker and there will be no leftovers to doctor up for lunch the next day. Ask the butcher to give you the trimmings with the meat; make soup with the bones and use the fat for frying.

To stretch the pennies as well as to add menu variety, use such meats as liver or kidneys once a week. They are rich in vitamins and minerals. Brains, giblets, hearts and tripe are also good buys.

Fish and cheese are usually cheaper than meat and good protein sources. Cottage cheese is especially good for dieters.

Serve dry beans such as navy, kidney, lima or soy beans. Don't forget dry peas and lentils.

Grades B and C are just as nutritious as grade A eggs, though much cheaper. If you don't care to fry them for breakfast use them in cooking.

Select the dark, whole grain, or enriched foods for their extra vitamins and iron. Day old bread is cheaper and better for toasting. Bread made with milk, or milk served with cereal make a high-quality protein combination. To be thrifty, don't buy costly ready-baked products. Get a good American cook-book and learn to blend together your own inexpensive flour mixes. While baking, save time and fuel by putting in several items to be cooked at the same time. For instance, when you are roasting meat you can also put in scrubbed potatoes to be baked in their jackets and a cake for dessert.

Instead of white sugar, use molasses, brown sugar and honey, more often in cooking. Molasses is a cheap source of iron, besides it adds flavor and food value to baked beans, bread, cookies, gingerbread and puddings. In between meals give the children raisins, dried apricots, prunes, fruits, raw carrot and celery sticks instead of candy. If you want to save on steep dentist bills, serve fruit juices and milk, in place of soft drinks. If possible, encourage the brushing of teeth after meals.

One last reminder—buy fresh seasonable foods and try cook-ing Chinese dishes whenever possible. They not only have more eye, taste and budget appeal, but they are also best for maintaining good health.

Cooking Utensils

A GOOD SUPPLY OF POTS AND PANS IN VARIOUS SIZES IS NECESSARY. Heavy pots are used for stewing. Thin pans are used for quick cooking. The Chinese use a "wak" for frying. It is a wide shallow bowl that can be used for sauté frying as well as deep frying. However, one can use a skillet for sauté cooking and a deep pan for deep frying and get as good results.

Every Chinese family owns a steamer. A double boiler is not quite the same thing since the steam does not get directly at the food. To make your own steamer for dry-steaming, simply punch holes in the bottom of an empty pound coffee can and place it upside down in a wide pot. Pour water up to half the can level before adding the dish of food on top of can to be steamed. Then cover and steam in high heat. For wet-steaming, just put bowl of food in wide pot containing an inch of water. Cover tightly and turn to high heat.

Slit, as well as regular ladles, are needed. Spoons, spatulas, and chopsticks are used in a Chinese kitchen. Even more important than a grinder is a good heavy chopping knife. There are chopping knives for vegetables and cleavers for meats. Both look the same in a Chinese kitchen. The difference is in the sharpness. Of course a heavy chopping block is also essential. You can make your own by sawing off a thick plank. It should be about 12 in. in diameter and 4-6 in. deep.

Glass jars are handy to store dried foods and will save you much time by having the needed ingredients close at hand.

If there's a choice whether to install a gas or other range, do by all means choose the gas range—that is if you plan to cook Chinese food occasionally or often. Chinese dishes require wide and quick changes of heat. Gas is so much easier to regulate.

Finally, use common sense. Don't do as the English lady did who went to a Chinese restaurant and found she liked fried rice so much she attempted to cook some herself the very next day—without a recipe! First she washed the rice, then dumped the wet rice into a hot-oiled pan. The grains popped up to the ceiling. She got flying, instead of fried, rice. That scared her out of "going Chinese" for good! I hope that won't happen to anyone else, for I know that a little eagerness to experiment, with common sense, will go a long way in launching this new adventure.

Cooking Preparations and Methods

A CHINESE CHEF PREPARES EVERYTHING AHEAD OF TIME. Quality rather than quantity holds first importance. Vegetables and meats are bought with care and cleaned. According to the recipes, meats are sliced paper-thin against the grain, diced, or ground. (To slice meat paper-thin have meat partly frozen before cutting.) Vegetables are cut diagonally, julienned, or chopped. All ingredients are neatly arranged on the kitchen table. Most foods are cooked as little as possible with little liquid to preserve maximum minerals and vitamins.

Common Chinese vegetables are water chestnuts, bamboo shoots, bean sprouts and exotic vegetables, such as east melons, bitter squash, bottle gourd, etc. (Though they are not always available, except in cans, they can be substituted with fresh celery, carrots, and onions or even omitted when necessary. In a pinch, ginger powder may be used in place of ginger root, olive oil instead of sesame oil, gin or sherry wine instead of rice wine, vegetable oil instead of peanut oil, etc.) The amount of meat, poultry, or seafood in most dishes should be about one third to one half the amount of mixed vegetables. That's why Chinese food is especially good for dieters.

Meats should be cut the same size and shape as vegetables to establish uniformity. All ingredients must be cut small into slivers, dices or shreds, because the Chinese use chopsticks instead of knives and forks. Using stock instead of water is one of the tricks used to enhance flavor.

There are three principal methods used in Chinese cooking. They are stewing (clear and red), steaming (wet and dry), and frying (sauté and deep frying).

Stewing is the simplest. In clear stewing, use no soy sauce but in red stewing use a little sugar and soy sauce which gives food a reddish tinge. After the liquid is brought to a boil turn to low heat and simmer until food is tender. Just make sure there's enough liquid in the pot so as not to burn the food.

In wet steaming, pour off all liquid and add barely enough stock to cover the substance. Steam till food is tender. Remove any surface fat and liquid. Steam a few minutes longer using high heat. Dry steaming takes the place of baking in most Chinese homes.

Deep frying is done over hot oil. Food is done when it floats.

Sauté frying consists of three parts—meat, vegetables and garnishes. This kind of frying should always be done over high heat. The oil must be hot enough to keep food from sticking but not so hot it flashes and imparts a burnt taste and a rancid smell to the food. All food should be stirred constantly either with a spoon or spatula so that each particle will receive an even amount of heat. This quick-cooking method is the most difficult but the most typical of Chinese cooking. To master it, is to master Chinese cooking.

Roasting, baking and broiling were not common home methods, because individual ovens were unsuitable to most Chinese homes. However, we have incorporated these methods in our ranch home with the greatest of ease.

Success in almost all things lies in accurate timing. This is doubly true in the art of cooking. No amount of good material, seasoning, or method of cooking can give perfect results unless the timing in its preparation is strictly observed. Timing is the one thing no cookbook or chef can relay to another with 100 per cent accuracy. For that perfect timing, one must rely on experience, common sense, and intuition. GOOD LUCK!

Hints

In this book all ingredients except rhinoceros are available in the U.S.A. Most recipes call for only easy-to-get ingredients. However, special recipes calling for exotic ingredients may be purchased from Chinese groceries by mail.

A Chinese cook wastes nothing. Celery leaves are used for salads and soups. Outer cabbage leaves are cooked in soups, or fed to animals. Ham skins are removed after roasting, boiled till soft and cut up into small pieces and put back into stews. Even chicken and duck feet are stewed, or fried into very delicious dishes. Giblets are considered delicacies. Tripe is cut up and cooked in congee. Pig intestines are used to stuff sausages. Fats from roasts, stews, and cooking are saved for future use. They are, however, never mixed into one container. Chicken fats go into one can, pork fats into another, and beef into a third can, etc. Leftovers are all put immediately into the refrigerator to be warmed up for lunch, or to be mixed up to make "ice box" soup. Bones are saved from roasts to make stock or soup. Fish heads are cooked in congee. Chicken necks and backs are used for broth. Watermelon rinds are sautéed with meat and its seeds are roasted. Tangerine peels are dried and used for seasoning. Used tea leaves are cooked with eggs. Stale breads are used to make bread crumbs, or steamed into a delicious freshness. Leftover rice is used for fried rice, or put into soups.

Chop suey is not an authentic Chinese dish. It was invented by a Cantonese in California 90 years ago. Nor are those brittle fried noodles real chow mein. A good cook can make

34

them taste similar to Chinese food, but they are not Chinese dishes.

And no matter how nutritious certain foods are, they will not be appetizing unless prepared in a way appealing to the eyes and nose as well. That is why the Orientals are very particular about the correct combination and blending of colors in their meals.

Cooking Terms

Bake — To cook by dry heat in an oven.

Baste — To spoon liquid over meat while roasting in oven.

Batter — An egg mixture that is pourable.

Beat — To mix thoroughly.

Blanch — To immerse in boiling then in cold water.

Blend — To mix evenly.

Boil — To cook liquid to a bubbling stage.

Braise — To brown food in a little oil, then to cover and cook for some time in a little liquid.

Breaded — Coated with fine bread or cracker crumbs before frying.

Broil — To cook over or under direct heat.

Chop — To cut into tiny uniform pieces.

Chopsticks — Two sticks used for picking up food.

Chow — To fry.

Combine — To mix together.

Cook — To prepare food by fuel.

Cream — To soften to a smooth batter.

Crumble — To crush into brittle pieces.

Crush — To compress out of shape.

Cube — To cut into squares.

Debone — To remove bones.

Dice — To cut into tiny squares.

Dissolve — To melt.

Dough — A mixture of flour and liquid that is thick enough to be rolled or kneaded. When rolled out it is called "skins" by the Chinese.

Dust — To coat lightly with flour.

Evaporate — To cook until water dries.

Fry — To cook in oil till brown and soft.

Fu Yong — Omelet.

Garnishes — Decorations.

Grate — To rub against a grater.

Grill — An outdoor stove.

Grind — To cut into fine pieces or crush to a powder.

Infuse — To steep in boiling water.

Julienne — To cut into thin shreds.

Knead — To press repeatedly with dusted hands.

Marinate — To soak in liquid and chill.

Mash — To crush to a pulp.

Mein — Noodles.

Melt — To heat to a liquid.

Mince — To chop very fine.

Mix — To blend ingredients evenly.

Monosodium glutamate * — A white taste powder made from an extract of wheat flour, which enhances the flavor of food.

Pan-broiled — To cook in an uncovered pan, draining off excess fat.

Peel — To skin.

Roast — To cook without cover in an oven.

Sauté — To stir food in a little oil till brown, then to add a little liquid, cover pan, cook quickly, and mix thoroughly.

Score — To cut diamond-shaped gashes.

Shred — To cut into matchsticks.

Sift — To separate with a sieve the fine flour or sugar from the coarse.

Simmer — To cook just below the bubbling point.

Steam — To cook food covered above boiling water till soft.

Stock — A broth from cooked bones, meat, or vegetables.

Unmold — To take out of the mold before serving.

* Good cooks don't use M.S.G. very often. If it is used indiscriminately all dishes will begin to taste the same and there will be a drop in appetite. I always save the bones to make stock and refrigerate for future use. Even the liquid from cooked vegetables makes good stock. However, bouillon cubes are good substitutes to have on hand.

How to Serve Chinese Meals

Family Dinners

THE BIG DIFFERENCE BETWEEN FAMILY MEALS AND DINNER parties is the variety and quantity of food, of course. But at Chinese meals you can tell which kind of Chinese meal you have been invited to by looking at the table. If the dishes to be served are all on the table, then you may assume it's a quiet family affair. There are usually as many dishes as people present. Even in the most humble home, however, there will be at least four dishes on the table. These will be the basic four— one meat, one fish, one vegetable, and one soup. Everyone sits down to a setting with a bowl of rice, a pair of chopsticks and a china spoon. Each one helps himself to the central dishes. He eats the food and the rice simultaneously. At the end of the meal, hot tea will be served. Don't expect dessert.

Banquets

A CHINESE BANQUET USUALLY INCLUDES TWELVE PEOPLE AT A round table. The more people invited, the more tables will be set. The number of dishes served will far outnumber a family dinner. Delicate flavor is the first prerequisite, which of course means elaborate preparation. According to old Chinese custom five main courses are required at a banquet. There are: four cold "hors d'oeuvres" such as ham, chicken, abalone, and asparagus with rice wine; four minor fried vegetables or meat dishes such as pepper steak, egg fu yong, sweet and sour fish and almond chicken; six major dishes such as red stewed bear's

paw, squid, rabbit, venison, pheasant, squabs with rice; a
cauldron of soup, perhaps birds' nest; and finally a sweet bowl
such as almond gruel. But in this modern trend of "easier
living," most people have reduced a feast to one "hors
d'oeuvre" such as cold abalone with wine; four major dishes
such as chicken, duck, lobster and pork with rice wine; a
tureen of soup—maybe shark's fin soup; and the sweet bowl
of almond gruel. Small sauce plates with different sauces and
spices are placed at individual settings.

In a banquet the different dishes are served one at a time.

The host makes a toast and guests toast their thanks. Later
the host may propose the finger game. The loser has to drink
the agreed upon amount of rice wine. This game is one means
of breaking the ice in a large group. The host helps the guests
to food. When the guest of honor starts to eat the others also
eat.

An outstanding banquet provides stimulating conversation
besides an abundance of delicacies, expert cookery and fine
chinaware.

Besides the regular festival dishes, auspicious food may be
inserted for different occasions. On a birthday celebration, for
instance, long noodles and peaches are served. Long noodles
signify longevity and peaches mean congratulations. At the
Harvest Moon Festival, moon cakes are added in honor of the
moon.

Rice is served at the beginning of the major course even at
a banquet.

Tea comes before and after the banquet as it is the main
beverage in China. Before the feast it's used to whet the
appetite, after the banquet it's one means of reviving the
sluggish.

It is my opinion the Chinese are basically a democratic
people. All feasts are served at round tables. The only distinc-
tion is that the host gets a lower seat and the guest of honor
has the upper one.

Main and Miscellaneous Meals

ORDINARILY MOST CHINESE EAT THREE MEALS A DAY. IN OUR family, however, three meals do not seem like a square deal, so we usually have four square meals daily.

Breakfast is usually Chinese sausages on rice and hot tea, on cold winter mornings. In the summer, or when we are dieting, as little as a bowl of rice gruel with a boiled egg will suffice. If we have guests, breakfast must be more leisurely and elaborate with fried "Chiao-Tzu," congee, and tea.

Lunch is a hearty beef rice, fried rice, if friends are present, a tureen of pot noodles, or last night's warmed-up leftovers if the cook is ornery.

Brunch on Sunday mornings is an elaborate tea with many pastries and tidbits called "Diem Sum" meaning to touch the heart.

Dinner at night is our main meal. At least the basic fours must be served for a family and more if the cook is happy and energetic that day.

Midnight snacks served late in the evening are our favorite meals. They consist of such special dishes as Cantonese "Chow Mein," "Yat-Koi Mein" (individual noodle soup), fish congee, "Won Ton" (ravioli in chicken soup), etc. These dishes are usually sent up from the restaurants so even the cook may enjoy them thoroughly.

Simple Menu Suggestions for Chinese Meals in Western Style

Sunday

Birds' Nest Soup
Rice
Roast Duck
Chicken Salad
Baked Grapefruit
Tea

Monday

Piggies in Blanket
Rice
Sweet and Sour Spareribs
Spinach Salad
Almond Cake
Tea

Tuesday

Broth
Rice
Beef Barbecued
Cold Asparagus
Preserved Kumquats
Tea

Wednesday

Vegetable Soup
Rice
Bean Curd Sautéed with
*   Scallions*
Garden Peas
Candy Peels
Tea

Thursday

"Hot" and Sour Soup
Rice
Red Stewed Lamb
Sweet and Sour Cabbage
Sesame Candy
Tea

Friday

Cold Abalone
Rice
Cantonese Lobster
Raw Celery Cabbage
Canton Fruit Cup
Tea

41

Saturday

Stuffed Celery
Rice
"Egg Fu Yong"
Bean Sprouts
Steamed Sponge Cake
 Tea

Lichee nuts used to be served at Chinese-American restaurants after meals. They seem to have made a hit.

PART II

Exotic Foods

Different and Unusual Foods

PHEASANT AND MALLARD ARE COMMON FEAST FOODS. SEAFOODS come in wide varieties from fish to shell fish to seaweeds to "sea cucumbers." Pork is the most common meat used in China, but among Chinese Mohammedans and Jews only lamb or beef are eaten. Rabbit and venison are festival foods as is bear meat when available. Bear meat (mostly paws) is usually dried and has to be soaked in water to soften before cooking in soy sauce.

Bean products sort of take the place of dairy products in the East. Soy beans contain 18% fat, 35% carbohydrate, 35% protein and many of the essential amino acids which are found only in yeast and meat products. Bean curd, white and red "cheeses," and soy bean jam for which Bovril may be substituted are all made from soy beans, not to mention soy sauce, the major flavoring sauce for the Chinese people.

The Chinese use so many different vegetables even in this country that I confess I do not know the English name for many of them. As a child I loved our east melon and "Loofah Gourd" in soups. Later, I learned to enjoy stuffed bitter melons and a thick green bitter cabbage. (Whenever I want to make dishes calling for this bitter cabbage I substitute broccoli.) Then there is a vegetable called "bottle-gourd." It somewhat resembles a giant pear and is slightly sweet and crisp when cooked in stews. Chinese radishes are similar to those grown here.

By now many Westerners are familiar with the snow peas and Chinese cabbage (somewhat like celery cabbage but with dark green leaves). Of course, most people know about the

45

bean sprouts, bamboo shoots, and water chestnuts which are aquatic bulbs, widely cultivated in Asia. Potatoes and yams are used too, but prized are the taro roots we call "Wu-Tao." It resembles a grey potato. Chinese mushrooms are dried. If they are too expensive in a Chinese store, buy mushrooms in season. String them through caps and stems and hang them in the sun to dry for 4 days then store them for future use in a cool, dry spot.

Other things the Chinese cook are dried fungus, vermicelli, bean curd sticks, black hair seaweed, dried lilies, called golden needles in Chinese, chrysanthemums, lotus roots and seeds, etc.

It is said the orange and peach trees came from China, so of course their fruits were our most familiar ones from birth. Pears, plums, grapes, bananas, apricots, apples and persimmons are common fruits at home, not to mention the less common pomegranate. During New Year's all the citrus fruits including fresh kumquats but not lemons are eaten. Summer fruits include watermelon, sugar cane, star apples and mangoes. All year round there are the savory dried fruits.

Walnuts, chestnuts, peanuts, almonds, melon and sesame seeds are used in Chinese cookery. Almonds are usually used as garnishes, and sesame seeds are used mostly to make oils. Peanut oil is used like butter in Chinese cooking. Whenever a recipe calls for vegetable oil it means peanut oil to a Chinese. Sesame oil is strong and delicious. A few drops is enough to improve a salad immensely. Hence the magical term "open sesame" was coined.

Bean Curd

BEAN CURD IS MADE FROM SOY BEANS. THE PROCESS IS SO COM-
plex, a book is needed to describe each step. Below a brief
account is given of it.

Soy beans are soaked in cold water for several hours. They
are then ground in a water stone-grinder. These ground soy
beans are cooked with calcium powder for 5 hours; then
filtered through a cloth. The liquid which comes through into
a bowl is allowed to harden into a solid mass, tied in a piece
of cloth, and boiled. The finished product is bean curd.

Bean curd has the same nourishing value as soy beans, but
it is much more palatable and digestible. It is inexpensive and
simple to cook and can be purchased from Chinese grocers.
Almost any meat, fish, eggs, or vegetables go well with bean
curd.

WHITE (BEAN CURD) CHEESE

1 qt. bean curd, cut into 1" x 1½" bricks
Gin
Salt
Pt. jars, sterilized

Divide bean curd into jars. Fill each jar one fourth full of
gin. Salt to taste. Seal jars. Let age at least a fortnight before
using. Serve with rice, or cook with string beans.

(RED) "SOUTHERN CHEESE"

To make "Southern Cheese" use red bean curds made from red soy beans. Wrap red cheese in cloth. Press 5 days. Unwrap. Scrape off the mold. Put cheese into sterilized jar. Fill jar one fourth full of gin, or rice wine. Season generously with salt. Seal jar. Age 2 weeks before using.

Soy Sauce

Soy sauce is one of the most important ingredients in Chinese cookery. It is essential in most Chinese dishes and enhances the flavor of many American dishes, such as hamburgers, chops, roasts, and steaks. For thousands of years, soy sauce has been the favorite condiment of the Chinese people. It is quickly catching on in American supermarkets, because it contains no vinegar, starch, or spice except salt, and never sours or molds. Soy sauce brings out the best in good food.

At this point I would like to explain how it is made. Of course it's impractical to reproduce in small quantities at home when it's so inexpensive and available at most grocery stores.

SOY SAUCE

Soy beans
Salt

Boil soy beans in low heat for 6 hours. Strain. Expose liquid in big pot to the hot sun. The liquid will turn brown and form a layer on the surface. Skim off this covering and other coverings till no more coverings can be formed. Add salt to taste and boil some more. There's your soy sauce.

Sesame

SESAME PLANTS ARE TROPICAL HERBS THAT THRIVE UNDER THE same conditions as cotton. They produce seeds which have a nutty taste when cooked. As late as the 1930's the U. S. used these seeds primarily as a source of vegetable oil. Now the seeds are used as toppings on breads and cookies, as a paste in candies, and as a flavoring oil for chicken and shrimp curry dishes, mashed turnips, poultry stuffings, plus icings.

TOASTED SESAME SEEDS

Raw sesame seeds

Roast raw seeds in 350° oven for 20 min. to brown.

SESAME OIL

Sesame seeds, toasted

Grind seeds with stone grinder and collect in pan. Remove sesame oil on top.

PEANUT OIL

Peanuts, shelled and skinned

Fry raw peanut to a golden yellow. Place peanuts in hollow block of heavy wood with hole in one end and smaller holes around. Crush peanuts with stick in large hole. Peanut oil will come through smaller holes.

Bean Sprouts

PURCHASE SOME TINY GREEN "MUNG" BEANS FROM ANY CHINESE grocers. Use a large clay flower pot. Scrub clean inside out. Place a layer of clean pebbles to line bottom of pot. Put one layer of beans over pebbles. Pour enough water over all beans to wet thoroughly. (Excess water will run out through pebbles down hole in center of pot onto saucer.) Cover beans with damp, black cloth. Put in warm spot. Rinse with fresh water daily. In 8 days when all beans have sprouted, they should be washed and cooked. These crisp, tender, white sprouts are an asset to dishes such as "Chow Mein," "Egg Fu Yong" and other vegetable recipes. They contain 21-25% protein, 64% carbohydrate, 1½% fat, and may be purchased in cans or bought fresh from Chinese stores.

Spices

PRACTICALLY EVERY KITCHEN HAS A SPICE CABINET. SPICES ARE so common nowadays, probably every conceivable kind can be found in any grocery store. However, spices were not always so readily available. Centuries ago they were worth their weight in gold. To obtain spices, pirates overran the high seas to plunder ships, countries fought bloody wars, and the whole European continent competed to find new routes to the East. This desire for spices was one of the major driving forces of modern history.

Spices are as old as the hills. When Europe was still a forest, India was cultivating pepper fields. And China was planting ginger and anise long before any Caucasians knew what they were. Confucius (550 or 551-479 B.C.) said, "There should be a little ginger in one's food."

It was not until Marco Polo (C. 1254-1324) came home with his fabulous stories that the powers of Europe, while striving to find new ways to the far lands, discovered the Americas.

Nowadays spices come from all over the world. From India we get pepper (black and white), cinnamon and curry; from Malaya, mace, nutmeg and tumeric; from Zanzibar, cloves; from South America, all-spice and vanilla; from Europe, caraway, dill, mustard, sage and thyme; from China, star anise, ginger root, spicery powder, Chinese red pepper, and Chinese parsley.

In Cathay spices were used principally to preserve food and to counteract any gamey taste. Later spices everywhere were used mostly to flavor food. The flavor comes from aromatic oils in the plants. These oils come from different parts of the plants depending on the kind, i.e.: cloves and capers are flowerbuds of trees, vanilla; pepper, dill, and anise are fruits; nutmeg is the seed; mace is the external covering of nutmeg; thyme, sage and bay are leaves; sassafras is the bark of a root; and ginger * and licorice are roots.

While spices are a necessity in a Chinese kitchen they should be used with discretion, i.e. they should enrich rather than overpower the flavor of the food itself. The Chinese believe that a little spice in foods stimulates the appetite and aids digestion.

Today spices are used not only as seasoning agents but are also widely employed in medicines, candies, soaps and perfumes. The great variety obtainable in any American supermarket is sufficient to constitute one of the spices of life for any kitchen artist—professional or otherwise.

* Where a recipe calls for ginger root, and this is not readily accessible, ginger powder may be substituted.

Food Preservation

THE CHINESE PRESERVE FOOD BY SALTING, DRYING, PICKLING, candying, canning and smoking. For example: shrimplet are salted, pork and duck are dried, vegetables are pickled, ginger is candied, abalone are canned and fish and tobacco are smoked.

Many foods are salted in China because there is little refrigeration. As a matter of course, Mother used to salt all fresh meats, fish or eggs not to be used up within a few days even though we always had refrigeration in Boston.

Drying was the next method she used in preserving foods. Things were cleaned, cooked and hung out to dry in the sun, then in the wind, on our roof. Uncut Chinese leafy vegetables were pickled in vinegar. Hunks of ginger root were preserved in syrup and eaten like candy. As far as I recall, abalone always came out of cans during the New Year's holiday or festive occasions.

Smoking seemed to be the most interesting method in preserving fish. Usually herring-like species of fish were chosen for smoking. This procedure varies a bit from region to region but mainly the small fish are washed, then cooked in boiling, salted water. Thereupon they are spread out to dry in the sun for 2 hours. The dried fish are then placed in small, round bamboo trays so constructed as to permit circulation through the bottom. The fish are placed one layer deep, head down at a bit of an angle so the rows overlap. These trays are placed over a round opening in the top of a long concrete furnace which contains a series of such openings. Several trays are piled one on top of the other. A tightly woven cover is placed over the top tray. Smoke comes from a smoky fire. Smoking takes 5-6 hours or longer if the fish are for exportation. Trays are shifted in place during this time. The fish are sold in market places by the trayful.

Rice

RICE IS CHINA'S STAPLE FOOD THOUGH WHEAT IS PREFERRED IN the northern provinces. There are two kinds of rice—the long and the short grain. The Chinese seem to like the long grain because it's more simple to cook.

A rice harvest is both colorful and ancient. Water buffaloes help out in the preparation of the land but it is human labor alone that does the planting, reaping and threshing. (That is why Chinese adults are careful not to waste one grain of rice and the children are warned to clean their rice bowls to avoid marrying a pocked face partner.) The buffaloes are used to tramp the earth down to a clean, hard threshing floor while the wind blows away the chaff.

Rice is planted in small blades that reflect in the water of the paddies. As the rice plants grow, they turn a darker green. Before long the water is hidden by these wavering blades. The farmers must stir the freshly fertilized soil.

As soon as the rice "heads" and opens, it is flattened on the ground and hand-cut. The grain is threshed by crude hand machines, then spread on the dirt threshing floor to be separated from the chaff.

Harvest time is a happy time. If it should rain, thatched shelters are placed over the rice. The minute the rain stops, busy fingers begin their work anew.

When a kernel of rice leaves the thresher it is enclosed by the husk and is known as rough rice. Some rough rice is fed to livestock or used as seed, but the greater part of it is milled for food. Frequently milled rice is coated with vegetable oil to improve its looks. By-products include bran, and polish used to feed livestock; broken rice used for distilling besides the manufacture of flour and starch; husks used for fuel and packing; straw for feed, bedding, thatching roofs, mats, garments and brooms, and rice is even used in fish-farming. (Many farmers from the South raise fish in their irrigated rice paddy fields. Around 400 small carp, grown in hatcheries, are put into an acre of ten-inch water-covered land. The carp grow very big during the 4 months the rice is maturing. When the rice is harvested the fish yield is close to 100 lb.) Nothing is wasted. Rice is our staff of life.

Tea

IT WAS IN THE "ERH YA," THE CHINESE DICTIONARY ANNOTATED by Kuo P'o, a renowned Chinese scholar of about 350 A.D., that the first definition of tea was found. But the tea of Kuo P'o's time was really a medicinal concoction. Not until the latter part of the 6th century did the Chinese generally regard tea as a refreshing beverage.

Tea, according to the author of "Kuen Fang P'u" was first used as a beverage in the reign of Emperor Wen Ti 589-601 A.D. of the Sui Dynasty. However, not until 780 A.D. did writer Lu Yu first publish in his famous "Ch'a Ching" (Tea Classic) the horticultural aspect of tea-growing and its manufacture.

Yu Lu was more than a writer, he was a tea expert. It was he who formulated a Code of Tea from which the Japanese later developed the Tea Ceremony.

By the Sung Dynasty (960-1280 A.D.) the "Kuen Fang P'u" stated that tea was served throughout China, and that whipped tea was popular among tea connoisseurs. Dried leaves were ground to a powder and whipped in hot water with a small bamboo whisk. Salt was no longer employed as a flavoring agent. Now tea was enjoyed for its own delicate flavor and aroma.

During the Ming Dynasty (1368-1644 A.D.) the second tea book appeared. It was entitled "Ch'a P'u" by Ku Yuan-ch'ing, another scholar. It is evident from this book that the Chinese of the 9th century infused tea leaves much as they do today.

Tea is the most common beverage in Chinese homes. When visitors come, hot tea is always served. Cake and cookies may accompany it but never sugar, cream, or lemon.

58

There are two main kinds of tea—green and black. They are really not from different plants. The difference is due to the methods of drying the leaves. This information can be gleaned from encyclopedias so I shall not go into that aspect. Each has its special flavor. All things being equal, the quality is about the same in both varieties of tea.

POPULAR CHINESE TEAS

"Dragon Well" green unfermented teas are light in color and fresh in flavor.

"Gunpowder," a green, unfermented tea, is basket or pan fired.

"Jasmine" is a delicate flower scented, semi-fermented tea mixed with its blossoms.

"Keemun," a spicy tea, is one of the best Chinese black fermented teas.

"Lapsang Souchong" is a very smoky black fermented tea.

"Lichee" is a faintly sweet black fermented tea.

"Oolong" is a Formosan tea that is neither green nor black with long, daintily-tipped tea leaves.

PART III

Seasonable and Festival
Recipes with Stories

Chinese New Year's*

New Year's is the great day for the Chinese whether in China or abroad. It is equal to Christmas, birthday, and holiday, all rolled up in one. Such being the case, New Year's cannot be celebrated in one day. Indeed, we Cantonese in America take a week to a fortnight, to complete the big celebration.

In our home, my parents start months before the day, ordering Chinese groceries from Hong Kong. The imported staples consist mostly of dried commodities or canned goods, including dried mushrooms, squid, shrimp, birds' nest, canned abalone, lichee nuts, bottled oyster sauce, and sesame seed oil. All are distinctly oriental and exotic.

Then my mother begins her big housecleaning. All the windows must be cleaned till the panes gleam. Every curtain is washed, starched and pressed, then rehung looking as frothy as new. The oak floors are scrubbed and waxed so smooth and slippery that the children slide on them when no adult is near enough to object. All the closets, drawers, shelves and seldom-looked-into places are taken apart, scoured and relined with fresh white paper, where needed. The household god will not overlook one place in the house, no matter how obscure, and neither will Mother.

Father is far from idle. Being a well respected citizen of the Chinese community we live in, he begins early to go over his books. To all who owe him money, he sends out notices of payment due. He must also find some way to repay his debts,

* Since the founding of the Chinese Republic, October 10, 1911, the Gregorian calendar has been adopted in China, but old holidays such as New Year's are still observed according to the old calendar of China.

no matter how difficult. Every reputable Chinese starts the New Year with a clean slate.

The older girls sew gay new garments for themselves and shop for the younger children, while young boys practice the dragon dance. The dragon is an imaginary head of a beast that is both gorgeous and terrifying, with artificial eyes that are as big and shiny as large flash lights. The opened mouth, large enough to swallow a man, is painted bright red with a flapping tongue. His body and tail consist of just a piece of soft material that is equally handsome studded with jewelry and brilliant colors. Inside the hard shell of the skull is a boy dressed in gay, flashy colors to match this splendid creature. At the rear is another lad in identical costume. This couple will perform the dragon dance until they are relieved by a fresh pair. The older boys polish up on their jujitsu, a favorite pastime during the New Year's holiday. Other young men are indulging in an Eastern kind of fencing in which no one ever hurts his opponent. Some bachelors are rehearsing nightly for the various operas performed only at this season. Those taking the female parts have to learn to sing in an unnatural falsetto.

A week ahead, the Chinese ladies get together in each other's houses and help prepare the many kinds of sweets and hors d'oeuvres for New Year's. All sizes, shapes, colors and tantalizing smells are conjured up in those hectic days. Everywhere and everything seem a hopeless hodgepodge. But every year, very mysteriously, order reigns once more on the Day.

On New Year's Eve the long anticipated fun begins. All females retire to the kitchen. Incense burns on a table against a wall. Also on this table are platters of grapefruits, oranges, tangerines and kumquats in pyramid style. Little potted orange trees decorate the home the way wreaths are displayed at Christmastime. Appropriately, orange blossoms signify fruitfulness and abundance for the New Year. On the center of the table is a lazy susan laden with tidbits and delicacies. Red scrolls painted in jet black ink with propitious sayings in my father's best calligraphy hang on the wall. One by one, we kneel and with bowed heads and closed palms do honor to the kitchen god for another year.

The men and boys are off to their vegetarian dinner in the various clan societies. Only males are allowed at these affairs. On entering, the members go immediately before an altar. At the center hangs a painting of Confucius surrounded by beautiful poetry embroidered in silk cloth. Beneath the painting is a table piled with bowls of citrus fruits and burning joss sticks. Each individual kowtows three times before this august image. In paying homage to Confucius one is symbolically paying respect to all the ancestors too. No meat is allowed on this one occasion, but that does not prevent the Chinese from eating one vegetable dish molded into the form of a lifelike chicken.

At midnight, from everywhere, firecrackers sputter with alacrity. Then the dragon dance begins. Teen aged youths dressed in colorful costumes of red, green, and gold get under a make-believe dragon. They turn, twist, writhe; shake, and jump under this animal. The dragon will flap its wide, wide mouth and bare two sharp fangs. Its glass eyes beam like headlights. Thus this ferocious serpent parades throughout the town accompanied by loud drums and cymbals. It stops at each store to wolf down a head of lettuce (dollar bills) tied on a pole above the door. (This money goes for charity.) Adolescents light the way with pretty paper lanterns. The procession stops at the Chinese Chamber of Commerce Building. With a final barrage of fireworks from the Mayor, the dragon gives a great leap, bows and flees into his lair up in the municipal building.

Few adults retire. Many men stay up all night without sleep, playing cards and making merry. The women are busy with last-minute preparations.

In the morning the children are up with the sun. Everyone has taken a bath, cut and washed his hair the day before, so all one needs to do this day is to put on smart new clothes from head to toe. The girls wear their most stunning costumes.

Before breakfast the children of the family line up to wish father and mother a happy new year. In return the parents give each child his first red envelope for the New Year, usually containing two coins. Two pieces are necessary because the Chinese believe everything good must come in twos, though it is not important that they are identical. Thus, the Chinese character for 'good' consists of a girl and boy together.

Around 9 o'clock the children go in groups to every store in the Chinese district to wish every proprietor a prosperous new year. In each case they are rewarded with more tiny packages of lucky money and oranges.

After lunch every one goes out. The housewives call on each other briefly and exchange presents of steamed pastries, "Diem Sum" (delicacies that touch the heart) and fruits. All the men go to their own family clubs to see old relatives and friends. There they chew watermelon seeds, drink pale Chinese tea, gossip, and gamble. The children are seen everywhere, playing in their fine clothes.

Dinner on New Year's Day is a family feast within the immediate family. The big banquet comes at the end of the holiday celebration when relatives and friends are also invited. Every family has its own special recipes. Our family's favorite hors d'oeuvre is Chinese dried oysters marinated overnight in wine, then ground up with the choicest pork, fried, and wrapped in tender, crisp lettuce leaves. Then different chicken dishes are served. Every family serves the simple white-cut chicken with oyster sauce, birds' nest soup intact in a chicken, squab, shark's fins, fried lobster in the shell, cold abalone, honey-glazed duck, crisp skinned chicken, vermicelli, octopus, seaweed soup, snow pea vegetable, sea cucumber, and many other indescribable dishes followed by "Oolong" Tea.

After the meal some men will usually play the finger challenge. It's more or less an odd and even game. The loser has to down more "Ng Ga Pei" (pronounced eng gar pee), a very potent rice spirit, every time he shoots out the wrong number of fingers. This noisy game keeps up till one player becomes incapacitated.

In the evening nearly everyone goes to the opera. Sometimes the company is a local one but often the talent is imported. Frequently the opera cannot be completed in one evening, but to the easy-going Chinese that is insignificant. They will come back the following night. If not, they may attend a Chinese movie. The night after, there's a fencing bout to see and on the following night one mustn't forget the jujitsu match if one isn't busy attending the rounds of mah-jong and domino parties. You see, Chinese New Year's does not "open" for at least another week.

1. January 31—Thursday: Chinese New Year's

"CHIEN TZU" (PASTRY)

½ C. brown sugar   1 C. coconut shreds, or
⅔ C. boiling water   peanut butter
1 C. glutinous rice flour *   ½ C. sesame seeds
            Oil

Melt sugar in boiling water and bring to a boil again. Remove from heat. Stir in flour till dough forms. Cool. Shape dough into in.-wide sausages. Break into in.-long pieces. With clean palms of scrubbed hands, roll into balls and flatten. Put in scant t. coconut shreds or peanut butter in center of balls. Wrap dough around filling and reroll into balls. Sprinkle sesame seeds all over balls. Slip balls into hot deep fat. Fry till golden brown. Serve warm.

* Glutinous rice flour is called "Nor My Fun" in Cantonese. It's available in Chinese groceries.

2. February 1—Friday

DOUBLE DOUGH (CLAMS)

36 fresh clams	½ C. sugar
1 clove garlic, minced	½ C. vinegar
2 T. oil	3 T. wine
1 t. salt	¼ C. cornstarch
¼ C. soy sauce	1 pt. water

Wash clams. Steam till shells open.

Heat oil. Put garlic in oil and brown, then discard garlic. Put shelled clams and broth in oil. Blend rest of ingredients together and add to oil. Cook 5 min. Serves several lucky people.

3. February 2—Saturday

SHARK'S FINS SOUP WITH EGGS

2 lb. dried fins	1½ qt. stock
3 cloves garlic	1 T. cornstarch
2 slices ginger root (or ½ t.	1 t. soy sauce
ginger powder)	¼ C. water
2 T. lard	½ C. ham slivers
3 qt. water	2 eggs, boiled and quartered
2 t. M.S.G.	Parsley
Vinegar	

Soak dried fins in water for 3 hrs.

Boil fins with garlic and ginger in saucepan. Change water 3 times. Put in pot. Add lard and 2 qt. water with 1 t. M.S.G. Bring to a boil, then simmer ½ hr. Pour off liquid. Into another pot, put fins and another qt. water with ½ t. M.S.G. Boil. Discard liquid again. Into a third pot put fins and 1½ qt. stock with ½ t. M.S.G. Boil. Make a gravy by blending together water, cornstarch, soy sauce, and salt. Stir into cooking soup. Garnish with ham slivers, egg wedges, parsley, and dash of vinegar. Serves 6.

4. February 3—Sunday

BIRDS' NEST * SOUP

2 C. dried birds' nest	3 T. cornstarch
3 pt. chicken stock	¼ C. water
1 slice ginger root (or ½ t. ginger powder)	4 drops sesame oil (or olive oil)
¼ C. ham slivers	1 t. salt
¼ C. chicken slivers	½ t. pepper

Soak birds' nest in cold water for 1 hr. Wash. Put in pot. Cover with water. Add ginger. Bring to a boil and simmer 1 hr. Discard liquid. Put in stock. Simmer ½ hr. Garnish with ham and chicken. Blend together cornstarch, water, sesame oil, salt and pepper. Stir into soup. Bring to a boil. Turn off heat. Serves 6.

VARIATION: While boiling, stir in 2 eggs beaten, to form flowers.

* Birds' nest is the saliva of sea swallows found in South China.

5. February 4—Monday

CHINESE PORK STRIP

2 lb. fresh shoulder	1 t. salt
4 t. honey	⅓ C. stock (or hot water)
4 t. sugar	4 drops of red food-coloring
1 T. soy sauce	liquid (opt.)

Cut shoulder into several long strips. Mix honey, sugar, soy sauce, salt, stock, and food coloring if desired, in roasting pan. Put pork in and marinate for 4 hrs. turning several times.

Roast in 350° oven 1½ hrs., basting from time to time. Slice pork and serve with Plum Sauce. Serves 6-8.

6. February 5—Tuesday

BEEF WITH TOMATOES

¼ lb. flank steak	1 t. sugar
4 medium tomatoes	¼ C. water
1 T. cornstarch	1 t. soy sauce
½ t. salt	1 T. oil

Cut beef into narrow strips, and slice paper thin against the grain. (Remember to slice meat as thin as possible, have meat partly frozen before cutting.)

Heat oil. Fry beef quickly. Remove meat from pan. Skin tomatoes; cut into wedges, and put in pan. Heat through and put beef back into pan. Blend together cornstarch, salt, sugar, water, and soy sauce. Pour into pan. Stir. When mixture is translucent turn off heat. Serves 4.

7. February 6—Wednesday

SNOW PEA * VEGETABLES

1 lb. snow peas or very young, tender peas with pods
3 T. peanut or vegetable oil
1 t. salt
½ C. boiling water

String snow peas. Do not discard shells. Heat oil in pan. Put in clean peas in pods and salt. Sauté. Add water. Stir. Cover 5 min. Serves 4.

* Snow peas are known as sugar peas in this country.

8. February 7—Thursday

"CHIAO-TZU" WITH LAMB STUFFING

DURING CHINESE NEW YEAR'S THERE ARE USUALLY LOTS OF visitors in the regular household. After the New Year's feast, house guests still have to be fed for a day or more. One of the ways a Chinese hostess solves the feeding problem on days after the big dinner, is to have a meal of "Chiao-tzu." In this way all the guests' and even the children's help is enlisted. Everyone is kept busy and entertained talking, while preparing this inexpensive and delicious meal.

"Chiao-tzu" is a sort of ravioli. It is made by wrapping a small piece of thin dough around some meat stuffing to form a turnover. These little turnovers are usually cooked by boiling. In northern China these "Chiao-tzu" often constitute the main food of a meal. Below is the common recipe for making "Chiao-tzu."

CRUST

3 lb. wheat flour
3 C. water

Combine the flour and water gradually. Knead into a smooth, non-sticky dough. Divide into 5 dozen lengths. Shape dough into long sausages. Cut into equal lumps. Roll out little pie crusts of about ⅛" thickness and 3" diameter. These crusts are called "skins" in Chinese.

STUFFING

1½ lb. lean lamb, or pork
3-4 lb. spinach, or cabbage
½ C. soy sauce

3 slices ginger root (or ½ t. ginger powder)
3 T. peanut oil (or vegetable oil)

Grind the meat through a medium fine chopper. Do the same with the vegetables. Drain juice of vegetables. Mix all ingredients well.

From here on, round up all available persons in the house to help "wrap" these tidbits. Everybody scrubs his hands. Adults won't need coaching, but tell the youngsters who can help to take a pr. of chopsticks and place about 2 t. stuffing on the "skin." Then fold it into a turnover and pinch the edges 'till the stuffing is securely sealed in. Make every ready-to-boil "Chiao-tzu" stand separately on a flour dusted cookie sheet.

Boil 1 gal. water over high heat. After the water begins to bubble, put in all the "Chiao-tzu." This stops the boiling for awhile. When the bubbling begins again, dump in 1 pt. cold water and switch to medium heat. On the third bubbling, pour in still another pt. of water. This 10 min. dripping method strengthens the edges of the "Chiao-tzu." Immediately after this third dripping, take the "Chiao-tzu" out with a slit ladle. Save the good soup to serve in individual rice bowls last.

The drained "Chiao-tzu" are served along with a sauce of mixed vinegar, soy sauce and minced garlic, or they may be eaten plain. No other dish is necessary, though one may have relish dishes, such as pickles or hot peppers, on the side.

They are wonderful shallow fried for breakfast the next morning along with congee and tea.

9. February 8—Friday

ABALONE * SALAD

1 can abalone, drained (save liquid for soup)	2 t. sugar
	2 t. salt
2 bunches celery hearts	2 t. sesame oil (or olive
1 T. soy sauce	oil)

Cut abalone into shreds. Wash and drain celery hearts. Cut into thin oblique pieces. Mix all ingredients well. Chill. Serves 6.

* Abalone is a shell animal belonging to a specie of the mollusks of the genus Haliotis. Its shell is used to make mother of pearl buttons and inlaying in furniture.

10. February 9—Saturday

SPRING ROLLS (HORS D'OEUVRE)
(ALSO KNOWN AS EGG ROLLS)

Stuffing
½ C. celery, minced
1 C. cabbage, shredded
2 T. oil
½ C. cooked shrimp, diced
½ C. cooked meat, diced
½ C. water chestnuts, chopped (or canned water chestnuts)

½ C. bamboo shoots, shredded (or canned bamboo shoots)
2 small onions, minced
1 t. salt
½ t. pepper
¼ C. soy sauce

Cook celery and cabbage. Drain. Heat oil. Warm shrimp and meat. Add vegetables and seasoning. When cooked throughout turn off heat and let cool.

"SKINS" *

1 lb. wheat flour
2 T. cornstarch
1 t. salt
1 large egg

1 t. sugar
1 qt. water
½ C. oil
1 egg white

Sift together flour, cornstarch and salt. Beat in egg and sugar. Add just enough water to beat to a smooth light batter. Put in enough oil to grease a 6″ pan well. Ladle ¼ C. batter into pan. Tilt to spread batter all over. When pancake shrinks from edges, deftly turn over. Stake cooked pancakes on plate. Cool. Take one pancake at a time and place on board. Scoop up 3 T. stuffing and spread neatly into oblong mound. Fold one long side of pancake over stuffing. Next fold both short ends. Last, brush remaining long side with egg white and seal.

* Spring roll "skins" may be purchased from Chinese noodle factories.

Heat 2" oil in 10" pan. Fry rolls to a golden crispness. Drain on absorbent paper. Serve hot with mustard or Plum Sauce. Serves 6-8.

11. February 10—Sunday

ROAST DUCK

4-5 lb. duckling, dressed	*1 t. salt*
3 T. chicken stock	*½ t. pepper*
4 t. honey	*1 T. soy sauce*
4 t. sugar	*¼ C. water*

Wash duck. Mix all other ingredients in a roasting pan. Marinate duck in mixture for 1 hr., turning once. Roast in 350° oven 2 hrs., basting now and then. Serves 4 or 5 plain, or with Plum Sauce.

12. February 11—Monday

MALLARD

4 T. oil	*2 C. water chestnuts, peeled*
1 mallard, dressed	*½ lb. pork ground*
1 C. soy sauce	*1 C. barley*
Salt	*½ C. "gingko" nuts, shelled*
2 C. chestnuts, shelled and	*and skinned*
skinned	

Soak chestnuts and barley in cold water an hr.

Open back of mallard with 4" cut. If possible remove bones without tearing meat too much. Rub mallard inside and out with soy sauce. Salt evenly.

Heat oil. Put in mallard and fry 10 min. Add gin, turning mallard often. Place mallard in big bowl. Fill mallard with chestnuts, water chestnuts, "gingko" nuts, barley and juice from frying pan. Put bowl in huge steamer containing water. Cover steamer tightly. Steam 2½ hr. Serves 8.

13. February 12—Tuesday

BEEF AND CABBAGE SOUP

1 lb. flank steak, sliced thin,   *1 t. pepper*
   diagonally   *3 qt. stock*
¼ C. vegetable oil   *1 head cabbage, sliced diag-*
2 T. soy sauce   *onally*
2 t. salt   *1 onion, minced*

In a bowl, blend together oil, soy sauce, salt, and pepper. Put meat into bowl to marinate whole morning, or overnight in refrigerator.

Bring stock to a boil in big pot. Add cabbage and onion. When it starts to bubble again put in beef mixture. Cook 5 mins. Turn heat off and serve 10-12.

14. February 13—Wednesday

SCRAMBLED EGGS WITH SHARK'S FINS

2 lb. shark's fins   *2 T. soy sauce*
Water   *½ t. M.S.G.*
1 t. soda   *2 T. oil*
1-2 pt. red stewed stock   *6 eggs*
                      1 t. salt

Cover shark's fins with cold water. Boil 1 hr. Drain. Wash away any foreign objects. Cover with water again, adding soda. Boil several hrs. Drain and soak in clear warm water. Drain.

Cook stock in pot with softened fins 10 min. Add soy sauce and M.S.G. Serve soup first.

Beat eggs lightly. Heat oil. Put in drained fins. Add salt. Pour in eggs. Scramble eggs with fins over low heat. Cook till eggs set. Serve hot. Serves 4-6.

15. February 14—Thursday: "Yuan Hsiao," *
or Lantern Festival

"YUAN HSIAO" (BOILED STUFFED DUMPLINGS OR SNOWBALLS)

1 lb. glutinous rice flour   *¼ C. sesame seeds, toasted*
¼ C. walnut meat, ground   *(or caraway seeds)*
¼ C. almond meat, ground   *½ C. sugar*
        1 T. shortening

Mix nuts with seeds and shortening. Form into ½" balls.

Use large tray about 2' in diameter. Cover tray with generous layer of glutinous rice flour. Moisten nut balls by immersing in water. Place balls on tray and tilt back and forth so nut balls will snowball into a larger size. When balls are too dry to increase any more, wet thoroughly again. Repeat rolling method till all flour is used up. On the final rolling, don't re-wet snowballs till boiling time.

Slip balls into 1 qt. boiling water. Keep bubbling for 5 min. Now watch balls float to surface. Add another C. cold water. Boil several min. more. Serve four or more balls to each person with the liquid. Enough for 6-8.

* "Yuan Hsiao" is a dumpling eaten after the New Year's celebration. This festival occurs every year on the first full moon of the old Chinese calendar. That would make it the 15th Day of the 1st Month. On that day too, fancy lanterns are lit in the homes and streets, so people may see as they travel to visit the sick and the aged.

16. February 15—Friday

LOBSTER FLAKES

¼ C. oil
5-6 lb. lobster
2 C. bamboo shoots (or
    canned bamboo shoots)
2 C. water chestnuts (or
    canned water chestnuts)
2 C. celery
1 onion

2-3 slices ginger root, minced
    (or ½ t. ginger powder)
1 T. rice wine or gin
1 C. stock
1 T. cornstarch
1 t. soy sauce
¼ C. water
1 t. salt

½ t. sugar

Boil lobster until shell becomes red. (About 6 min.) Remove shell and cut up meat. Heat 2 T. oil in pan. Stir lobster with ginger and wine, or gin, in high heat for 5 min. Put in a dish.

Cut vegetables in thin strips. Heat remaining oil in pan. Stir vegetables for 3 min. Add stock. Cover. Cook 10 min. Add lobster. Blend cornstarch, water, soy sauce, salt and sugar together. Pour into lobster mixture. Stir. When juice thickens, turn off heat and serve hot. For 4-6.

17. February 16—Saturday

"EGG FU YONG"

3-4 eggs, depending on size
3 C. cooked meat, cubed
1 T. oil
½ lb. mushroms
½ C. bean sprouts (or canned
    bean sprouts, drained)

¼ lb. water chestnuts,
    chopped (or canned water
    chestnuts)
1 onion, chopped
1 stalk celery, chopped
1 t. salt

½ t. pepper

GRAVY: *1 T. cornstarch*   *1 t. soy sauce*
       1½ C. (chicken)   *1 t. salt*
          stock   *½ t. pepper*
             ¼ t. sugar

In big bowl beat eggs lightly. Add all ingredients except those for gravy. Melt oil in heated pan. Ladle one fourth egg mixture into pan and fry over low heat till golden on bottom. With spatula turn carefully and do the same for the other side. Turn into warm plate. Then repeat this process 3 times till all the mixture is used. Serve plain or with gravy. Gravy is made by blending cornstarch to (chicken) stock, soy sauce, salt, pepper and sugar. Cook over medium heat, stirring constantly. When it boils and thickens, turn off heat. Pour over omelets. Serves 4.

18. February 17—Sunday

RED STEWED CHICKEN

5-6 lb. fowl, dressed and cut   *2 T. rice wine, or sherry*
    into small pieces   *1 bunch scallions, cut into 6"*
3 C. stock, or water   *lengths*
½ C. soy sauce   *1 T. sugar*
     3 slices ginger root (or ½ t. ginger powder)

Put clean pieces of chicken into big pot. Add stock. Cover and bring to a boil. Add all ingredients except sugar. Turn to low heat and simmer for 3 hrs. Add sugar and continue cooking for 20 min. Serves 6.

19. February 18—Monday

CHINESE PORK SAUSAGES *

Outside lining of small intes- 3 T. salt
tine of pig 1 T. rice wine, or gin
1 lb. pork 3 slivers orange peels, grated
1 T. sesame oil

Wash lining of small intestine thoroughly with salt water. Let stand in hot water 10 min. Tie bottom end. Blow air from loose end. Tie. Dry in strong sunlight.

Cut pork in ¾" cubes. Add all other ingredients. Mix well. Untie one end. Use a funnel to push seasoned pork into pig lining. Tie lining every 6". Punch tiny holes into lining with needle.

Expose to bright sunshine for 1 day then air in windy place several days. Put in porcelain jar to age for 1 week. Steam for ½ hr. before serving on top of hot fried potatoes.

* These sausages called "Larp Cheong," may be purchased in Chinese groceries; however, if you want to make them yourself, it would be best to do so during the fall or winter when the air is dry.

20. February 19—Tuesday

ONION STEAK

2 T. oil 3 slices ginger, minced (or
3 large onions, cut into rings ½ t. ginger powder)
1 lb. flank steak, cut into 2 T. soy sauce
strips then into paper thin 1 t. salt
slivers diagonally ½ t. pepper

Heat oil in pan. Fry onion rings. Season with salt and pepper. Stir constantly. When rings are tender turn to high heat and add meat slivers and ginger. As the meat browns, add soy sauce. Mix well. Turn off heat and serve on hot, flaky rice. Serves 4.

21. February 20—Wednesday

RICE

½ *lb. rice*
Water

Wash rice thoroughly rubbing between the hands. Change water four times. Add enough water to cover over back palm of hand resting on top of rice. Place uncovered pot over high heat. When rice boils, turn to low heat and after water evap-orates, cover pot. Cooking time is about 20 min. Turn off heat and let stand 10 min. before uncovering pot. Stir the rice just before serving. The Chinese eat a great deal of rice, so this will only be enough for a couple of men, but if this amount is served to Americans, who eat very little rice, there will probably be enough for 4-6 people.

22. February 21—Thursday

LAMB "CHOW MEIN"

1 lb. long egg noodles   *1 C. mushrooms, sliced*
2-3 T. oil   *2 C. bean sprouts*
1½ C. lamb, cut into thin   *½ T. cornstarch*
  slices against the grain   *1 t. salt*
1 C. onion, shredded   *½ t. pepper*
1 C. celery heart, sliced   *½ t. M.S.G.*
  diagonally   *¾ C. water*

Place noodles in boiling water. Boil 8 min. Rinse with cold water. Drain.

Heat oil. Sauté lamb 1 min. Add vegetables. Cook 5 min. Blend together cornstarch, salt, pepper and M.S.G. in water. Add to pan. Stir till juice thickens. Pour over noodles. Serves 6.

23. February 22—Friday

STEAMED FISH

2 lb. butterfish	½ t. pepper
1 scallion	4 slices ginger root (or ½ t.
2 T. soy sauce	ginger powder)
1 T. rice wine, or sherry	1 clove garlic
1 t. salt	3 T. oil

Clean fish. Salt all over. Let stand 15 min. Wash. Put in bowl. Mince garlic. Distribute over fish. Chop scallion and ginger, fine. Sprinkle over fish. Season with salt, soy sauce and pepper. Add wine to fish dish. Place dish in pot and steam 15 min. Boil oil. Pour over fish. Steam another 5 min. Serve 1 fish per person with hot, boiled rice. Serves 4.

24. February 23—Saturday

EGG CUSTARD

4 extra large eggs, beaten	1 C. small shrimp, or lobster
1½ C. stock	flakes
½ t. salt	1 t. soy sauce
1 scallion, minced	1 T. oil

Mix all ingredients, except oil, in deep bowl. Put 1″ water in wide pot, then place deep bowl of batter inside. Cover pot tightly and steam 15 min. Heat oil very hot and pour over custard. Steam 5 more min. Serves 4.

25. February 24—Sunday

CHICKEN MUSHROOM SOUP

½ C. egg noodles

6 C. chicken stock

1 C. mushrooms, sliced

½ C. cooked chicken, diced

½ C. celery cabbage, cut diagonally into shreds

1 t. salt

Heat stock. Put in noodles, vegetables, chicken and salt. Cook for 10 min. Serves 6.

26. February 25—Monday

PORK AND CABBAGE

2 lb. pork chops (center pieces), cubed

1 head cabbage, shredded

1 pt. stock

½ C. soy sauce

¼ C. rice wine or sherry

½ t. salt

2-3 slices ginger root (or ½ t. ginger powder)

1½ C. mushrooms, quartered

Put bones and meat in pot with stock. Bring to a boil. Add wine, soy sauce, salt and ginger. Simmer 1¾ hrs. Add mushrooms and cabbage. Cook another ¼ hr. Serves 4-6.

27. February 26—Tuesday

CANTONESE BEEF SLIVERS

1 lb. steak, cut into thin slivers

4 t. cornstarch

¼ C. water

4 t. salt

2 egg whites

4 stalks celery, sliced thin diagonally

2 onions, shredded

oil for deep frying

2 T. fat

5 T. soy sauce

4 T. wine

2 T. sugar

½ t. pepper

½ t. M.S.G.

1 T. cornstarch

2 T. water

Mix cornstarch and egg whites. Coat beef slivers with egg-white mixture.

Melt salt in ¼ C. water.

Blend 1 T. cornstarch with 2 T. water, soy sauce, wine, sugar, pepper and M.S.G.

Heat oil in deep pan. Deep-fry beef till it is browned. Take meat out and drain.

Melt fat. Sauté celery and onion 1 min. Add meat, salt solution and cornstarch mixture. Mix thoroughly and turn off heat. Serves 4.

28. February 27—Wednesday

THIN BISCUITS
(WHEAT BISCUITS BAKED FROM UNRAISED DOUGH)

1½ C. flour
¾ C. very hot water
⅛ C. vegetable oil

Mix together flour and water. Dough will divide into a dozen pieces. Form each piece into a round flat 3″ biscuit, and moisten one side with a generous amount of oil. Form another piece in similar fashion. Put on top of first piece. Under rolling pin roll out a double 6″ biscuit. Repeat process 5 times more.

Heat griddle and cook each double biscuit a few min. each side. Stack biscuits on warm plate and cover with a clean, cloth napkin. Yields 12 biscuits.

29. February 28—Thursday

LAMB CASSEROLE *

4-5 lb. lamb breast (have *1 can green beans, about 2 C.*
butcher chop into small *1 t. salt*
pieces) *½ t. pepper*
1 can tomatoes, about 2 C. *1 clove garlic, minced*
   1 onion, quartered

Wipe meat. Season. Brown meat with garlic. Pour off excess
oil. Put meat in 3 qt. casserole. Add tomatoes and bean liquid,
then onion and cover. Put in 325° oven and bake 3¾ hrs. Add
canned beans and stir. Cook 15 min. more. Serve with sauce
on hot rice. Serves 6.

* This is my very own recipe, but I'm sure my ancestors would have come
up with a similar recipe if they had had my handy oven.

30. March 1—Friday

OYSTER SAUCE *

1 pt. raw oysters
3 T. soy sauce

Grind oysters. Add liquid. Put in pot. Bring to a boil. Turn
to low heat and simmer ½ hr. Strain. Mix in soy sauce.
Bottle. This is a good dipping sauce for chicken, eggs, or beef.

* Oyster sauce may be purchased from Chinese groceries if you haven't the
time to make it yourself. It doesn't require refrigeration.

31. March 2—Saturday

SCRAMBLED EGGS WITH OYSTER SAUCE

6 extra large eggs, beaten   *1 T. Oyster Sauce*
3 T. oil   *¼ C. cooked ham, shredded*
1 t. salt   *Parsley*
                       ½ t. pepper

In big bowl mix eggs with salt, pepper and 1 T. oil. Heat rest of oil in pan. Pour in the batter. Keep turning with spatula. When eggs are set, turn off heat and add Oyster Sauce. (It's not good to cook Oyster Sauce much.) Stir once more. Garnish with ham shreds and parsley. Serves 6.

32. March 3—Sunday

SESAME ROAST CHICKEN

5 lb. capon   *2 dashes cloves, ground*
½ C. sesame seeds   *½ t. cardamom, ground*
4 T. onion, minced   *½ t. ginger, ground*
2 cloves garlic, minced   *6 T. melted chicken fat, or*
2 t. salt   *butter*
2 dashes dried chili pepper, *3 T. water (opt.)*
ground

Mix together sesame seeds, onion, garlic, salt, chili pepper, cloves, cardamom, ginger and chicken fat. Brush onto chicken. Put in roasting pan and roast in 350° oven 2 hrs., or till capon is tender. Put in water to stop burning, if necessary. Baste and turn chicken every now and then. Serves 6-8.

33. March 4—Monday

CHINESE SAUSAGES * WITH CABBAGE

1 lb. sausages, cut diagonally   *1 t. salt*
1 head cabbage, cut into strips   *½ t. pepper*
1 T. oil   *½ C. stock*

Heat oil in pan. Put in cabbage, salt and pepper. Stir in high heat 5 min. Add sausages, then stock. Cover and cook 15 min. Serve with piping hot rice. For 4.

* Bacon may be substituted for sausages. If bacon is used, omit oil. Fry bacon 3 min. before adding cabbage, then stock. Cover. After 15 min., uncover. Stir for 2 more min. then serve.

34. March 5—Tuesday

CHINESE ROAST BEEF

5 lb. rib roast   *1 t. salt*
1 clove garlic, minced   *½ t. pepper*
3 T. soy sauce   *2 T. rice wine or sherry*
2 T. oil

GRAVY: *6 T. beef dripping*   *3 T. soy sauce*
        6 T. flour   *2 C. stock*

Mix garlic, soy sauce, wine, salt and pepper together. Spoon all over roast. Marinate in refrigerator overnight if possible. Brush on oil. Roast in 350° oven 2-2½ hrs., basting occasionally. Put all gravy ingredients into pan. Stir constantly and cook to a smooth sauce. Serve with roast. Enough for 8.

35. March 6—Wednesday

PLUM SAUCE *
(SOMETIMES CALLED DUCK SAUCE)

12 oz. plum jelly   *4 t. sugar*
6 oz. Chutney, chopped fine   *5 t. vinegar*

Blend in all ingredients evenly.

* This is a popular dipping sauce for Duck, Pork Strip, Cured Pigs' Feet, Egg Rolls, etc.

36. March 7—Thursday

RED STEWED LAMB

6 lb. lamb breast (have   *½ C. soy sauce*
butcher chop into small   *1 t. salt*
pieces)   *3 slices ginger root (or ½ t.*
1 qt. water or lamb stock   *ginger powder)*
1 big onion, cut into wedges

Brown lamb in pot. Pour off oil. Add water. Bring to a boil. Add onions, soy sauce, salt, and ginger. Simmer in low heat 4 hrs. Serves 8.

37. March 8—Friday

OYSTER SAUCE BEAN CURD

1 T. oil   *½ C. water*
1 qt. bean curd, cut into 1"   *⅛ C. soy sauce*
cubes   *1 scallion, cut in 1" lengths*
1 T. cornstarch   *¼ t. M.S.G.*
     ⅛ C. Oyster Sauce

Heat oil. Sauté bean curd gently for several min. Blend together cornstarch, soy sauce, M.S.G., and water. Add to bean curd. Cook till juice thickens. Turn off heat. Add Oyster Sauce. Mix well. Serves 4.

38. March 9—Saturday

SALT DUCK EGGS *

1 C. rock salt, or regular salt
½ gal. water
1 doz. duck eggs

Pour water in big pot. Add salt. Bring to a boil. Melt salt. Cool. Put salt water in wide-mouth gallon jug. Slip in raw duck eggs. Cover. Age 1 month. Hard-boil the eggs before serving with steaming rice.

* Duck or chicken eggs are both preserved. Some are salted, others are buried in black ashes, still others are preserved in lime. The older the preserved egg, the more it is prized as a delicacy.

39. March 10—Sunday

FRIED CHICKEN

2 chicken breasts
1 egg, slightly beaten
½ C. buttered bread crumbs
1 t. soy sauce
½ C. oil

1 C. pineapple juice
1 T. cornstarch
¼ t. curry powder (opt.)
1 T. sugar
¼ C. almonds, chopped

Remove bones by slitting the breasts. Immerse chicken meat in egg. Roll in bread crumbs. Season with soy sauce. Sauté in hot oil till brown. Drain off oil. Blend together cornstarch (curry powder), juice and sugar. Pour over chicken. Cook gently for 25 min. Garnish with almonds. Serve on buttered toast with asparagus spears. Serves 4.

40. March 11—Monday

PORK SAUSAGES ON RICE

1½ C. rice
1 qt. water
6 Chinese sausages

Wash rice several times. Add water and bring to a boil. Turn to low heat. Meanwhile, cut dried sausages into thin diagonal slices. Put on top of partly dried rice. Cover. Cook over low heat till all water has evaporated. Serve on a brisk, winter morning, with tea. Enough for several husky people.

41. March 12—Tuesday: Chinese Arbor Day *

PRESERVED KUMQUATS

1½ lb. hand picked kumquats   *½ C. preserved ginger,*
1 pt. water   *minced*
1 C. sugar   *Juice of 1 lime*

Punch each clean kumquat in four places with a large needle. Pour water, kumquats, sugar, ginger and juice, into saucepan. Simmer till liquid becomes thick and translucent. Seal into several sterilized pt. jars.

* On this day pupils go with their teachers to an empty plot. They carry young trees with them. After planting these trees they all sing a plant tree song to commemorate this occasion. It is only fitting that we favor this day using a fruit recipe of a native tree.

42. March 13—Wednesday: This, the 12th Day of the 2nd Moon, is the Queen of All Flowers' Birthday

LOTUS ROOTS

2 T. oil
½ t. salt
¼ lb. meat (pork or beef), sliced thin against the grain
1 T. soy sauce
1 t. gin

¼ lb. lotus roots, cleaned, peeled, sliced thin along the grain
¼ t. M.S.G.
¼ t. sugar
½ T. cornstarch

¼ C. water

Heat oil in skillet. Add salt. Put meat in oil to brown. Pour in soy sauce and gin. Add lotus roots. Cover. Cook 5 min. Sprinkle on M.S.G. and sugar. Blend together cornstarch and water. Add to pan. Stir until mixture is translucent. Serves 2-3.

43. March 14—Thursday

LAMB SAUSAGES

Outside lining of small intestine of pig
2 lb. lamb, cubed

2 T. rice wine, or gin
6 slivers orange peel, grated
1 t. M.S.G.

⅓ C. salt

Wash lining of small intestine well with salt dissolved in hot water. Keep in water for another hr. Fasten bottom end. Blow from other end. Tie. Dry in bright sunlight.

Mix all other ingredients thoroughly. Untie one end of pig lining. Force seasoned lamb into lining with the help of a funnel. Tie every 6". Punch holes into lining. Sun in bright sunshine 1 day. Air in windy spot several days. (Best time of year for these climatic conditions seems to be the fall and winter.) Place in china jar to age 1 week. Steam ½ hr. before serving.

44. March 15—Friday

SQUID *

2 T. oil
3 lb. squid
1 scallion, cut in 1" sections
2 slices ginger or ½ t. ginger powder
1 T. gin
2 T. fat

1 C. celery, sliced diagonally
2 C. cabbage, sliced diagonally
2 C. mushrooms, sliced
1 C. stock
1 T. cornstarch
2 T. soy sauce
2 T. water

Soak dried squid 45 min. Wash well. Pull out center bones. Remove skin and clean out insides. Cut into 1½" squares. Score the squares. Marinate squares in gin and ginger.

Melt fat in skillet. Put in celery, scallion, mushrooms, and cabbage. Mix well. Pour in stock. Cover. Cook 15 min.

In another pan heat oil till very heat. Put in squid squares. Stir constantly till squares roll up like cigarettes. Add the cooked vegetables with juice. Mix well. Blend together cornstarch, soy sauce and water. Add to pan. Stir till liquid thickens. Serves 6-8.

* Squid is dried in China.

45. March 16—Saturday

FRIED RICE

½ lb. bacon, cubed
4 C. cold cooked rice
1 onion, chopped

2 T. soy sauce
2 eggs, beaten lightly
½ t. salt
¼ t. pepper

Fry bacon, then onions and eggs, a little on both sides. Add all other ingredients. Mix well. Keep stirring several min. Serves 4.

46. March 17—Sunday: Saint Patrick's Day

GREEN PARSLEY DUCK

4½ lb. duckling, dressed   1 clove garlic, minced
1 C. soy sauce   1 T. rice wine, or gin
1 t. sugar   1½ C. chicken stock
1 pt. oil for deep frying   Parsley enough to cover dish
1 C. small button mushrooms   up to 1"
1 slice ginger root, minced or   1 C. cooked ham, cut into
   ¼ t. ginger powder   shreds

GRAVY: 2 T. cornstarch   2 t. soy sauce
           ½ C. water

Wash duck. Cut back of duck down to 4". Mix soy sauce with sugar. Rub duck inside and out with soy sauce and sugar mixture. Let duck marinate in remaining liquid while deep fat is heating.

Drain duck thoroughly. Brown duck in hot oil on each side for minutes, or until it turns a golden brown.

Place duck in a pan. Put rack inside a very wide pot. Add 2" water to pot. Then put pan with duck on top of rack. Cover duck with mushrooms, ginger, garlic, rice wine and stock. Cover pot tightly. Steam for 3 hrs. (Replenish water in bottom of pot as it evaporates.)

Take duck out and place on top of parsley dish.

Pour duck liquid into sauce pan. Blend together cornstarch, soy sauce, and water. Add to duck liquid in pan. Stir constantly in high heat till juice thickens a little. Take this gravy and pour it over the duck. Garnish with ham shreds. Serves 6-8.

47. March 18—Monday

GOLD AND SILVER SAUSAGES *

Outside lining of small intes-   *6 T. salt*
   tine of pig   *2 T. rice wine, or gin*
1 lb. pork, cubed   *6 slivers orange peel, grated*
1 lb. pork liver, cubed   *1 t. pepper*

In hot salt water, wash lining well. Let stand in salt solution. Tie bottom. Blow through opening. Tie and dry in strong sunlight. In large bowl mix all other ingredients. Undo one end of lining. Tie every 6″. Poke holes into lining with needle. Dry in hot sun 24 hrs. Air in windy place 3 days. Let age in porcelain jar 1 week. Steam 30 min. before serving.

* This should wind up the sausage making season. The air is too damp to attempt this project during the spring and in the summer there's not enough wind.

48. March 19—Tuesday

BRAISED BEEF WITH PEAS

2 lb. chuck beef, cubed   *2 T. oil*
2 pkg. frozen peas (use fresh   *1 t. salt*
   peas whenever seasonable)   *½ t. pepper*
½ C. stock   *2 t. soy sauce*

Heat oil. Brown beef. Add seasoning and stock. Cover. Simmer 1¾ hrs., adding more stock if needed. Uncover and stir in peas. Cook 10-15 min. till peas are tender. Serves 8.

49. March 20—Wednesday: Spring *

"KUM WO CHAR"
(A LICORICE TEA TO SOOTHE SORE THROATS)

1 pkg. ¼ oz. tea
1 C. boiling water

Put in brick package of tea in hot, rinsed teapot. Pour boiling water over it. Steep 15 min. Serves 1.

* We don't have any molasses and sulphur spring tonic, but we do have plenty of tonics. I shall pause here and record some tonic recipes handed down through the ages. Some of them may have more than face value but all are interesting and not hard-to-take tonics, as far as tonics go. Of course all ingredients except rhinoceros may be purchased in Chinese drugstores. It is possible to procure these ingredients through mail order.

50. March 21—Thursday

"LU JUNG"
(DEER ANTLERS FOR INCREASING WEIGHT)

IF YOU WOULD BUBBLE WITH GOOD HEALTH AND ACQUIRE A FEELing of well-being you should consider taking a course of the Chinese tonic call "Lu Jung" (pronounced loo yung). It costs about $100.00 owing to import duties and middle man's profits, but modern science recognizes the hormonic effects of the tonic which is derived from the soft core of the young antlers of a certain species closely related to the Wapiti deer of the North American continent. They are prominent in Manchuria and shed their antlers annually in the late fall or winter. New ones begin to grow in the spring. While the antlers are still soft, about six or seven in. in height, the deer are shot. The soft cores of these antlers are buried in heated, white sand for preservation. By the time the cores have dried they have shrunk to the size of walnuts. The Chinese pharmacist chops them into many portions. An order of this material carries a fancy price tag, but the fact that present day science acknowledges its hormonic effects can be checked in some very reputable pharmaceutical journals under "Deer Antler." Other scientific data on this subject can be gleaned from such sources too.

To prepare this costly tonic, one must purchase from a Chinese shop a special clay urn with two separate vessels designed solely for this purpose.

Place the chopped antler in the inner vessel. Add some water. Then seal with the outer vessel. It is very necessary to see that nothing else gets inside. Tie tightly with a string and fix urn in the center of a pot. Pour water up to three in. of the urn. Bring water to a boiling point then simmer for ten hrs. The pieces of antler will not melt entirely away in this process.

After taking this tonic one must undergo a strict diet of boiled rice and salt chicken, or pork for three weeks. Under no circumstances should one eat anything sweet or sour, during this period. Even vegetables are tabooed.

The therapeutic value of this tonic is internal. Many have testified to its absolute worth. One becomes the picture of good health and feels wonderful immediately afterwards. Some say sterile couples have been known to produce children thereafter. And thin and poor eaters have gained unprecedentedly good appetites as well as body weight.

51. March 22—Friday

TURTLE SOUP
(TONIC FOR BETTER APPETITE)

NEW YORK'S TURTLE MARKET ALWAYS DOES A LIVELY BUSINESS. The merchants who specialize in diamond back and golden coin turtles make a considerable profit. Turtles are sold in shell sizes ranging from five to seven in. in diameter. $1.25 per in. is the general price advertised in the New York Chinese newspapers.

Delicious as turtle meat is, to some Chinese the merit of

this delicacy lies not in its pleasing taste but its sole value as a tonic.

Usually three 6″ turtles are crated and sold to an average family of five or six members for $22.00. The reason why three turtles are necessary is obviously because so little of a turtle is edible.

The preparation of these turtles is complicated. To concoct this delicacy, first fill a dish pan half full of water. Heat on top of the stove. When water boils, place live turtles into bubbling water without turning off high heat. As turtles swim round and round the hot bath, they will not only slowly get cooked but their bladder content will empty out into the pan. Great care must be taken not to break the bladder since that will ruin the meat for eating.

Next slip off the outer skin of the turtles' legs.

Now invert the cooked turtles. With a very sharp kitchen knife loosen the meat from the shells in a circumferential scraping. When the shells are separated from the meat, cut off the intestines. That leaves only the feet and six other side bits of the turtles for eating. Save the shells for further boiling to obtain every last bit of meat sticking to them.

Dump the turtle meat in a huge pot with a large stewing chicken. Cover with water. Bring water to boiling point, then turn to low heat and simmer for 8 hrs. All the value is in the soup. As a tonic it is claimed this soup is reputedly as good as a shot in the arm and much more pleasant to take.

The turtle shells can be saved for souvenirs, or ash trays.

52. March 23—Saturday

"GIN SENG"
(HERB, GOOD FOR COLDS)

"GIN SENG" IS ANOTHER TONIC USED BY THE CHINESE. IT IS A perennial herb found in the Appalachian Mountains and the State of Connecticut in the U.S.A. It contains glucose. The

Chinese chop up this hard, yellowish herb and brew a tea with it whenever anyone has a cold in the family. This tea is bitter-sweet and refreshing. It gives out a faint, sweet scent. There was a superstition that since the "Gin Seng" is shaped like a man, it must give healing powers. Furthermore, this tonic became fashionable because in olden times it was used by the imperial household.

53. March 22—Sunday

"WHY SHON" SQUAB
(TO REBUILD STRENGTH OF CONVALESCENTS)

6 squabs, dressed	1 T. salt
½ C. pork, cut into slivers	1 t. pepper
¼ C. "Why Shon" (Chinese herb)	1 qt. stock

Wash squabs, pork and herbs. Put in bowl. Place a trivet in a large pot. Fill bottom of pot with an in. or two of water. Place bowl on top of rack. Add stock, salt and pepper in bowl. Cover pot. Steam about 2 hrs. over low heat.

Skim off excess oil on top of liquid. Use liquid as soup.

Remove squabs and serve with soy sauce. Enough for 6 servings.

54. March 25—Monday

RHINOCEROS
(FOR RESTORING LOST VITALITY)

MANY ORIENTALS BELIEVE EVERY PART OF THE RHINOCEROS' body to have medicinal values. Properly prepared, rhinoceros is considered a specific for restoring lost vitality.

The horn commands the highest pricetag. Ground to powder, it becomes a powerful aphrodisiac in some Chinese

minds. Rhinoceros horn cups, believed to render poison harm-
less, were for centuries used by Eastern emperors. These cups
still figure in some oriental religious ceremonies.

55. March 26—Tuesday *

ICE BOX SOUP
(FOR ANYONE NOT HUNGRY, BUT WHO MUST EAT)

½ lb. leftover *roast beef, cut*   ½ t. *pepper*
   into thin slivers   2 T. *cornstarch*
1½ qt. *stock*   1 C. *water*
2 T. *soy sauce*   3 T. *vinegar*
1 t. *salt*   2 *extra large eggs, beaten*

In a saucepan bring stock to a boil. Mix together cornstarch,
water, salt and soy sauce. Add to stock. Stir eggs into stock.
Last, add pepper, vinegar, leftover roast beef and a good wish.
Serves 6-8.

* We have had enough of tonics and after this we shall resume our regular
schedule.

56. March 27—Wednesday

SPINACH * AND VERMICELLI

10 oz. pkg. *washed spinach*   1 t. *soy sauce*
2 T. *peanut or vegetable oil*   ¼ C. *water*
1 t. *salt*   ½ lb. *Chinese vermicelli*

Wash spinach again. Put in pot with all other ingredients
except vermicelli. When it begins to boil, turn to low heat and
add vermicelli. Cover. Cook 2 min. more. Serves 4.

* The Chinese were the first to mention spinach. It was enjoyed in China
way back in 647 B.C. They cook it for a very short time (no more than 5
min.), and with hardly any liquid.

57. March 28—Thursday

LAMB SAUSAGES AND CHIPS

*1 lb. Lamb Sausages, cut
diagonally*
*2 big potatoes, peeled and cut
into strips*

1 t. salt
½ t. pepper
1 C. oil

Steam sausages in dish for ½ hr. on top of a trivet in a covered pot. Meanwhile, heat oil and deep fry potatoes till golden brown. Drain on absorbent paper and season. Line large plate with these chips then place sausages on top of them. Serves 4.

58. March 29—Friday

MUSHROOM SHRIMP

2 t. oil
1 C. mushrooms, sliced
*1 lb. shrimp, shelled and
sliced into two layers
horizontally*

1 t. salt
½ t. pepper
½ C. stock
2 T. cornstarch
2 t. soy sauce

¼ C. water

Heat oil. Sauté shrimp 5 min. Add mushrooms, salt and pepper. Pour in stock. Cover. Turn to low heat. Cook another 5 min. Blend together cornstarch, soy sauce and water. Stir till juice thickens. Serves 4.

59. March 30—Saturday

SHRIMP OMELET

2 T. fat
6 eggs, beaten
*1 lb. shrimp, shelled and
sliced into two layers
horizontally*

1 lb. pork, cut into thin shreds
1 C. onion, shredded
*½ C. celery hearts, sliced
diagonally*
1 qt. oil for deep frying

Melt fat. Fry pork over medium heat 1 min. Add shrimp and vegetables. Cover. Cook 5 min. Put in bowl of beaten eggs and mix.

Pour oil in deep pan and heat till very hot. Ladle out ¾ C. batter and slip into oil. Take out each omelet with a slit spatula as soon as it turns to a golden brown. Stack on a plate. Serves 6.

60. March 31—Sunday

CHICKEN DISH

2 T. oil
3 lb. fryer, chopped into bite-sized pieces
2 C. water chestnuts, chopped fine (or canned water chestnuts)
2 C. mushrooms, chopped fine

SAUCE: 2 T. cornstarch
2 t. soy sauce
1 t. salt

2 C. bamboo shoots, chopped fine (or canned bamboo shoots)
½ t. ginger powder
½ t. gin
1 C. stock
1 head lettuce, shredded
¼ C. ham, diced
½ t. pepper
½ t. sugar
¼ C. water

Heat oil. Put in chicken. Brown well. Add vegetables, ginger, gin and stock. Cover. Simmer 15-20 min. Blend together cornstarch, soy sauce, salt, pepper, sugar and water. Add to mixture. Stir till juice thickens. Serve on lettuce. Garnish with ham. Serves 6.

61. April 1—Monday

PORK SAUSAGES * AND GREEN BEANS

1 lb. sausages, cut diagonally　*1 T. oil*
1 lb. green beans, strung and　*1 t. salt*
*　broken into 1½" pieces*　*½ t. pepper*
½ C. stock

Wash beans.
Heat oil. Put in beans and add seasoning. Stir 5 min. Add sausages and stock. Cover pan tightly. Simmer 15 min. more. Serves 6.

* Bacon may be substituted. If bacon is used omit oil. Fry bacon till transparent, before adding beans to be fried for 5 min. Pour in stock and cover. Cook 15 min. longer.

62. April 2—Tuesday: Silkworm Maiden Day * (Thread specialist)

MEAT THREADS

1½ lb. rump steak, cut into　*2½ T. soy sauce*
*　1½" shreds or threads,*　*3 T. oil*
*　diagonally*　*1 t. salt*
1 large onion, shredded, or　*½ t. pepper*
*　large scallion cut into 1"*　*1 clove garlic, minced*
*　lengths*　*1 T. rice wine or gin*

Mix all ingredients except oil and onion. Heat oil. Fry onion or scallion and seasoned meat over high heat. Stir constantly 3-4 min. Serves 6.

* This, the 3rd Moon of the 3rd Day, is reserved for the worshipping of the Silkworm Maiden. Meat threads will be eaten on this day.

Silkworm Maiden

Long ago there was a princess named Sang Nu (Silkworm Lady) who loved her parents dearly. On the year she was 15, enemies kidnapped her father. Sang Nu became sad with grief. Her waking hours were spent in the stable with her father's favorite steed because he too seemed to be waiting patiently for the Emperor's return. Soon she refused her meals and had difficulty sleeping. Her imperial mother feared for her daughter's life. Henceforth she issued a decree stating that anyone who could bring the Emperor back alive should wed the Princess Sang Nu.

Many, many tried but to no avail. A year passed and still the missing Emperor could not be found.

Sang Nu continued to visit the stables. The noble steed was her only companion now. As she stroked the horse's mane she sobbed out her hopelessness.

"Though my mother has offered me as wife to anyone who can bring dear Papa back, no man can find him. You who have borne him so often on your strong back, can you not bring him home once more?"

To her utter surprise the steed neighed, burst out of his stable and galloped off before the grooms realized what was happening.

Two days later the horse cantered gracefully towards the palace with his majesty astride him.

Then celebration filled the empire. The wining and dining showed how very happy everyone was over the Emperor's return.

Only in the stables were there notes of discord. The heroic

horse who was responsible for his master's return neighed endlessly.

The choicest oats put before him were spurned. The Empress told the Emperor of her decree to save their child's life during his absence.

"But we cannot have our princess wed a horse," scoffed the Emperor.

In a fit of temper he shot an arrow through the whinnying steed. Then he ordered the grooms to skin the animal and dry its hide as a memento.

For some inexplicable reason as Princess Sang Nu walked near the drying hide she paused for a moment beside it. Mysteriously the hide blew up and enveloped the princess within. Together they flew into the sky and disappeared behind a cloud.

Once again sorrow filled the land. For a fortnight the royal pair gazed up at the heavens praying for a return of their beloved daughter. At last their prayers seemed to be answered. A servant reported breathlessly that the Princess had returned and was at the mulberry tree that very minute.

The royal pair ran to the mulberry tree. As they neared the scene a miracle unfolded before their eyes. The Princess stepped out of the hide and turned into a worm. Immediately it began to nibble away at the mulberry leaves.

Day after day the Emperor and Empress came to visit the fat grey worm. It seemed senseless for them to beg it to resume their daughter's form, but still they could not keep away. One morning instead of the worm just eating leaves, they saw it regurgitating a fine thread into which it wound itself. Then it was seen no more.

The Emperor and Empress were stricken with grief at the loss of their only child again. In their sorrow they prayed more than ever for comfort. As they faced heaven one day they saw their daughter with their horse among the clouds.

She rode down to them and bade them to grieve no more.

Because of her love for her parents the Jade Emperor had invited her to live in his heavenly kingdom.

"To you, my Imperial Mother, I give the task of teaching our people how to make silk," she said. "Unwind the threads which the silkworm spins. Twist them into strong strands and there you will get shining cloth."

With that she disappeared with the horse. It was said that was how the first silk came into being.

63. April 3—Wednesday

YAMS WITH SYRUP THREADS

Oil for deep frying   ¼ *C. sugar*
1 lb. yams   ¼ *C. oil*
             1 T. water

Peel and cut yams into large chunks. Fry in deep fat till golden brown.

Put oil, sugar and water in saucepan. Stir mixture over moderate heat till sugar dissolves. Cook 2 more min. till it turns yellow and forms a syrup. Add fried yams. Mix well. When yams are lifted, the syrup will form "threads." Serves 6-8.

64. April 4—Thursday: Children's Day *

SESAME SEED CANDY

2 T. oil   ¼ *C. cornstarch*
1 lb. sugar   *10 oz. water*
       ½ *C. sesame seeds*

* Today the schools will hold a children's assembly. Families are invited to come and watch a children's program of singing, dancing, and story telling. It is a day of kite flying for the children too. The boys will have their annual kite battles. Each one will try to hook his kite behind another and then draw both kites to the ground. Then the winner may claim both kites.

Heat oil. Pour in water, sugar and cornstarch. Cook until water evaporates. Line tray with sesame seeds. Pour syrup over seeds. When cool, cut into bars. Roll in sesame seed tray till candies are completely coated with seeds.

65. April 5—Friday: "Ching Ming" or Clear Bright *

SWEET BUNS

1 lb. red lentils	*2 lb. flour (4 C.)*
½ C. shortening	*Cold water*
1 C. sugar	*1 t. salt*
	2 t. baking powder

Cook lentils in water 3 hrs. Mash. Pour in water so that the lentil skins float to the surface. Remove skins. Filter lentils through several layers of cheese cloth. Dry. Cream with sugar and shortening.

Sift flour. Mix flour with enough cold water to make a thin dough. Roll dough out thin. Cut to bun size. Fill each piece of dough with dried lentils. Wrap dough around lentils to form ball. Let buns stand in double boiler 10 min. before turning on heat. Steam 45 min.

* This is a solar period at which the Chinese worship at the graves. It roughly corresponds to our Easter time about April 5th. On this day the families bring buns and rice wine to their cemeteries. Before the grave mounds they light a small fire to heat their pot of wine. When warmed, they fill the wine into tiny cups. They they pinch off bits of bun and throw them to the ancestors while pouring wine over the graves. Finally they eat the buns and drink the wine themselves.

66. April 6—Saturday

CHINESE CHEWS

½ C. butter or shortening   ½ t. salt
1 C. sugar   1 pkg. dates, chopped
2 eggs, beaten   1 C. nuts, chopped
1 C. flour   1 t. vanilla ·
1 t. baking powder   Powdered sugar

Cream butter and sugar. Add eggs. Sift flour, baking powder and salt, together twice. Blend into batter. Add dates, nuts, and vanilla extract. Pour into greased 7" x 11" pan. Bake 40 min. in 375° oven. Cut into fingers. Sprinkle with powdered sugar.

67. April 7—Sunday

QUAIL

¼ C. oil   3 slices ginger, minced or ½
4 quails, dressed and cut   t. ginger powder
   into small pieces   1 C. stock
2 C. water chestnuts,   2 T. cornstarch
   chopped   2 t. soy sauce
2 C. mushrooms, chopped   1 t. salt
2 C. bamboo shoots,   ¼ C. water
   chopped   1 head lettuce, shredded
1 t. gin   1 C. ham, diced

Heat oil. Fry quails till brown. Put in water chestnuts, mushrooms, bamboo shoots, and ginger. Mix well. Pour in stock and gin. Cover. Cook 15 min. Blend together cornstarch, soy sauce, salt and water. Then add to quail pan. Stir till juice thickens. Put mixture on top of lettuce shreds. Garnish with diced ham. Serves 6-8.

68. April 8—Monday

RED STEWED PORK CHOPS
(WITH VERMICELLI)

2-3 lb. pork loin cut in chops   *1 t. salt*
½ lb. vermicelli* (opt.)   *1 t. sugar*
1 pt. water   *3 slices ginger root or ½ t.*
2 T. rice wine, or sherry   *ginger powder*
½ C. soy sauce

Dice meat. Put meat and bones in pot with water. Bring to a boil. Add wine, soy sauce, sugar, salt and ginger. Cover. Simmer for 1 hr. Add vermicelli and cook another hr. Serves 4-6.

* Chinese vermicelli is a pea-starch noodle called "Fun Hsu." It may be purchased from Chinese groceries by mail.

69. April 9—Tuesday

CHINESE ALMOND CAKES

2½ C. butter, or shortening   *1 egg*
1 C. sugar   *½ t. almond extract*
2 C. flour   *Almonds for cake centers*

Cream butter and sugar. Add egg. Sift flour and blend into batter. Add flavoring and knead dough till very smooth. Form into small balls. Press middle with nut. Bake in 400° oven 15 min. Yields 3 dozen.

70. April 10—Wednesday

SESAME SEED COOKIES

½ C. butter
1 scant C. sugar
2 C. flour, sifted
1 t. baking powder, double
    acting
Dash of salt

1 egg, beaten
1½ T. sesame seeds, roasted
2 T. water
½ t. nutmeg
Sesame seeds, roasted, for
    sprinkling over cookies

Cream butter and sugar. Beat in egg and sesame seeds. Sift in flour with baking powder, salt, and nutmeg, alternating with water. Chill several hrs. Drop dough from teaspoon onto cookie sheet. Press to thin wafers with damp cloth covered over bottom of glass. Sprinkle with sesame seeds. Bake in 375° oven 10 min. Yields 3 dozen.

71. April 11—Thursday

LAMB HASH

2 T. oil
1 lb. lamb, ground
1 C. water chestnuts,
    chopped fine (or canned
    water chestnuts)
1 C. bamboo shoots,
    chopped fine (or canned
    bamboo shoots)

1 C. mushrooms, chopped
    fine
½ head of lettuce, shredded
1 C. cooked ham, shredded
    (opt.)
½ T. gin
¼ t. ginger powder
½ C. stock

Heat oil. Fry lamb. Add ginger mixed in gin. Put in water chestnuts, bamboo shoots and mushrooms. Mix evenly. Pour in stock. Cover. Cook 10-15 min. Spread lettuce shreds on four plates. Put lamb hash on top. Serve plain or garnish with ham shreds.

72. April 12—Friday

SHRIMP AND VEGETABLES

¼ C. oil
1½ lb. fresh shrimp
½ C. onions, sliced
1 t. salt
½ t. pepper
2 C. celery, sliced
1 C. stock

¼ C. bamboo shoots, sliced
¼ C. water chestnuts, sliced
¼ C. bean sprouts
¼ C. mushrooms, sliced
⅛ C. cornstarch
¼ C. water
⅛ C. soy sauce

1 t. sugar

Heat oil. Fry onions for 3 min. till translucent. Add shrimp and stir 8 min. Put in celery, bamboo shoots, water chestnuts, bean sprouts, and mushrooms. Pour in stock. Mix well. Cover. Cook 5-10 min. Blend together cornstarch, water, soy sauce, and sugar. Add to pan. Stir constantly till juice thickens. Serves 4-6.

73. April 13—Saturday

EGG AND SOY SAUCE

4 extra large eggs
1 onion, chopped
2 T. oil

½ t. salt
¼ t. pepper
2 T. soy sauce

Heat oil. Brown onion. Beat eggs lightly. Scramble eggs by stirring 3 min. Season with salt and pepper. Turn off heat. Add soy sauce. Mix well. Serves 4.

74. April 14—Sunday

FRIED SQUAB

6 squabs
1 C. soy sauce

1 T. garlic salt
Oil for deep frying

Clean squabs. Marinate squabs in soy sauce and garlic salt ¾ hr. Drain. Fry in deep fat till golden brown. Drain on absorbent paper. Serves 6.

75. April 15—Monday

BARBECUED MAPLE SPARERIBS

3 lb. fresh spareribs
⅓ C. maple syrup
1½ T. salt

½ t. sugar
3 T. soy sauce
1 T. rice wine, or sherry

1 clove garlic, minced

Wash ribs. Chop into 1½" pieces. Mix all ingredients. Marinate ribs overnight. Broil under medium heat for ½ hr. Turn to low heat and cook one more hr. Serves 6-8.

76. April 16—Tuesday: Today is our son's 8th birthday. He shall have his favorite dish.

SNOW PEAS' STEAK

1 lb. rump steak, cut into
strips, then cut into thin
slivers against the grain
1 lb. snow peas (or very
young peas in pods may be
used)
2 T. soy sauce

1 T. wine
4 T. oil
1 t. sugar
1 t. salt
1 T. cornstarch
½ t. pepper
2 T. stock

Marinate meat in mixture of soy sauce, wine, cornstarch, sugar, salt, pepper and stock.

String snow peas and wash. Heat 2 T. oil. Put in peas and stir constantly for 3 min.

In another pan add the other 2 T. oil. Heat. Pour in meat mixture. Brown meat by stirring constantly for 2-3 min. Add snow peas and cook together another min. Serves 4-6.

77. April 17—Wednesday

CONGEE

1 C. rice
1 qt. water
dash of soda

Wash rice as usual. Put rice in pot and add water and soda. Bring to a boil, then turn to low heat. Simmer till rice turns into a porridge. Serve 4-6 with thin biscuits, perhaps?

78. April 18—Thursday

SCALLOPED LAMB

¾ C. buttered bread crumbs
4 hard-boiled eggs, chopped fine
1½ C. cooked lamb meat, chopped
GRAVY: *2 T. cornstarch*
       2 t. soy sauce
       ½ C. water
       1½ C. lamb broth from boiling lamb bones

Sprinkle bottom of baking dish with ⅓ crumbs, half the chopped eggs, and meat. (Make gravy by blending together cornstarch, soy sauce, and water. Heat broth. Add gravy to the hot broth and stir till liquid thickens.) Now pour ½ gravy over top of meat in dish. Repeat whole process. Cover top with crumbs. Bake in 375° oven till crumbs are browned. Serves 4.

79. April 19—Friday

FISH CONGEE

1 C. rice	*½ lb. very fresh fillet of*
1 qt. water	*haddock, flaked*
Dash of soda	*1 extra large egg*
	1½ T. soy sauce

Wash rice several times. Put rice in pot with water. Boil. Turn to low heat. Simmer till a gruel forms. Stir in a beaten egg. Slip in raw fish flakes immediately. Put in ½ t. soy sauce per bowl. Stir and serve boiling, in heated bowls. Serves 4-6.

80. April 30—Saturday

EGG SAUCE SHRIMP

1 lb. shrimp, shelled and	*1 T. carrots, chopped*
washed	*1 T. onions, chopped*
2 T. oil	*1 C. stock*
1½ t. salt	*1 egg, beaten lightly*
Dash of pepper	*2 T. cornstarch*
½ lb. pork, chopped	*¼ C. water*
1 T. celery, chopped	*2 t. soy sauce*

Mix together chopped pork, celery, carrots, onions, salt and pepper. Heat oil. Put pork mixture and shrimp into oil. Brown. Pour in stock. Cover. Cook in medium heat 10 min. Turn to high heat and stir in egg. Blend together cornstarch, soy sauce and water. Add to pan. Stir till juice thickens. Serve over steaming rice. Serves 4.

81. April 21—Sunday: Easter

EASTER HAM AND DUCK

3 lb. duckling, dressed *1 pt. stock*
1 lb. ham *1 C. rice wine, or gin*

Debone duck. (Save carcass to make duck stock for future use.) Boil duck meat 15 min. Now boil ham slice 15 min. Cut duck and ham meat into small slivers. Mix both meats in bowl. Add boiling stock from duck and ham, then wine. Get steaming kettle. Put in trivet. Add 2″ water in kettle. On top of trivet place bowl of duck and ham. Cover kettle tightly. Steam 2½ hrs. Serves 6-8.

82. April 22—Monday

STEAMED MEAT CAKE

1 lb. lean pork, ground *1 t. soy sauce*
3 water chestnuts, peeled and *½ t. salt*
 chopped fine *¼ t. pepper*
½ lb. mushrooms, chopped *1 egg, beaten*
 fine

Grind pork in medium chopper. Mix with water chestnuts, egg, mushrooms, soy sauce, salt and pepper. In a round plate form mixture into a flat pie, slightly smaller than plate. Place a trivet in a steaming kettle. Add 1″ water. Place meat cake on top of trivet. Cover steamer. Steam 1½ hrs. Serves 4.

83. April 23—Tuesday

BEEF RICE

1 qt. cooked rice	*1 lb. top round beef, cut into*
3 T. oil	*strips then into slivers*
1 onion, minced	*against the grain*
1 clove garlic, mashed and	*3 T. soy sauce*
minced	*1 C. boiling water*
½ t. salt	*½ lb. mushrooms*
¼ t. pepper	*2 t. cornstarch*
	¼ C. water

Warm up rice.

Heat oil. Fry onion and garlic. Add salt and pepper. Put in beef and stir 3 min. Add mushrooms, soy sauce and hot water. Bring to a boil. Blend cornstarch and water. Add to beef mixture. When sauce thickens, pour hot mixture over warmed rice. Serves 4.

84. April 24—Wednesday

SAUTÉED DANDELION GREENS

1 lb. dandelion green	*½ t. salt*
2 T. peanut oil, or	*2 t. sugar*
vegetable oil	

Only the greens are good for cooking. Wash out all sand from dandelions. Drain. Heat oil. Put clean, dry dandelions in pot and add salt and sugar. Stir constantly for 5 min. Serves 4.

85. April 25—Thursday

MUTTON * AND MUSHROOMS

3 T. oil

1½ lb. mutton, sliced paper-
thin against the grain

1 lb. mushrooms, sliced

2 C. canned bamboo shoots,
sliced

4 slices ginger, minced or ¾
t. ginger powder

1 C. stock

1 t. salt

1 T. cornstarch

1 t. soy sauce

¼ C. water

Heat oil. Sauté mushrooms, bamboo shoots and ginger for
10 min. Add mutton. Continue to stir constantly for 5 min.
Pour in stock. Cover. Cook till only half the stock remains.
Blend together starch, soy sauce, and water. When juice
thickens, turn off heat. Serves 6.

* In China lamb and mutton are considered the same.

86. April 26—Friday

FRIED SHRIMP IN SHELL

1½ lb. fresh shrimp, washed
and drained

½ C. catsup

1 T. cornstarch

1 T. soy sauce

1 T. sugar

¼ C. water

2 t. salt

1 scallion, chopped

4 slices ginger root, minced
or ¾ t. ginger powder

½ T. rice wine, or sherry

¼ C. oil

Heat oil. Fry shrimp 5 min. in oil. Add salt, catsup, scallion,
ginger and wine. Stir another 5 min. Blend together cornstarch,
water, soy sauce, and sugar. Add to pan of shrimp. Stir till
juice thickens. Serves 6.

87. April 27—Saturday

CRAB OMELET

⅓ C. oil
2 crabs, or 7 oz. can crab meat
4 eggs, slightly beaten

1 scallion, cut into 1" pieces
1 t. salt
1 can bamboo shoots, julienned

Heat oil. Put in scallion and eggs. Stir. Add crab meat, bamboo shoots and salt. Fry together 2 more min. Serves 4.

88. April 28—Sunday

CHICKEN GIZZARDS AND HEARTS

¼ C. oil
1 lb. giblets and hearts, sliced ¼" thick
1 bunch scallions
½ lb. mushrooms
1 C. celery
1 C. cabbage
½ C. water

½ t. salt
1 T. soy sauce
1 T. gin
½ t. sugar
½ t. M.S.G.
4 drops sesame, or salad oil
1 T. cornstarch
¼ C. water
1 t. soy sauce

Heat 2 T. oil. Fry meat in heated oil. Add salt, soy sauce and gin. Stir 5 min. Place on plate and put aside. Heat rest of oil. Fry scallions, mushrooms, celery and cabbage. Stir constantly 5 min. Add water. Cover. Cook for 10 min. more. Add sugar, M.S.G. and oil. Pour in meat and mix thoroughly. Blend together cornstarch, soy sauce and water, then add to pan. When juice thickens, turn off heat. Serves 4-6.

89. April 29—Monday

STUFFED STEAMED MUSHROOMS

1 T. oil	*1 T. cornstarch*
½ lb. fresh mushrooms	*1 t. salt*
½ lb. fresh pork	*1 t. sugar*
½ lb. shrimp	*2 T. soy sauce*
4 water chestnuts, canned or fresh	

Wash and cook mushrooms. Clean shrimp. Grind shrimp, pork and water chestnuts. Put in bowl. Blend cornstarch, salt, sugar and soy sauce, then mix with ground shrimp, pork and chestnut mixture.

Remove stems from mushrooms. Fill whiskey glass with ground mixture and unmold onto mushroom caps. Place stuffed caps on dish. Get steamer. Put rack inside. Fill steamer with 2" water. Put dish on top. Cover. Steam ¾ hr. Serves 4.

90. April 30—Tuesday

OXTAIL SOUP

3 lb. oxtail, chopped into pieces	*1 t. salt*
1 qt. water	*½ t. pepper*
	2 C. tomatoes
1 onion, cut in 6 wedges	

Parboil oxtail with enough water to cover. Drain. Add fresh water and bring to a boil. Season with salt and pepper. Simmer 5 hrs. Add tomatoes and onion. Cook another ½ hr. Serves 6.

91. May 1—Wednesday: May Day *

BLOSSOM TEAS

*4 t. jasmine, chrysanthemum, orange blossom, or rose blossom
tea †*
1 qt. water

Boil water. Rinse clean teapot with hot water. Put in tea
leaves. Pour in boiling water. Infuse 5-10 min. Serves 4.

* On May Day there's dancing in the streets to welcome the return of
warm weather. Serve one of the blossom teas to visitors and remember for
Chinese tea, no cream, sugar, or lemon are used.
† Jasmine tea is a superb, semi-fermented "Foo Chow" tea. It is toasted in
alternate layers with the jasmine blossoms.
Chrysanthemum tea is the dried up petals of this flower.
Orange blossom tea is a fragrant tea blended with equally fragrant orange-
blossom buds.
Rose blossom tea is a tea blended with rose petals.

92. May 2—Thursday

BRAISED LAMB HEART

2 T. oil	*1 t. salt*
1 lb. lamb heart, sliced	*½ t. pepper*
1 clove garlic, minced	*½ t. M.S.G.*
1 T. soy sauce	*1 C. lamb stock*

Wash lamb heart thoroughly with warm water. Remove
membrane.

Heat oil. Put in garlic, onion and heart slices. Brown meat.
Add soy sauce, salt, pepper and M.S.G. then stock. Cover.
Simmer 1½-2½ hrs. Serve with gravy from pan over steamed
rice. Serves 4.

93. May 3—Friday

SHELLFISH AND SAUCE

¼ C. brown sugar
2 T. cornstarch
½ t. salt
¼ C. vinegar
1 T. soy sauce

1¼ lb. canned pineapple chunks
1 green pepper, shredded
2 onions, shredded
1 lb. cooked prawns

2-3 slices ginger, minced or ½ t. ginger powder

In sauce pan, blend together vinegar, soy sauce, ginger, syrup from pineapple, sugar, cornstarch and salt. Stir constantly till liquid thickens a bit. Add green pepper, onion, pineapple chunks and simmer 2 min. Finally put in prawns and bring mixture to a boil, stirring all the while. Serve with hot, steaming rice. Serves 4.

94. May 4—Saturday

GOLD POND LOBSTER

6 extra large eggs
3 lb. lobster
1 t. salt

1 T. cooked ham, shredded
Parsley
1 T. soy sauce

2 T. oil, heated

Cook lobster 6 min. Shell. Cut meat into shreds. Mix eggs with an equal amount of cold water. Beat well. Add salt. Pour batter into a bowl. Sprinkle lobster on top. Steam in steamer 20 min. Garnish with ham and parsley. Pour soy sauce and hot oil on top. Serves 6.

95. May 5—Sunday

PINEAPPLE DUCK

4-5 lb. duckling	1 green pepper, cut in pineapple chunk sizes
2 t. salt	
2 T. oil	2 T. cornstarch
1½ C. pineapple chunks	2 t. soy sauce
2 slices ginger or ¼ t. ginger powder	⅛ t. pepper
	6 T. pineapple juice

Wash and quarter duck. Put in pot with 2 pt. water and salt. Bring to a boil, then simmer ¾ hr. Take duck out and drain. Save stock.

Heat oil in big pan. Brown duck on both sides for about ¼ hr. Add 1½ C. stock, pineapple chunks, ginger and green pepper. Cover and cook another ¼ hr. over medium heat. Take duck out and place in warm spot. Blend together cornstarch, pepper, soy sauce and juice. Pour into pineapple mixture. Stir till juice thickens. Put duck back into pan. Cook over low heat 10 min. more. Serves 5.

96. May 6—Monday

STUFFED MUSHROOM CAPS

2 T. oil	1 T. onion, minced
24 large thoroughly washed mushroom caps, with stems removed	1 T. water chestnuts, cut fine
¾ lb. pork, ground	1 t. salt
1 t. melted fat	½ t. pepper
1 T. soy sauce	1 t. flour
	¼ C. stock

Mix pork well with all ingredients except mushrooms, oil and stock. Form into small balls and press into each mushroom cavity.

Heat oil. Place stuffed mushrooms in pan. Pour in stock. Cover pan. Simmer 20 min. Serves 4.

97. May 7—Tuesday

BEEF SOUP WITH CELERY CABBAGE

1 qt. beef stock
½ lb. flank steak, sliced thin
* diagonally*
1 C. celery cabbage,
* shredded*

1 onion, minced
2 T. oil
1 T. soy sauce
1 t. salt
½ t. pepper
4 drops salad oil

Combine oil, soy sauce, salt and pepper. Marinate beef shreds in this mixture entire morning, or overnight.

Bring stock to a boil, and add cabbage and onion. When liquid boils again, add beef mixture. After 5 min. add salad oil. Serves 6.

98. May 8—Wednesday

BEAN CURD * AND SPINACH SOUP

2 sq. bean curd, sliced ¼"
* thick*
1 lb. spinach

6 C. vegetable stock, or
* water*
2 T. salt
1 t. M.S.G.

Wash spinach well. Heat stock or water to a boil. Put in spinach and bean curd. Simmer 2 min. To clear soup, skim. Add salt and M.S.G. Stir. Serves 8.

* Bean curd may be purchased in any large Chinese community. It's called "Doe Fu" and comes in white cubes.

99. May 9—Thursday

STEWED LAMB

4 lb. lamb breast, chopped   *1 clove garlic, minced*
     into small pieces   *1 t. salt*
       1 bunch scallions, chopped up

Brown lamb. Drain off excess fat. Put lamb into big pot. Add 1½ pt. water. Bring to a boil. Add scallions, garlic and salt. Simmer 3 hrs. Serves 6.

100. May 10—Friday

CHINA TUNA

2 T. oil   *½ C. green pepper, chopped*
¼ C. onion, chopped   *1 C. stock (chicken)*
7 oz. can tuna fish   *¼ C. soy sauce*
1 C. celery, chopped   *4 oz. fine noodles*
¾ C. mushrooms   *1 T. cornstarch*
       ¼ C. water

Heat oil. Fry onion 3 min. Flake tuna and stir into pan. Add celery, mushrooms, pepper, stock and soy sauce. Cover. Simmer 15 min.

Boil noodles from 8-10 min. (Don't overcook.) Drain and season with salt.

Blend cornstarch with water. Stir into tuna mixture. When juice thickens, turn off heat and serve with noodles. Serves 4.

101. May 11—Saturday

BEAN SPROUT OMELET

2 T. oil   *2 t. soy sauce*
6 eggs, slightly beaten   *1 t. salt*
1 lb. bean sprouts   *½ t. pepper*
2 T. scallion, chopped   *6 slices toast*

Heat oil. Fry scallion 1 min. Add sprouts, soy sauce, salt and pepper. Pour eggs into frying pan. Scramble and cook over low heat until eggs are done. Serve on buttered toast with small pork sausages. Serves 6.

102. May 12—Sunday

SAUTÉED CHICKEN AND MUSHROOMS

3 T. oil	½ t. M.S.G.
1 lb. fresh boneless chicken breast, sliced into shreds	2 T. soy sauce
	1 t. salt
2 C. celery heart, sliced diagonally	½ t. pepper
	1 T. cornstarch
1 lb. mushrooms, quartered	¼ C. water

Heat oil. Sauté chicken 2 min. Add celery, mushrooms, soy sauce, salt and M.S.G. Stir a min. or two. Cover. Cook 5 min. Blend cornstarch and water together. Add to pan. Stir till juice thickens. Serves 4.

103. May 13—Monday

NOODLES WITH SOY BEAN JAM *

6 oz. pork, diced	½ C. soy bean jam, or Bovril
¼ C. scallion, diced	
3 T. peanut oil	¼ C. boiling water
1 T. sesame oil	1 lb. thin spaghetti †

1 cucumber, cut in slivers

Heat peanut and sesame oil in pan. When smoke arises, add pork and scallion. Stir till brown. Add soy bean jam or

* Soy bean jam is called "Min Seeh" in Cantonese stores. It resembles a brown bean sauce. If not available substitute with Bovril.

† Spaghetti was introduced into Italy from China by Marco Polo (c. 1254 1324) upon his return to Venice in 1295.

Bovril, then boiling water. Cook over high heat stirring constantly for 6 min. till water has evaporated and sauce is
glossy. Pour in serving dish and garnish with cucumber slivers.

Cook spaghetti 15 min. Drain. Put in warm dish.

Each one helps himself to both dishes. Serves 5.

104. May 14—Tuesday

SWEET AND PUNGENT MEAT BALLS

1 lb. round steak, ground　　*4 pineapple slices, cut into 6*
1 egg, beaten　　　　　　　*wedges each*
2 T. flour　　　　　　　　*3 T. cornstarch*
1 t. salt　　　　　　　　　*1 T. soy sauce*
½ t. pepper　　　　　　　*½ C. sugar*
½ C. oil　　　　　　　　*½ t. M.S.G.*
1 C. stock　　　　　　　*½ C. vinegar*
2 green peppers, cut into　*½ C. pineapple juice*
pieces

Form beef into 18 balls. Mix egg, flour, salt and pepper.
Heat oil. Immerse meat balls in batter, then fry balls till
brown. Take out balls. Keep in warm dish. Pour off all but
1 T. oil from pan. Add ½ C. stock, pineapple and green
peppers. Cover and cook 10 min. Blend together cornstarch,
soy sauce, sugar, M.S.G., vinegar, rest of stock and juice. Add
to pan stirring constantly. As soon as juice thickens, put balls
back into pan. Stir a few min. more. Serves 4.

105. May 15—Wednesday

SPRING ASPARAGUS SALAD

1 bunch asparagus　　　*1 T. soy sauce*
1 pt. boiling water　　　*½ t. sugar*
　　　½ T. sesame oil, or salad oil

Wash and cut away white part of asparagus. Cut edible part of asparagus diagonally. Put asparagus in boiling water. Boil 2 min. Drain. Chill in refrigerator.

Mix soy sauce, sugar and sesame oil. Marinate asparagus in this mixture till serving time. Serves 4.

106. May 16—Thursday

SPRING LAMB AND ASPARAGUS

1 bunch asparagus	1 clove garlic, minced
1 lb. tender lamb	1 C. stock
3 T. oil	1 tomato
1 t. salt	1 T. cornstarch
½ t. pepper	¼ C. water
1 onion, chopped	1 T. soy sauce

Slice asparagus diagonally. Pour boiling water over it. Let stand 2 min. Slice lamb against grain. Heat oil. Put in lamb. Add salt, pepper, onion and garlic. Stir constantly 10 min. Put in asparagus. Pour in stock and tomato wedges. Cook 2 min. Blend together cornstarch, water and soy sauce. Keep stirring. When juice thickens turn off heat. Serves 4.

107. May 17—Friday

SHRIMP SWIRLS

1 lb. fresh washed shrimp, with feelers removed, but not shells	1 bunch scallions, cut in 1" pieces
½ t. garlic salt	2 T. vinegar
½ t. pepper	2 t. sugar
2 T. stock	1 t. salt
2 or 3 slices ginger, minced or ½ t. ginger powder	2 T. oil
1 clove garlic. minced	1 t. cornstarch
	¼ C. water
	½ t. soy sauce

Put shrimp in bowl and season with pepper, garlic salt and stock. Add ginger, garlic, scallions, vinegar, sugar, and salt.

Heat oil. Fry shrimp 1 min. each side. Pour in liquid mixture. Blend together cornstarch, water and soy sauce. Add to mixture. Stir constantly till juice thickens in 2 min. Serves 4.

108. May 18—Saturday

LOBSTER "FU YONG"

6 extra large eggs, beaten   *1 lb. bean sprouts*
½ t. salt   *6½ oz. can lobster meat*
¼ t. pepper   *½ C. onions, minced*
         2 T. oil

Put eggs in large bowl. Add all other ingredients except oil and mix well. Heat ½ t. oil in skillet each time. Ladle in ½ C. egg batter and fry till eggs set. Take out and stack on a plate. Serves 6 (2 omelets per person).

109. May 19—Sunday

VENISON

¼ C. oil   *2 C. chicken meat, chopped*
2 lb. venison, sliced into   *coarsely*
   slivers   *2 t. salt*
2 C. water chestnuts,   *½ t. pepper*
   chopped coarsely   *3 slices ginger, minced*
2 C. mushrooms, chopped   *1 C. stock*
   coarsely   *1 T. gin*
2 C. bamboo shoots,   *3 pieces sugar cane, 3" long*
   chopped coarsely   *unpeeled*

Heat oil. Fry venison stirring constantly. Season with salt, pepper and ginger. Add water chestnuts, bamboo shoots, mushrooms, canes and chicken. Stir 5 min. Pour in stock and bring to a boil. Transfer contents of pan to deep bowl. Sprinkle gin on top. Put in large steamer with water inside and steam with cover on for 2 hrs. Serve with small saucers of salad oil and soy sauce. Serves 6-8.

110. May 20—Monday

PORK AND BEAN SPROUT

3 T. oil	*2 t. salt*
3 C. pork, shredded	*3 slices ginger, minced*
2 C. bean sprouts	*1 T. wine*
⅛ C. soy sauce	*1 t. sugar*

Soak meat in ginger, wine, sugar and half of soy sauce.
Heat 2. T. oil. Sauté pork 2 or 3 min. Take out and keep warm.
Heat remaining 1 T. oil. Sauté sprouts with salt and remaining soy sauce another 2 min. Put in meat again and stir 1 min. more. May be served wrapped in thin biscuits, or with hot boiled rice. Serves 6.

111. May 21—Tuesday

ASPARAGUS STEAK

¼ C. oil	*1 t. salt*
1 lb. round steak, cut into strips then sliced very thin against the grain	*½ t. pepper*
	1 onion, minced
	1 clove garlic, minced
1 lb. asparagus, sliced diagonally after discarding hard white part	*⅓ C. stock*
	1 T. cornstarch
	⅓ C. water

Heat oil. Put in beef, garlic and onion. Brown beef. Pour in stock. Add asparagus. Cover. Cook 5 min. Blend together cornstarch and water. Add to pan. Stir till juice thickens. Serves 4.

112. May 22—Wednesday

CHINESE CABBAGE *

2 T. peanut oil or vegetable   1 t. salt
oil   ½ t. pepper
1 bunch Chinese cabbage,   3 slices ginger root, minced
sliced diagonally into strips   ¼ C. water

Heat oil and put in clean cabbage. Stir constantly for 5 minutes. Add salt, pepper and ginger. Mix well. Add water and cover pan tightly. Cook over medium heat 10 min. Uncover. Stir till water is almost evaporated and vegetable is tender. Serves 6.

* Chinese cabbage is not celery cabbage. It has dark, green leaves and no trace of the bitterness present in other cabbages. However, if it is inconvenient to buy this vegetable in a Chinese grocery, use celery cabbage and don't complain about what you've been missing when you have the opportunity to discover the real McCoy.

113. May 23—Thursday

SAVORY LAMB STEW

2 T. oil   ½ C. mushrooms
2 lb. lamb breast, chopped   4 carrots, quartered
into small pieces   1 doz. small onions, quartered
1 t. soy sauce   1 stalk celery
½ t. pepper   5 potatoes, cubed
1 clove garlic   3 T. wine
2 T. flour   1 C. peas
2 T. tomato paste   1 bay leaf
1 pt. water   Few sprigs parsley

Heat 1 T. oil. Rub garlic and soy sauce into lamb. Season with pepper. Brown meat. Turn to low heat. Sprinkle with flour over lamb. Cook gently until all flour is absorbed.

Pour in water and paste. Bring to a boil. Add bay leaf. Put in 3 qt. casserole. Cover. Bake ½ hr.

Heat the other T. oil. Fry mushrooms 3 min. Take out. Add quartered carrots and onions to pan. Sprinkle sugar over to glaze vegetables. Cook long enough for vegetables to glisten.

Add mushrooms, carrots, onions and potatoes to casserole. Cover. Bake another hr. Add wine, peas, and parsley. Cook 20 min. more. Serves 8.

114. May 24—Friday

LOBSTER CANTONESE

2 T. oil	3 T. soy sauce
2 live chicken lobsters	1 t. sugar
1 t. moist baby black beans,*	1 t. salt
mashed and minced (opt.)	1 t. pepper
1 clove garlic, mashed and	1 egg, beaten
minced	1½ C. boiling stock
1 onion, minced	1 T. cornstarch
½ lb. pork, ground	¼ C. cold water

Wash lobsters. Break and crack claws. Discard heads and feelers. With cleaver, chop lobsters through shell full length, then sideways into 1″ cubes.

Heat oil. Put in baby black beans, garlic and onion. Brown. Add pork and brown. Mix soy sauce, sugar, salt, pepper and stock. Stir into pan. Add lobsters. Cover and cook about 10

* Baby black beans are called "Dow Sea" in Cantonese. They may be purchased in Chinese groceries. If it's too much bother to send for them just omit; however, they do make quite a bit of difference in the taste of the dish.

min. Blend together cornstarch and water, then add to pan. When juice thickens, turn off heat and quickly stir in egg. Serves 4.

115. May 25—Saturday

TURKEY OMELET

2 T. oil	*1 scallion, chopped*
4 extra large eggs	*1 stalk celery, sliced thin*
1½ C. cooked turkey	*diagonally*
½ lb. mushrooms	*1 t. salt*
1 C. bean sprouts	*½ t. pepper*

In large mixing bowl, beat eggs. Mix in all other ingredients except oil. Heat 6″ pan with a little oil. Ladle in ½ C. egg batter. Fry until egg sets on one side. Turn carefully and fry other side. Repeat process with remaining egg batter. Serves 4.

116. May 26—Sunday

CHINESE ROAST DUCKLING

5 lb. duckling, dressed	*2 drops sesame oil*
1 t. celery salt	*1 t. salt*
1 C. soy sauce	*1 C. hot water*

Soak duckling in hot water for 2 minutes before adding celery salt, soy sauce, sesame oil, and salt. Mix. Turn duck few times. Drain. Reserve liquid for further use. Stuff as desired. Roast in 325° oven about 2½ hrs. Baste occasionally with liquid. Serves 6.

117. May 27—Monday

ROAST PORK

2 lean pork fillets

½ C. soy sauce

3 T. sugar

⅛ C. onion, minced

2 cloves garlic, minced

4 slices ginger, minced

¾ C. sesame seeds

⅛ C. oil

Wash and dry strips of pork. Mix with soy sauce, sugar, onion, garlic, ginger and sesame seeds. Marinate pork in this liquid several hrs., turning often. Oil oven pan. Put in pork strips. Roast in 375° oven ¾ hr. Heat liquid and use as sauce for pork. Slice pork against grain to serve with hot rice. Serves 4.

118. May 28—Tuesday

BEEF AND VEGETABLES

2 T. oil

2 lb. top round steak, sliced very thin diagonally

2 C. green pepper, cut into 1" strips

1 C. celery sliced diagonally

1 C. bean sprouts

3-4 slices ginger root

½ t. gin

1 C. beef steak

1 t. flour

4 drops sesame or salad oil

1 T. cornstarch

¼ C. water

1 t. soy sauce

Mix beef with flour, sesame oil, ginger and gin. Heat 1 T. oil. Brown meat in oil. Put in warm dish. Heat rest of oil. Fry celery, sprouts, and peppers for 5 min. Pour in stock. Add beef. Cover. Cook 10 min. more. Blend together cornstarch, soy sauce and water. Add to pan. When juice thickens, turn off heat. Serves 8.

119. May 29—Wednesday *

FLOURISHING CAKES

1 lb. rice flour, called "Jim   *1 lb. sugar*
My Fun" in Cantonese   *2 T. baking powder*
stores   *1 qt. water*

Mix all ingredients. Let stand overnight. Fill greased cup-
cake tins with mixture. Place tin pan in large steamer. Carefully pour boiling water up to 1" below pan in steamer. Cover.
Steam ½ hr. in high heat. Yields 3 doz.

* May is house moving month for many people. Before this month ends,
Flourishing Cakes is a Chinese housewarming gift any friend or neighbor
can whip up for those with new addresses.

120. May 30—Thursday

SPRING LAMB IN RICE GRUEL

¼ C. rice   *1 T. salt*
1 qt. water   *dash of garlic salt*
½ C. lamb slivers, sliced very   *1 T. soy sauce*
thin against the grain

Boil rice and water for 20 min. Add seasoning, soy sauce
and meat slivers. Cook another 5 min. and serve for breakfast.
Serves 4.

121. May 31—Friday

ASPARAGUS SHRIMP

1 bunch asparagus, cut   *½ lb. mushrooms, sliced*
diagonally   *1 C. stock*
1 lb. shrimp, shelled   *1 t. salt*
1 egg   *½ t. pepper*
⅛ C. flour   *3 T. cornstarch*
⅓ C. oil   *¼ C. water*

Beat egg. Stir in flour. Soak shrimp in batter.

Heat oil. Put in shrimp. Brown 5 min. each side. Drain on absorbent paper. Remove all but ⅛ C. oil from pan. Add mushrooms, salt and pepper. Pour in stock and put in asparagus. Cover pan. Cook 5 min. Blend together cornstarch and water. Add to pan. Stir constantly till liquid thickens. Serves 4.

122. June 1—Saturday *

EGG AND WATERCRESS DIP

6 hard-boiled eggs, chopped
1 bunch watercress, washed and chopped
½ C. salad oil
3 T. vinegar
¾ t. soy sauce
¾ t. dry mustard
4 drops sesame oil
1 t. paprika
Chives
1 bunch celery hearts, cut into slender sticks
1 t. sugar

Mix together eggs and watercress. Blend together oil, vinegar, soy sauce, sugar, mustard and sesame oil. Add to mixture. Sprinkle with chives and paprika. Wash celery hearts. Either stuff celery, or use slender stalks as dippers.

* This is the month of weddings for the Chinese too. Betel-nuts are served at Chinese wedding celebrations.

The betel-nut is a fruit of the areca palm, and the leaf is the product of betel vine. This palm is native to Malaya and is cultivated in southern India, Ceylon, Thailand and the Philippine Islands. The fruit is the size of a pullet egg, and within its fibrous rind is the nut; the albumen is hard and has a mottled grey and brown look. These nuts are cultivated mainly for use as a masticatory. They are annually gathered between August and November. First they are sliced, then boiled in water and finally dried in the sun till they turn a dark brown or black color. For chewing, a small piece is wrapped up in a leaf, with a pill of shell lime, or cardamon. It has a licorice taste. Mastication causes a free flow of brick red saliva which dyes the lips, mouth and gums. Red signifies happiness to the Chinese. That is why betel-nuts are used at weddings.

123. June 2—Sunday: This, the 5th Day of the 5th Moon, is Poet's Day, or the Dragon Boat Festival *

SWEET RICE DUMPLINGS

5 lb. glutinous rice (Called "Nor My" in Cantonese)
½ C. alkaline solution
Dried bamboo leaves, soaked in water
String
Sugar

Soak glutinous rice 2 hrs. and drain. Mix with alkaline solution. Wrap 1½ C. glutinous rice in bamboo leaves. Tie well

* Poet's Day is celebrated in honor of Chu Yuan, a Chinese poet and statesman who lived 300 B.C. He was drowned in the Mi Lo River. Every year on the 5th Day of the 5th Moon the Dragon Boat Festival is held in his honor. Huge canoes shaped like dragons with as many as eighty paddlers search for his body. Rice dumplings are scattered on the water to appease his spirit.

Boat races are held in the afternoon. The dragon boats that enter these races are long, narrow, with curved ends carved into dragon shapes. Thirty strong men sit behind the oars. The head boatman saddles himself on the neck of the dragon. He waves the flag to direct the men which way to paddle. The winning boat gets the prize tied to a tall bamboo pole. This prize is usually a bolt of fine silk.

Tea and rice dumplings are served at the races. However, one must not forget in the heat of the races why rice dumplings are the traditional food on this day.

Long ago there lived a poet named Chu Yuan. He earned his living as an important official of the state. All went well under his administration till his Emperor fell in with evil men. They weaned him away from the "straight and narrow" path with flatteries and filled him with lies about the faithful Chu Yuan. The Emperor began to go soft. To obtain every comfort he began to spend lavishly. His people were taxed to the hilt. Discontent spread like fire. Chu Yuan pleaded with the Emperor to stop bleeding the angry people. The Emperor had already sunk beyond repentance. Chu Yuan became depressed. He thought the Emperor would not reform because his wicked friends had poisoned the Emperor's mind to such an extent that anything Chu Yuan asked, the Emperor would never grant. "Perhaps the Emperor would come to his senses if I were not around," thought Chu Yuan. With that thought he flung himself into the river.

The people grieved over this sad news. A searching party immediately set out to find him. They dragged the river without success. To appease his spirit they threw food into the river so he wouldn't be hungry. They were going to dump more in the next morning when one of his colleagues said, "Stop! Chu Yuan appeared in my dreams last night. He said he could not get the food

with string. Put in huge pot. Cover with water. Bring to a boil. Simmer 4 hrs. Replenish water if necessary. Cool. Unwrap dumpling and cut into pieces before serving. Coat dumpling generously with sugar before eating. Yields 1 doz. dumplings.

---

we threw in the river because the fish got it first. Why don't we wrap it in palm leaves to keep it dry and intact?"

To this day the Chinese always eat rice dumplings wrapped in green leaves all tied up on the 5th Day of the 5th Moon in memory of the good Chu Yuan.

124. June 3—Monday

SALTY RICE DUMPLING

5 lb. long grain rice, soaked 2 hrs.
1 lb. cooked pork, shredded
1 lb. cooked ham, shredded
1 C. walnut meat, chopped coarsely
1 C. peanut meat
Dried bamboo leaves, soaked in water to soften
String

Mix rice, pork, ham, and nuts. Scoop up 1½ C. rice mixture and wrap in bamboo leaves. Tie. Put in huge pot. Cover with cold water. Bring to a boil. Simmer 4 hrs. Cool. Unwrap dumplings before serving. Yields 12-14 large dumplings.

125. June 4—Tuesday

MUSHROOM STEAK

1 lb. round steak, cut into strips then sliced very thin against the grain
1 lb. mushrooms, sliced
2 T. oil
1 t. salt
½ t. pepper
1 onion, minced
1 clove garlic, minced
½ C. stock
2 T. cornstarch
2 t. soy sauce
¼ C. water

Heat oil. Add beef. Season with salt and pepper. Add onion and garlic. Stir until meat is brown. Put in mushrooms and stock. Cover. Cook 10 min. Blend together cornstarch, soy sauce and water. Add to pan. When juice thickens turn off heat and serve with rice. Serves 4.

126. June 5—Wednesday

CORN (FLOWER) SOUP

2 C. canned corn, cream style   1 T. salt
1 qt. water, or vegetable stock   ½ t. pepper
1 egg, beaten (opt.)   2 T. scallion, chopped
½ t. M.S.G.

Bring stock to a boil. Add corn (stir in egg). Season with salt, pepper and M.S.G. Turn to low heat. Sprinkle scallion on top. Simmer 4-5 min. Serves 4.

127. June 6—Thursday

INSTANT BOILED MUTTON
(A FAMOUS PEKING MEAL)

5 lb. tenderloin lamb, sliced paper thin against the grain
½ lb. salted cabbage, or drained sauerkraut
1½ qt. boiling stock
1 T. salt
2 lb. celery cabbage
1 lb. egg noodles, boiled 10 min. and drained
½ lb. vermicelli, boiled
Mix and divide this sauce into 10 bowls: 1 C. soy sauce
½ C. vinegar
1 C. onion, minced
1 C. wine
1 C. peanut butter

Put stock in huge chafing pot over electric hot plate. Salt. Put in salted cabbage or sauerkraut. Add 2 or 3 slices of fat lamb shreds. Put in celery cabbage. Keep broth simmering. Each guest takes several slices of lamb between a pair of chopsticks. Hold in broth. (Count 10 mentally.) Take out, then plunge into piquant sauce to cool and flavor, before eating.

The cooked egg noodles and vermicelli are put in the soup at the end of the self-cooked meal. With the lost pieces of lamb in the pot, the soup gets better than ever. To finish up the delightful meal, the host ladles a scant cupful of noodle soup into the 10 sauce bowls for 10 satisfied people.

128. June 7—Friday

SAUTÉED SWORDFISH

2 T. oil
2 lb. fresh swordfish, cut into 4 pieces
2 T. soy sauce
3 slices ginger, mashed and minced

1 clove garlic, mashed and minced
1 t. salt
½ t. pepper
½ t. sugar
1 scallion, chopped

Wash swordfish. Drain. Salt both sides and let stand 15 min. Wipe off salt. Heat oil. Put in swordfish. Sprinkle with ginger, garlic, salt, pepper, sugar and soy sauce. Sauté gently 10 min. each side. Add scallion and cook another min. Serves 4.

129. June 8—Saturday

STUFFED EGGS

6 eggs
1 can 6½ oz. crab meat, flaked fine

⅛ C. ham, chopped fine
2 scallions, chopped fine
2 T. sesame oil

1 C. soy sauce

Mix together crab, ham, chicken and scallions.

Oil 6 egg cups. Break eggs into cups, putting whites in first. Finally let the yolks float on top. Steam eggs 5-10 min.

Scoop out yolks carefully and save, to make Egg Relish Salad. Fill egg cavities with meat mixture and scallions. Steam 20 min. Serve with sesame oil and soy sauce. Serves 6.

130. June 9—Sunday

CANTONESE FRIED CHICKEN

1 qt. oil for deep frying	*½ C. stock*
3 lb. fryer, cut up	*3 slices ginger, minced*
2 T. chicken fat	*2 T. scallion, chopped*
2 T. soy sauce	*¼ C. wine*

Clean chicken. Rub fat and soy sauce onto chicken. Heat oil. Fry chicken till golden. Pour off oil and reserve for future use. Add stock, wine, ginger and scallion to chicken. Cover. Cook ½ hr. turning occasionally. Serve with hot, boiled rice. Serves 4.

131. June 10—Monday

WATERCRESS SOUP

2 C. pork, diced	*2 T. onion, chopped*
1 qt. pork stock	*½ C. celery, cut diagonally*
2 t. salt	*2 C. watercress*

Put meat in with stock. Bring to a boil. Add salt, onion, and celery. Simmer 20 min. Add watercress. Stir. When it boils again, turn off heat. Serves 6.

132. June 11—Tuesday

VEAL AND VEGETABLES

2 T. oil
1 lb. veal, cut thin against
    the grain
1 t. salt
½ t. pepper
1 C. onion, minced

1 C. celery, sliced
    diagonally
2 C. mushrooms, sliced
½ C. stock
2 T. cornstarch
2 t. soy sauce

¼ C. water

Heat oil. Put in onion and veal to brown. Season with salt
and pepper. Add celery, mushrooms and stock. Cover skillet.
Cook over low heat 10 min. Blend together cornstarch, soy
sauce and water. Add to skillet. When juice thickens turn off
heat. Serves 4.

133. June 12—Wednesday

SAUTÉED BEAN SPROUTS

1 lb. fresh bean sprouts
1 T. vegetable oil

1 T. soy sauce
¼ t. salt

⅛ t. pepper

Wash bean sprouts. Drain. Heat oil. Fry sprouts for a few
min., then add soy sauce, salt and pepper. Cover. Simmer 5
min. Stir another min. or two. Serves 4.

134. June 13—Thursday

LAMB ASPIC RING

4 lb. leg of lamb
1 scallion, chopped

½ C. soy sauce
1 t. salt

3 C. water

Cut lamb into small pieces. Put in pot. Pour in water. Boil. Add scallion, soy sauce and salt. Simmer several hrs. Cool. Remove all bones. Put lamb meat in cake ring which has been rinsed in cold water. Pour liquid mixture to brim. Place in refrigerator overnight. Next day, when liquid has jellied, carefully scrape off the top layer of fat. Unmold over platter of lettuce, by inverting ring and placing hot dish cloth over it. Lunch or supper is awaiting 8 lucky people.

135. June 14—Friday

COCKTAIL CRABMEAT SPREAD

6½ oz. can crabmeat
½ C. cottage cheese
2 t. chives, chopped
6 olives, chopped
1 t. horse-radish

1 t. soy sauce
1 clove garlic, minced
3 T. chili sauce
2 large cucumbers, peeled
    and cut into discs

Discard unedible membrane from crabmeat. Flake. Mix thoroughly with cottage cheese, chives, olives, horse-radish, soy sauce, garlic and chili sauce. Yields 1½ C. Chill. Spread on cucumber rings.

136. June 15—Saturday *

TEA EGGS

1 doz. eggs, hard-boiled
1½ pt. boiling water
1 t. aniseed
4 T. soy sauce

5 T. inexpensive tea leaves
    (plain orange pekoe will
    do)
2 T. salt

* The picnic season is upon us. Tea Eggs is a good recipe for picnics, or even breakfasts.

Shell eggs carefully. Pour boiling water over aniseed, soy sauce, tea, and salt. Put eggs in this mixture. Simmer 90 min. Serves 6.

137. June 16—Sunday

SESAME CHICKEN

2 lb. Spring chicken breast	¼ C. wine
1½ pt. boiling water	¼ C. sesame oil
1 scallion, minced	2 t. sugar
2 slices ginger, minced	2 smidgens (pinches) salt
1 t. pepper	1 scant t. vinegar

⅔ C. soy sauce

Cover chicken with boiling water and boil for ¼ hr. Chop chicken against the grain, through bones into ¾″ strips. Divide chicken on 4 plates. Sprinkle on ginger and scallion. Blend together wine, sesame oil, sugar, salt, vinegar and soy sauce, then pour over chicken. Season with pepper. Serves 4.

138. June 17—Monday

PIGGIES IN BLANKET

1 can water chestnuts, or use fresh ones if available
½ lb. bacon
Colored toothpicks

Cut bacon strips into thirds. Wrap around water chestnuts. Fasten with picks. Fry till bacon becomes crisp. An interesting, hot hors d'oeuvre for cocktail guests, n'est-ce pas?

139. June 18—Tuesday

CUCUMBER BEEF LIVER

1 lb. beef liver, sliced	*⅛ C. fat*
2 t. cornstarch	*5 cucumbers, quartered and*
1 t. salt	*sliced in rings*
½ t. pepper	*1 t. soy sauce*
¼ C. oil	*½ C. stock*
Parsley	

Put liver, cornstarch, salt, pepper and oil in mixing bowl. Mix well.

Heat fat till it melts. Put in liver mixture. Brown evenly. Add cucumbers, soy sauce, and stock. Cover. Cook at medium heat till cucumbers are tender (about 5 min). Garnish with parsley. Serves 4.

140. June 19—Wednesday

TEA PEAS *

½ lb. dried peas	*6 T. sugar*
5½ C. water	*2 T. cornstarch*

Soak peas in warm water overnight. Using water, peas were soaked in, boil peas for 2½ hrs., or till tender. Press through sieve with remaining liquid. Add sugar and cornstarch. Mix thoroughly. Return to burner and boil ¼ hr., stirring constantly. The mixture will be gummy when it's done. Pour into pan up to 1" deep. Chill. Cut into 1" cubes. Place on a plate, speared with colored picks.

* These are served at afternoon teas outdoors.

141. June 20—Thursday

LAMB STEAK

1 lb. tender lamb	*½ t. salt*
1 T. soy sauce	*1 small onion, chopped*
2 t. wine	*2 T. oil*

Slice lamb paper-thin against the grain. (Remember, to slice meat as thin as possible, have meat partly frozen before cutting.) Marinate meat in soy sauce, wine, salt, and onion 40 min. Drain.

Heat oil till hot. Put in seasoned meat. Stir 2 min. Serves 4.

142. June 21—Friday

GOLDEN BATS
(STUFFED FROGS' LEGS)

2 lb. frog legs, cleaned and chilled	*¼ C. flour*
	1 t. salt
1 C. turkey drumstick, cut into matchsticks	*½ t. pepper*
	½ t. M.S.G.
1 egg, beaten	*oil for deep frying*
Oyster Sauce	

Mix egg with flour, salt, pepper and M.S.G. Pull out bones from legs and replace with turkey matchsticks. Dip legs in egg batter.

Fry eggs into golden bats. Drain on absorbent paper. Serve with Oyster Sauce. Serves 6.

143. June 22—Saturday

DE LUXE EGG CUSTARD

3 extra large eggs	2 onions, minced
1 t. salt	2 cabbage leaves, shredded
1 C. water	½ C. stock
4 mushrooms, sliced	¼ t. salt
1 can bamboo shoots, sliced	1 t. soy sauce
¼ C. ham slivers, cooked	2 T. oil

Beat eggs in bowl. Mix with water and salt. Put bowl in large pot with water inside. Steam for 20 min. or till done.

Heat oil. Sauté onions, shoots, ham and mushrooms for 1 min. Add cabbage, soy sauce and salt. Stir another min. Pour vegetable mixture on top of egg custard. Serves 4.

144. June 23—Sunday

STEAMED CHICKEN

3½ lb. broiler, chopped into 1" cubes	4 mushrooms, chopped coarsely
2 T. soy sauce	2 Chinese dates,* chopped coarsely (opt.)
2 slices ginger, minced	
2 scallions, cut into ½" dices	1 T. cornstarch
1½ T. oil	

Put chicken, soy sauce, ginger, scallion, oil, mushrooms and dates in a big bowl. Blend in cornstarch last. Get a large pot and put a trivet or rack in it. Pour in 2" boiling water. Now put bowl on rack. Cover. Steam over moderate heat 40 min. Serves 6-8.

* Chinese dates are very expensive in Chinese groceries and California dates are too sweet for this dish, so omit if you wish.

145. June 24—Monday: Torch Festival

PORK IN LETTUCE
(HORS D'OEUVRE)

1 clove garlic, minced
2 T. oil
1 lb. lean pork, ground
½ C. peas, cooked
1 t. salt
¼ C. water
2 T. rice wine, or sherry

1 head lettuce
⅛ C. almonds, fried and ground
¼ C. water
1 T. cornstarch
2 t. soy sauce
1 t. sugar

Heat oil. Brown garlic then discard. Put in pork. Add water, salt, and wine. Cook meat well. Add peas. Blend together cornstarch, water, soy sauce, and sugar. Put into pan. Stir till juice is translucent. Empty into plate. Sprinkle with almonds. Place it next to a plate of drained lettuce leaves. Guests are supposed to scoop meat with a spoon into lettuce, then roll up leaf neatly and eat with fingers.

The Torch Festival of the Yunanese

LONG, LONG AGO IN THE TANG DYNASTY (618-909 A.D.) A CHIEF-tain in the Tali region of Yunan (south west China) coveted the beautiful bride of a neighboring prince. He invited the Prince to a feast and poisoned him. Thereupon the Chieftain set out to win the Princess. The Princess, realizing the treach-ery of the Chieftain, resolved on revenge. When the Tyrant proposed marriage, she stalled for time and said that a year must pass after her husband's death before she could remarry in good taste. She also made the condition that he must build her a wooden tower in which to hold the wedding cere-mony. The wedding date was set at June 24, the first anni-versary of the Prince's death. On that evening, she awaited the eager groom at the top of the nuptial tower. When he arrived, she locked herself in with him and ordered her ladies-in-waiting to set the tower in flames with their torches. Those two perished in the blazing fire.

This fidelity-festival is celebrated by many of the Yunan people. It is also a favorite wedding day.

146. June 25—Tuesday

MEATBALLS

1½ lb. hamburger meat	1 egg, beaten
1 onion, minced	1 t. salt
¾ C. oatmeal	½ t. pepper
½ C. milk	1 C. beef stock

2 T. oil

GRAVY: ¼ C. vinegar   2 T. brown sugar
         ¾ C. catsup   ⅛ C. soy sauce

Mix all ingredients except oil and stock. Form into 1″ meatballs. Heat oil. Brown balls all over. Add stock. Cover. Simmer 1 hour.

Blend together vinegar, catsup, brown sugar and soy sauce. Pour over meatballs. Serve with hot, boiled rice. Serves 6.

147. June 26—Wednesday

PEAS IN RICE

1 C. rice washed
½ lb. peas, shelled

Put rice in pot and add enough water to cover back palm of hand resting on rice. Put in clean peas. Mix. Bring mixture to a boil. Turn down heat. Cover. Simmer 20 min. till all water has evaporated. Let stand 10 min. after heat is turned off. (This dish goes well with any sautéed meat dish.) Serves 4-6.

148. June 27—Thursday

STEAMED MUTTON

2 lb. mutton, cut into small   ½ C. stock
   pieces   2 C. mushrooms
½ C. soy sauce   2 C. chestnuts, shelled and
½ t. sugar   peeled
1 t. salt   3 Chinese dates (opt.)
              1 C. gin

Parboil mutton 10 min. Marinate mutton in mixture of soy sauce, sugar and salt. Put in bowl. Add stock, mushrooms, chestnuts, dates and gin. Put in pot filled with 2″ hot water around a trivet. Cover tightly. Steam 1 hr., or till meat is tender. Skim fat from liquid. Serves 8.

149. June 28—Friday

LETTUCE SHRIMP

¼ C. oil

1 lb. shrimp, shelled, cleaned, and sliced horizontally

1 head lettuce, sliced into strips

½ t. salt

¼ t. pepper

½ C. stock

2 T. cornstarch

¼ C. water

2 t. soy sauce

Heat oil. Put in shrimp. When shrimps are pink add lettuce. Pour in stock. Stir 5 min. Blend together cornstarch, soy sauce, and water. Stir till juice thickens. Serves 4.

150. June 29—Saturday

YELLOW FLOW

2 dried mushrooms, soaked

2 T. dried shrimp, soaked

2 T. bamboo shoots, chopped

2 T. ham, chopped

2 water chestnuts, chopped

6 eggs, beaten

2 T. cornstarch

1 C. water

1 t. salt

2 t. wine

½ C. oil

Mix all ingredients except oil.

Heat oil very hot. Pour in batter. Stir till eggs form into a smooth pudding. Serves 4.

151. June 30—Sunday

CHICKEN SALAD

2 C. cooked chicken (white meat), sliced into slivers
1 bunch celery hearts, sliced diagonally
1 clove garlic, minced
1 T. soy sauce
1 t. salt
½ t. pepper
1 T. sesame, or olive oil
1 t. vinegar

Mix all ingredients. Chill. Serves 6 with steaming rice.

152. July 1—Monday

SAUTÉED SPARERIBS

4 lb. spareribs, chopped into 1½" lengths
¼ C. oil
1 egg, beaten
1 t. soy sauce
1 t. salt
2 t. cornstarch
2 t. sugar
1 C. gin
2 C. water
1 C. vinegar

Mix well the spareribs, egg, soy sauce, salt, 1 t. cornstarch, and 1 t. sugar. Heat oil and fry spareribs till brown. Add vinegar, gin, 1 t. cornstarch, 1 t. sugar and water. Cook until water has almost evaporated. Serves 6.

153. July 2—Tuesday

SHANGHAI SALAD

1 lb. cooked veal, diced
2 C. bean sprouts
½ C. sweet pickles, julienned
¼ C. onion, shredded
¾ C. mayonnaise
¼ C. French dressing
1 t. soy sauce
1 t. salt
½ t. pepper
¼ t. M.S.G.

Mix soy sauce and French dressing. Soak veal in this mixture and leave it for one morning, or overnight in refrigerator. Add bean sprouts, pickles, onions, salt and pepper. Blend mayonnaise in gently. Serve on garden-green lettuce. Serves 4.

154. July 3—Wednesday

GARDEN PEAS

1 lb. garden peas, shelled	*1 C. hot water*
3 T. vegetable oil	*2 T. cornstarch*
3 scallions, chopped fine	*1 T. soy sauce*
8 water chestnuts, sliced	*⅓ C. cold water*
	¼ t. M.S.G.

Heat oil. Add scallions. Stir 2 min. Add peas and water chestnuts. Pour in hot water. Cover. Cook until peas are tender in about 4-5 min. Blend together cornstarch, cold water, soy sauce and M.S.G. Add to pan. Stir until juice thickens. Turn off heat. Serves 6.

155. July 4—Thursday: Because we Chinese are American citizens, we celebrate with a picnic too.

CRAB PICNIC

6 doz. dark green crabs	*12 slices ginger, minced*
water	*1 qt. rice wine*
salt	*3 qt. boiling water*
2 C. Chekiang vinegar	*12 T. brown sugar*
	1 T. ginger powder

Wash live crabs in cold running water to remove all sand. Plunge crabs into huge tank ¾ full of boiling, salted water. Steam 20-25 min. till shells turn a firecracker red. Serve with Chekiang vinegar, ginger and wine. Finish with hot drink of brown sugar and ginger powder. Serves 12.

At crab picnics each guest has a saucer of Chekiang vinegar, mixed with minced ginger for dipping crab meat. (Make your own Chekiang vinegar by mixing 1 C. soy sauce to ½ C. vinegar and adding 1 t. sugar.) Each guest is served ½ dozen steamed crabs complete with crackers and pics. Rice wine is a must for each adult at these picnics. (The Chinese like contrasts. Seafoods are considered cold foods, so they must be followed by a hot drink.) End picnic by serving a hot drink to each person. Make hot drink by dissolving 1 T. brown sugar and ¼ t. ginger powder to 1 C. boiling water per person.

156. July 5—Friday

STRING BEAN SCALLOPS

¼ C. oil	½ t. pepper
1 lb. green beans, cooked to garden-green only	1 C. stock
	1 lb. tomatoes, quartered
1 lb. scallops	2 T. cornstarch
Flour	2 t. soy sauce
1 t. salt	¼ C. water

Heat oil. Roll scallops in flour and put into pan. Season with salt and pepper. Brown evenly. Pour in stock. Add string beans and tomatoes. Cook 2 min. Blend together cornstarch, soy sauce and water. Add to pan. Stir till liquid thickens. Serves 4.

157. July 6—Saturday

SCRAMBLED EGGS WITH SCALLIONS

2 T. oil	1 t. soy sauce
6 eggs, beaten lightly	1 t. salt
1 bunch scallions, chopped fine	½ t. pepper

Heat oil. Put in scallions and eggs. Season with salt, pepper and soy sauce. Scramble eggs over low heat till eggs set. Serve piping hot for 4.

158. July 7—Sunday

CHICKEN PEAS

¼ C. oil	1 onion, minced
½ lb. cooked chicken,	1 t. salt
shredded	½ t. pepper
1 lb. fresh peas, shelled	1 C. stock
1 C. celery, cut diagonally	2 T. cornstarch
½ C. mushrooms, sliced	¼ C. water
2 t. soy sauce	

Heat oil in pan and brown onion. Add chicken, salt, and pepper. Put in peas, celery, and mushrooms. Mix well. Add stock. Cover. Simmer 15 min. Blend together cornstarch, soy sauce and water. Add to mixture. Stir till juice thickens. Serves 4.

159. July 8—Monday

PORK SALAD

2½ lb. fresh shoulder	2 t. salt
2½ lb. string beans, strung	½ C. mustard
and broken into 2″ pieces	1 C. vinegar
Parsley	

Put pork in pot. Add water. Simmer 2 hrs. Cool. Cut into thin slices against the grain. Mix with half the salt, half the vinegar and all the mustard.

Boil string beans 10-15 min. till tender. Drain if necessary. Add rest of salt and vinegar. Let beans marinate for 2 hrs.

Put beans on plate. Place pork on top. Garnish with parsley. Serves 6.

160. July 9—Tuesday

STRING BEAN STEAK

1 lb. flank steak	1/4 C. oil
1 lb. string beans	1 t. sugar
1/2 C. stock	1 t. salt
2 T. soy sauce	1/2 t. pepper
1 T. rice wine, or sherry	1 T. cornstarch
2 T. water	

Slice flank steak into strips. Cut into paper-thin slivers against the grain. Mix meat with soy sauce, wine, cornstarch, sugar, salt, pepper, and water. Put aside.

String the beans. Break into 1½" pieces. Heat 2 T. oil in skillet and put in clean beans. Stir for a few min. Add ½ C. stock. Cover. Cook 10 min. till garden-green.

In another pan, heat remaining oil. Put in meat mixture. Stir constantly for a few min. Add beans and stir together for another min. Serves 6.

161. July 10—Wednesday

PICKLES
(VEGETABLES)

1 lb. garden fresh vegetables	4 chili peppers
(turnips, carrots, cabbage,	1" ginger root
string beans, and celery, or	1/3 C. salt
a combination of them)	2 t. brandy (opt.)
1 qt. boiling water	Sterilized jar

Wash vegetables thoroughly. Put in colander and pour boiling water through them. Dry well. With a sterilized knife, cut vegetables in strips then in ½" dices. Bottle them in a sterilized jar with whole peppers and a piece of ginger. Salt and seal. Let stand at room temperature for several days before serving. In the summer, the brandy will keep the vegetables from spoiling. After unsealing, keep jar in ice box. When serving, always use clean spoon to dish vegetables out from the jar. Liquid may be kept for the next pickling operation, only add peppers and salt for any additional use.

162. July 11—Thursday

FRIED MUTTON

3 lb. lamb	*1 t. salt*
¼ t. M.S.G.	*½ C. soy sauce*
2 cloves garlic, minced	*½ t. celery salt*
	Oil for deep frying

In pot put lamb, M.S.G., garlic and salt. Cover with water then cover pot. Cook 1 hr. Take out lamb. Marinate in soy sauce and salt. Heat oil and fry lamb till brittle. Chop lamb into small pieces. Serves 6.

163. July 12—Friday

TUNA SALAD

7 oz. can tuna	*1 C. celery*
1½ C. scallion, chopped fine	*2 C. bean sprouts*
½ C. green pepper, cut into	*1 t. salt*
small pieces	*½ t. pepper*
	¾ C. mayonnaise

Scald the tuna. When it is cooled, break into small pieces. Toss together and mix all ingredients gently. Serve on lettuce. Serves 4.

164. July 13—Saturday

ELEGANT EGGS

1 doz. eggs	*2 T. fat*
1 t. oil	*½ C. cooked ham slivers*
1 T. salt	*Parsley*

Pour oil and salt into bowl. Break eggs in it and beat well. Melt fat in skillet and turn to medium heat. Pour eggs in skillet and keep turning with spatula. When eggs set, garnish with ham and parsley. Serves 6.

165. July 14—Sunday

CATHAYAN SALAD

1½ lb. cooked chicken, shredded	*1 t. salt*
2 C. bean sprouts	*½ t. pepper*
2 C. celery, sliced diagonally	*¼ C. French dressing*
	1 C. mayonnaise
	½ C. water chestnuts, sliced

½ C. green pepper, cut into shreds

Place all ingredients in a bowl except water chestnuts. Mix well. Serve on lettuce, garnish with water chestnuts. Serves 6.

166. July 15—Monday

PORK SAUTÉED WITH WATERCRESS

1 lb. pork shoulder, sliced-thin against the grain	*1 clove garlic, minced*
3-4 bunches watercress	*3 T. soy sauce*
	¼ C. oil

Wash all sand from watercress. Dry. Heat oil. Fry pork and garlic. When pork is brown, add watercress and soy sauce. Bring to a boil. Cover and cook 2 min. more. Serves 6.

167. July 16—Tuesday

SPINACH STEAK

¼ C. oil
3 C. round steak, cut in slivers
against the grain
1 lb. spinach, cut into large
pieces
1 clove garlic, minced

1 C. onion, shredded
1 T. cornstarch
2 T. soy sauce
1 t. salt
½ t. M.S.G.
¼ C. water

Heat oil. Sauté beef for 1 min. Add garlic and onion. Put in spinach. Cook 2 min. Blend together cornstarch, soy sauce, salt, M.S.G. and water. Add. Stir several min. till juice thickens. Serves 6.

168. July 17—Wednesday

JELLY DESSERT
(EATEN ONLY IN THE SUMMERTIME)

½ lb. agar-agar *
2 t. alkaline solution

½ C. glutinous rice flour
water

Sugar

Boil agar-agar weeds with alkaline solution for 2 hrs. Strain. Save juice. Moisten glutinous rice flour with water. Gradually stir in agar-agar juice. Put in refrigerator. When it solidifies, serve with sugar.

* Agar-agar is a gelatin-like product of red seaweed made from Gelidium and other agar bearing plants. It is sold in Chinese stores. The name of the Jelly Dessert is called "Leong Fun."

169. July 18—Thursday

LAMB AND GREEN BEANS

1 lb. lamb, cut into thin slivers	½ t. pepper
	1 C. stock
1 lb. green beans, julienned	1 T. cornstarch
3 T. oil	1 t. soy sauce
1 t. salt	⅓ C. water

Cook beans 5 min. till garden-green.

Heat oil. Brown meat. Add stock. Cover pan 5 min. Add green beans. Blend together cornstarch, soy sauce, and water. Add to contents in pan. Stir constantly till liquid is translucent. Serves 4.

170. July 19—Friday

RAW FISH SALAD

7 lb. very fresh pike, skin and bones removed and cut in thin slices	1 T. salt
	1 T. lemon juice
	1 T. sesame seeds, toasted
6 carrots, shredded	1 t. salted almonds, pounded
2 C. green pepper, shredded	1 t. salted peanuts, pounded
1 large pickle, shredded	to a powder
2 t. ginger powder	3 T. salad oil
1 T. vinegar	

Wash and dry fish shreds with paper towel.

In a bowl, mix well ½ T. vinegar, ½ T. salt, 1 T. oil, ginger and carrots.

Mix other ½ T. vinegar, 1 T. oil, almond and peanut powder.

Sprinkle carrot and nut mixtures over fish shreds, along with other ½ T. salt. Add green pepper, pickle, and sesame seeds. Put in lemon juice and remaining 1 T. salad oil. Mix well. Chill. Serves 8.

171. July 20—Saturday

EGG DIPPED CLAMS

¼ C. oil   Dried bread crumbs, or
2 C. raw clams, shelled   Cracker crumbs
                    1 egg, beaten

CHEKIANG VINEGAR: ¼ C. soy sauce
                          2 T. vinegar
                          ¼ t. sugar

Wash clams. Drain well. Roll clams in crumbs. Dip in egg. Reroll in crumbs.

Heat oil. Put in clams. Fry till brown. Drain on absorbent paper. Serve with Chekiang vinegar. Serves 4.

172. July 21—Sunday

CHICKEN AND SPINACH

¼ lb. chicken meat, minced   1 lb. spinach, washed and
1 T. ham fat, minced   chopped fine
¾ C. chicken stock   ½ t. salt
5 egg whites, beaten very   ¼ C. chicken stock
   lightly   ½ t. M.S.G.
1 t. M.S.G.   1 t. cornstarch
1 t. salt   1 T. water
1 t. water   ⅓ C. oil

Stir chicken and ham fat till smooth in a bowl. Keep stirring while adding ¾ C. stock gradually. Add egg whites, then M.S.G., salt and water.

Heat 2 T. oil until hot in skillet. Add spinach, salt, ¼ C. stock, M.S.G. and cornstarch mixed with water. Stir constantly 1 min. Take out and place on one side of plate.

Heat remaining oil very hot in same skillet. Put in chicken

mixture. Stir till mixture sets and becomes white. Put on plate beside spinach. Serves several people.

173. July 22—Monday

ALMOND PORK

½ C. oil	1 C. mushrooms, diced
1½ C. pork, diced	½ C. almonds, shelled,
2 C. bamboo shoots, diced	blanched and chopped
2 C. celery, diced	3 T. soy sauce
2 C. peas	¾ t. M.S.G.
1 C. water chestnuts, diced	1 t. salt
1 C. stock	

Mix clean vegetables with cornstarch, soy sauce and M.S.G. Heat oil. Fry almonds till golden brown. Pour off most of the oil. Add pork. Stir 1 min. Put in vegetables and mix thoroughly. Add stock. Cover. Simmer 5-10 min. Serves 6.

174. July 23—Tuesday

FRIED BEEF SHREDS

2 T. oil	½ C. water
¾ lb. flank steak, cut into	1 T. cornstarch
strips then sliced paper-	1 t. soy sauce
thin against the grain	½ t. gin
1 bunch celery, cut obliquely	¼ C. water
2 C. bean sprouts	4 drops sesame oil, or salad oil
⅛ t. ginger	

Heat 1 T. oil. Fry meat 1 min., then take out and keep warm. Now heat remaining oil and fry celery and bean sprouts 5 min. Add water. Put beef back. Cover and cook 10 min. more. Blend together cornstarch, soy sauce, gin, sesame oil and ginger. Add to pan. When juice thickens turn off heat. Serves 4.

175. July 24—Wednesday

SPICED STRING BEANS

2 lb. string beans, strung and
   broken in 1½" pieces
1½ pt. boiling water
2 T. salt

1 T. aniseed
1 T. Chinese red pepper, if
   not available substitute
   black pepper

Put clean beans in boiling water with salt, aniseed and pepper. Bring to a boil again and boil till tender. Drain beans and cool. Serves 4.

176. July 25—Thursday

LAMB AND SCALLION

½ lb. lean, tender lamb, sliced
   thin against the grain
2 t. cornstarch
4 t. water

1 doz. scallions, chopped
Oil for deep frying
¼ C. fat
4 t. garlic, minced

2 t. ginger, minced

SAUCE: ⅓ C. soy sauce
      2 T. wine

2 t. salt
2 t. vinegar

Mix cornstarch with water. Rub into lamb. Blend together ingredients of the sauce.

Heat oil very hot. Brown lamb in oil. Take out and drain meat.

Melt fat. Add scallions and fry 1 min. Then put in lamb, garlic, ginger and sauce. Mix thoroughly before turning off heat. Serves 4.

177. July 26—Friday

STUFFED SQUASH

1 squash, halved	*Oil for deep frying*
2 lb. fish fillet, ground	*1 C. stock*
1 t. salt	*2 T. cornstarch*
¼ t. pepper	*2 t. soy sauce*
2 scallions, chopped	*1 t. sugar*
1 C. ham, diced	*¼ C. water*
1 C. salted almonds, diced	*4 drops sesame oil*

Put fish fillet in a small amount of water. Salt. Let stand 30 min. Mix with ham, scallions and almonds. Take seeds out of squash. Stuff with ham mixture.

Heat oil. Fry stuffed squash in deep oil till golden brown. Pour off oil and add stock. Cover. Cook 30 min. Blend together cornstarch, soy sauce, sugar, sesame oil and water. Put into pan with squash. Stir till liquid thickens. Garnish with parsley. Serves 6.

178. July 27—Saturday

NETTED EEL
(THE LARD WRAPPED AROUND EEL WILL GIVE EEL A NETTED LOOK)

4 lb. eel	*leaf lard—enough to wrap eel*
Oil for deep frying	*1 qt. water*
1½ C. chestnuts, shelled and	*2 T. cornstarch*
skinned	*2 t. soy sauce*
1 t. gin	*1 t. salt*
1 egg white	*¼ C. water*
	Parsley

Soak eel in warm water for 20 min. Wash. Cut into 1″ long pieces.

Heat oil. Fry eel till golden. Wrap each piece of cooked eel with lard. Paste together with egg white.

Put wrapped eel in pan. Cover with 1 qt. water. Add chestnuts, and gin. Cook until ½ liquid remains. Blend together cornstarch, soy sauce, salt and water. Add to pan. Stir till liquid is translucent. Garnish with parsley. Serves 8.

179. July 28—Sunday

STRING BEAN CHICKEN

3 T. oil	1 C. celery, sliced diagonally
2 C. cooked chicken, shredded	1 C. young cabbage, shredded
1 t. salt	½ C. mushrooms, sliced
½ t. pepper	1 C. stock (chicken)
1 C. fresh string beans, strung and broken into 1½″ pieces	2 T. cornstarch
	¼ C. water
2 t. soy sauce	

Heat oil. Put in chicken. Season with salt and pepper. Brown slightly. Add string beans, celery, cabbage, and mushrooms. Mix well. Pour in stock. Cover. Simmer 15 min. Blend together cornstarch, soy sauce, and water. Then add to pan. Stir till juice thickens. Serve piping hot over rice. Serves 4.

180. July 29—Monday

SPINACH AND HAM

3 T. oil	⅛ C. soy sauce
1½ lb. ham butt, shredded	1 t. salt
1 C. onion, shredded	½ t. pepper
1 clove garlic, minced	½ t. M.S.G.
1 T. cornstarch	¼ C. water

Heat oil. Fry ham with garlic and onion for a few min. Add spinach. Blend together cornstarch, soy sauce, salt, pepper, M.S.G. and water. Cover. Cook 5 min. in medium heat until juice thickens. Serves 6.

181. July 30—Tuesday

TURNIP STEAK

¼ C. oil	½ t. pepper
1 lb. white turnips, peeled and diced	1 onion, minced
	1 clove garlic, minced
1 lb. top round steak, cut into strips then sliced into slivers against the grain	1 C. stock
	2 T. cornstarch
	2 t. soy sauce
1 t. salt	¼ C. water

Heat oil. Put in meat, salt, pepper, onion and garlic. Brown meat. Add turnips and stock. Cover. Cook 10 min. Blend together cornstarch, soy sauce and water. Add to pan. Stir till juice thickens. Serves 4.

182. July 31—Wednesday

SPINACH SALAD

½ lb. spinach, washed and cut up in large pieces	1 T. salad oil
	4 drops sesame oil
¾ C. red onion rings	½ t. salt
¾ T. vinegar	¼ t. pepper
¼ t. M.S.G.	

Dry spinach with clean cotton towel. Put in all other ingredients and toss lightly. Serves 4.

183. August 1—Thursday

MUTTON AND MIXED VEGETABLES

2 T. oil
1½ lb. mutton, sliced-thin
    against the grain
1 C. mushrooms, sliced
2 C. onion, shredded
2 C. celery hearts, sliced
    thin diagonally
2 C. Swiss chard, cut
    diagonally

3 C. bean sprouts
1 T. cornstarch
1 C. water
1 t. M.S.G.
2 t. soy sauce
1 t. salt
½ t. pepper

Heat oil. Brown mutton by stirring 2 min. in oil. Add mushroom, celery, chard and sprouts. Blend together cornstarch, water, M.S.G., soy sauce, salt and pepper, then add to pan. Cover. Cook 10 min. When juice thickens, turn off heat. Serves 6.

184. August 2—Friday: Today, the 7th Day of the 7th Moon, is the Spinning Maid Day *—Needle Specialist.

GOLDEN NEEDLES AND SHRIMP CUSHIONS

4 C. fresh shrimp, ground
1 C. pork, ground
⅛ C. wine
⅛ C. soy sauce
2 t. sugar
1 t. salt

¼ C. water
2 T. oil
⅛ lb. dried lilies,† soaked in
    boiling water 30 min. and
    washed
⅛ C. soy sauce

2 C. water

* Chinese women in old China always celebrated the 7th Day of the 7th Moon as the Spinning Maid Day. They considered the Spinning Maid as the goddess of weaving. The females of the household would put bowls of water with floating needles in the courtyard sunshine. At high noon these women and girls believed they could forecast their luck in needlework for the year just by the shadows cast by their needles.

† Dried lilies are called "golden needles" in Cantonese stores.

Blend together shrimp and pork with cornstarch, wine, soy sauce, sugar, salt and water. Form mixtures into golf-ball sized cushions.

Heat oil and brown cushions gently.

Put drained dried lilies on bottom of frying pan. Place shrimp cushions on top. Pour in soy sauce and water. Cover. Simmer 20 min. Serves 8.

The Spinning Maid and the Cowboy

LONG AGO THERE LIVED A COWBOY IN CHINA. HIS WATER COW was his pet. After the animal finished pulling his plow for him, the cowboy would lead her to the greenest pastures to graze with plenty of water to suit any water cow. One day as he was habitually talking of his loneliness to his pet, he was startled with an answer from the cow who was really a fairy beast.

"Lead me to the river, good master, and there you might find something to cure that loneliness."

When they arrived there, they saw seven dazzling beauties swimming in the moonlight.

"These are heavenly princesses," spoke the fairy beast. "Those six playing in a group are delightful enough, but that seventh one bathing by herself is the most marvelous of all. She is the only one capable of spinning fleecy clouds to screen heavenly secrets from earth. Because of your great kindness to me, I shall tell you how to keep this spinning princess on earth so you may wed her and be lonely no more," continued the water cow.

"See that pink robe behind that rock? Hide it so she cannot ride back to heaven on the back of yonder crane," said the beast.

The cowboy was quick to obey the water cow. Soon six of the beauties slipped on their robes and mounted their cranes. As they flew up into the sky the seventh one was still searching for her lost robe. She was not sad for long. The cowboy she met was so charming, she soon fell in love with him and happily consented to stay on earth and marry him.

166

For seven years they lived blissfully together with their two children; however, trouble was brewing above. No more clouds floated in the sky to hide the doings in heaven from man. The Empress of Heaven quickly dispatched an order for the Spinning Maid's immediate return to her heavenly duties. Thus it was that when the cowboy got home one evening, he found his wife had disappeared. Once again he poured out his troubles to his beloved pet.

"Do not grieve, good master," said the water cow. "My soul will depart this earth very soon. When that has happened, skin me and wrap yourself in my hide. Together we shall journey to your Spinning Maid in heaven."

Several days later, the water cow died. Without delay the cowboy carried out the instruction of the fairy beast. In the cow's hide the cowboy floated up to the Spinning Maid's palace.

How glad the couple was to be united again. They sang, danced and feasted. The sky spinning wheel and loom lay idle once more. This time the Sky Empress' anger knew no bounds. In a flash she drew a line across the sky with her silver hairpin that became the Milky Way and cut the heaven in two. On one side stood the Spinning Maid (represented by the star Vega) and on the other the Cowboy (represented by the star Altair).

"If the Spinning Maid cannot tend to her spinning whenever the cowboy is around, they must be separated," stormed the raging Empress.

This cruel separation brought lamentations from all corners of the sky. The Emperor of Heaven beseeched his Empress to show some mercy.

"What harm can there be for these two sweethearts to meet once a year?" he asked.

To keep peace the Empress consented with reluctance. But she refused to do one thing more. Now even the magpies from earth took pity. To provide a bridge by which the Spinning Maid might cross the broad milky way, all the magpies of the earth gathered together and flew up to the sky. Each magpie grasped the feathers of one of the others in his firm bill. Then they made a bridge for the Spinning Maid as she ran across to her cowboy every Seventh Day of the Seventh Moon.

185. August 3—Saturday

EGG RELISH SALAD

6 extra large eggs, hard-
   boiled and chopped fine
1 C. carrots, grated
½ C. celery, minced

¾ t. salt
¼ t. pepper
¼ t. M.S.G.
¼ C. sweet pickle relish

6 T. salad dressing: 4 T. salad oil
                   4 drops sesame oil
                   2 T. vinegar
                   ½ t. sugar
                   ½ t. dry mustard
                   ¼ t. paprika
Lettuce cups, or toasted bread

Mix together eggs, carrots, celery, salt, pepper, M.S.G., and relish. Moisten with salad dressing. Divide into lettuce cups. (May be tucked between sandwich toast too.) Serves 4.

186. August 4—Sunday

SAUTÉED CHICKEN LIVER

3 T. oil
2 C. chicken livers, cut into
   small pieces
⅛ C. celery, diced
⅛ C. onions, diced
2 t. salt

1 t. pepper
1 C. chicken stock
2 T. cornstarch
2 t. soy sauce
¼ C. water
2 C. egg noodles

Boil water. Put in noodles. Boil 8 min. in salted water. Rinse with cold water. Drain. Put aside, but keep warm.

Heat oil. Sauté liver with celery, onion, salt and pepper for 5 min. Pour in stock. Cover. Cook another 5 min. Blend together cornstarch, soy sauce and water. Pour in and stir till juice thickens. Serve over noodles for 4.

187. August 5—Monday

RED STEWED RABBIT

5-6 lb. rabbit, dressed and cut up in small pieces	4 slices ginger
	2 T. wine
1½ pt. water	1 T. sugar
½ C. soy sauce	1 onion, quartered

Wash rabbit. Put in pot with water. Bring to a boil. Put in soy sauce, wine, ginger and onion. Turn to low heat. Simmer 3½ hrs. Put in sugar. Simmer another ½ hr., or till meat is tender. Serves 6.

188. August 6—Tuesday

STEAMED PICKLE STEAK

½ C. sweet pickles, shredded	⅛ C. soy sauce
4 C. round steak, cut into thin slivers against the grain	1 t. salt
	½ t. pepper
½ t. M.S.G.	⅛ C. salad oil
1 T. cornstarch	

Mix all ingredients thoroughly. Pour in a dish. Place trivet in pot. Fill pot up to 1″ of water. Put dish with meat mixture on top of trivet. Cover. Steam 30-40 min. Serves 8.

189. August 7—Wednesday

SWEET CORN *

1 doz. ears garden-picked corn
Water to cover

Husk corn, but leave on last four leaves. Cover with water. Boil 5 min. Leaving on those few leaves will sweeten the ears. To obtain true flavor, the Chinese serve corn without salt or butter. Serves 4-6.

* Anyone who doesn't consider the above an adequate Chinese recipe may consider the one below.

189A.

SAUTÉED CABBAGE

1 head cabbage, cut in thin   *¼ C. water*
   strips   *1 t. salt*
¼ C. vegetable oil   *½ t. M.S.G.*

Heat oil in pan. Add cabbage and salt and M.S.G. Stir for 5 min. Pour in water. Cover. Bring to a boil. Turn to low heat and simmer for 10-15 min. Serves 6.

190. August 8—Thursday

FRIED LAMB BRAINS

2 T. oil   *1 t. garlic salt*
2 pr. brains   *½ t. pepper*
1 qt. cold water   *1 egg, beaten*
1 qt. boiling water   *½ C. dried bread crumbs*
1 t. salt   *2 T. cornstarch*
1 T. vinegar   *2 t. soy sauce*
            ¼ C. water

Put brains in cold water. Let sit idle ½ hr. Pour off cold water and pour in boiling water. Add salt and vinegar. Cover and simmer ¼ hr. Rinse in cold water, then remove membrane. Season with garlic salt and pepper. Roll in bread crumbs. Immerse in egg and 1 T. water. Roll again in dried crumbs. Heat oil. Fry till brown. Blend together cornstarch, soy sauce and water. Add to pan. Stir till juice thickens. Serves 4.

191. August 9—Friday

SNAILS

4 T. oil	2 C. bamboo shoots, sliced
3 snails, washed, shell broken, meat taken out and sliced into slivers	1 C. celery, sliced
	¼ C. pork, sliced
	3 slices ginger, minced
2 C. water chestnuts, sliced	1 T. gin
2 C. mushrooms, sliced	1 C. stock

GRAVY: 1 T. cornstarch   1 t. soy sauce
¼ C. water

Heat 2 T. oil. Fry pork. Add water chestnuts, mushrooms, shoots and celery. Pour in half of stock. Cover and cook 15 min. Heat remaining oil. Put in snail meat. Add ginger and gin. Put in cooked pork and vegetables. Mix well. Add rest of stock. Blend together cornstarch, soy sauce and water. Put into pan. Stir till liquid thickens. Garnish with ham and parsley. Serves 6-8.

192. August 10—Saturday: This, the 15th Day of the 7th Moon, is Chinese All Soul's Day *

SAUTÉED EGGPLANT

2 lb. eggplant	1 clove garlic, mashed and
3 T. oil	minced
1 C. water	2 T. dried shrimp, or ¼ C.
2 T. soy sauce	fresh shrimp, sliced
½ t. salt	

Peel eggplants. Cut once lengthwise, now cut across into small pieces.

Heat oil. Sauté eggplant 1 min. each side. Put in garlic, then add soy sauce, salt, shrimp and water. Simmer for ¼ hr. Serves 8.

* All Soul's Day is known as the Feast of the Dead. Eggplants are eaten on this day. Each family makes simple sacrifices before the ancestral shrine within the family compound.

193. August 11—Sunday

ALMOND CHICKEN

½ C. almond	2 C. celery, diced
¼ C. oil and oil for deep frying	1 C. stock
	2 C. cooked chicken, diced
2 C. onion, diced	1 t. salt
1 can water chestnuts, diced	½ t. pepper
1 C. mushrooms, diced	1 T. cornstarch
2 C. broccoli, peeled and diced	1 t. soy sauce
	¼ C. water

Blanch almonds in boiling water. Dry. Heat oil for deep frying. Fry almonds in hot oil till golden brown. Drain and chop.

In large skillet, heat ¼ C. oil. Add vegetables, salt, and pepper, stirring constantly for 5 minutes. Pour in stock. Cover. Cook 10 min. Add chicken. Blend together cornstarch, water and soy sauce and add. Stir 4 more min. Turn off heat. Sprinkle with almonds. Serves 4.

194. August 12—Monday

CABBAGE, TOMATO PORK

2 T. oil	1 head cabbage, shredded
1 lb. pork, sliced into slivers	1 lb. tomatoes, quartered
1 t. salt	1 C. pork stock
½ t. pepper	2 T. cornstarch
1 clove garlic, minced	2 t. soy sauce
1 onion, minced	¼ C. water

Heat oil. Put in pork, garlic and onion. Brown pork. Pour in stock. Add cabbage and tomatoes. Cover. Cook 10-15 min. till cabbage is tender. Blend together cornstarch, soy sauce and water. Add to pan. Stir till juice thickens. Serves 4.

195. August 13—Tuesday

CUCUMBER STEAK

1 lb. rump steak, cut into strips then sliced paper-thin against the grain	2 t. salt
	½ t. pepper
	¼ C. oil
4-5 cucumbers, peeled and sliced into rings	1 T. onion, minced
	½ C. beef stock
2 t. cornstarch	2 T. fat

Blend together cornstarch, salt, pepper and oil. Marinate beef in the mixture ½ hr.

Melt fat. Put in beef and onion. Fry till beef is brown. Put in cucumbers and stock. Cover. Cook 5 min. Serves 4.

196. August 14—Wednesday

CUCUMBER SALAD

3 cucumbers   ⅛ *C. vinegar*
1 t. salt   ⅛ *C. sugar*
⅛ *C. soy sauce*   *1 T. sesame oil*

Peel cucumbers. Slice into thin discs. Mix gently with salt, soy sauce, vinegar, sugar and sesame oil. Chill in refrigerator. Serves 6.

197. August 15—Thursday

SAUTÉED LAMB WITH BROCCOLI

1 lb. lamb, cut into strips and   *1 t. salt*
sliced into thin slivers diag-   ½ *t. pepper*
onally   *1 clove garlic, minced*
1 lb. broccoli (remove outer   *1 C. stock*
husk of tough fiber and cut   *2 T. cornstarch*
into 1" cubes)   ¼ *C. water*
¼ *C. oil*   ½ *t. soy sauce*

Heat oil in skillet. Put in lamb slivers. Add garlic. Stir meat until cooked through. Put in clean broccoli and pour in stock. Cover and cook over low heat till broccoli is tender (about 15-20 min.). Blend cornstarch, water and soy sauce. Add to pan. Stir till liquid is translucent. Serves 4-6.

198. August 16—Friday

SALAD ORIENTALIA

2 C. cooked rice
4½ t. scallions, chopped
1 C. salad dressing: 5 t. salad oil
4 drops sesame oil
3 T. vinegar
1 t. sugar
½ t. dry mustard
½ t. paprika

1 can drained sardines	*2 T. chili sauce*
1 C. shrimp, cooked	*1 T. capers*
½ C. vinegar	*1 t. parsley, minced*
4 eggs, hard-boiled, sieved	*1 head lettuce, washed and*
4 small pickles, sieved	*drained*

Mix rice and scallions with ½ mixed salad dressing. Marinate sardines and shrimp in vinegar 10 min. then drain. Line platter with lettuce leaves. Heap rice on top to form a mound. Surround base with sardines and shrimp. Sprinkle eggs and pickles over mound. Mix chili sauce, capers and parsley with remaining dressing and serve with salad. Serves 4.

199. August 17—Saturday

EGGS AND TOMATOES

2 T. oil	*4 tomatoes, cut into wedges*
4 extra large eggs	*1 t. salt*
	½ t. pepper

Heat oil. Break eggs and beat. Put in pan and scramble. Add skinned tomatoes. Stir together 5 min. Season. Serves 4.

200. August 18—Sunday

PAN BROILED CHICKEN

3½-4 lb. broiler, split   1 T. rice wine, or sauterne
3-4 slices ginger, minced   ½ t. sugar
2 T. soy sauce   ¼ C. oil

DIPPING SAUCE: 4 t. tabasco
                ⅓ C. soy sauce
                2 cloves garlic, minced
                Dash of sugar

Mix together, ginger, soy sauce, wine, and sugar. Put chicken in mixture and marinate about 2 hrs. then drain.

Heat oil very hot in big pan. Put drained chicken on a large slit spatula to place inside pan. Pan broil 10 min. to a golden brown. Quarter chicken, then mix together tabasco, soy sauce, garlic and sugar. Serve chicken with saucers of Dipping Sauce. Serves 4.

201. August 19—Monday

PICKLED PIGS' FEET
(EATEN ONLY DURING THE SUMMER)

6 pigs' feet   1 t. salt
¼ C. aniseed   Water

Put pigs' feet covered with water, in pot. Add aniseed and salt. Boil ½ hr. Take feet out. (Reminds one of tired feet.) Rinse in cold water. Replace in pot with aniseed solution, and repeat process 4 more times. Chill in refrigerator till ready to use. Serve with Plum Sauce. Serves 6.

202. August 20—Tuesday

TOMATO STEAK

3 T. oil
1½ lb. round steak, cut into
strips then sliced into slivers
against the grain
8 garden ripened tomatoes,
quartered

1 C. onion, shredded
1 T. cornstarch
2 T. soy sauce
1 t. salt
½ t. pepper
½ t. M.S.G.

Heat oil. Sauté beef and onion 1 min. over high heat. Add tomatoes. Blend together cornstarch, soy sauce, salt, pepper and M.S.G. Add to beef and mix. Cover. Cook 5 min. till juice thickens. Serves 6.

203. August 21—Wednesday

WATERMELON WALLOW *

20 lb. watermelon
Salt to taste (opt.)

Test watermelon for ripeness, by thumping with knuckles. A ripe melon gives out a hollow ring. Also press end (opposite to stem) of melon with thumb. If the rind springs a little, it's ripe. Cut watermelon into generous slices. Eat plain, or sprinkle with salt, as most Chinese prefer their watermelon. They claim salt brings out the natural flavor of the water-melon. Serves 10.

* At watermelon shindigs among the Chinese only watermelon is served. Anyone who doesn't consider the above an adequate Chinese recipe may consider the one below.

204. August 22—Thursday

BEAN CURD SAUTÉED WITH SCALLION

1 qt. bean curd, cut into 1"   ⅛ *C. vegetable oil*
cubes   ⅛ *C. soy sauce*
8 scallions, cut into 1" sec-   *2 t. salt*
tions

Heat oil. Add scallion and stir a min. Put in bean curd and stir 2 min. Season with soy sauce and salt. Stir another min. Serves 6 immediately.

205. August 23—Friday

HALIBUT WITH TOMATO SAUCE

1 lb. fillet of halibut   *1 scallion, or onion, minced*
1 can tomatoes, or 2 C. fresh   *2 slices ginger root, minced*
tomatoes   *1 T. rice wine, or sauterne*
½ t. moist baby black beans,   *1 t. salt*
mashed and minced (opt.)   *1 T. soy sauce*
1 clove garlic, minced   *½ t. sugar*
2 T. oil

Wash fillet. Salt both sides generously. Let stand ½ hr. Wipe off salt. Put fish in bowl. Sprinkle with baby black beans, garlic, scallion, ginger, salt, soy sauce, wine and sugar. Add tomatoes. Place in a big pot. Cover tightly. Steam 20 min. Heat oil till hot. Splash over fish. Serves 3-4.

206. August 24—Saturday

EGGS STEAMED WITH FISH

4 eggs, beaten	1 t. soy sauce
3 lb. flounder, skin and bones removed, cut in ½" slivers	1 onion, minced
	1 small green pepper, diced
1 T. cornstarch	1 C. stock
2 t. salt	

Sprinkle starch, soy sauce, onion and green pepper over fish flakes in bowl. Mix together eggs, stock, and salt. Pour over fish. Place trivet in big pot and add water. On top of trivet place bowl with fish mixture. Cover pot. Steam over low heat 1 hr. Serves 4.

207. August 25—Sunday

PEPPER TOMATO CHICKEN

5-6 lb. fowl	2 t. salt
2 small green peppers, quartered	1 t. pepper
	1 C. stock
3 T. oil	⅛ C. cornstarch
4 large tomatoes, cut into wedges	2 t. soy sauce
	½ C. water

Stew fowl in salted water for 2 hrs. (Save liquid for stock.) Slice.

Heat oil. Put in chicken slices, salt and pepper. Brown chicken. Add peppers and tomatoes. Pour in stock. Cover. Cook 10-15 min. Blend together cornstarch, soy sauce and water. Add to pan. Stir till juice thickens. Serves 6.

208. August 26—Monday

COLD LUNCHEON MEAT

6 lb. fresh pork shoulder   *1½ pt. water*
¼ C. salt   *1 T. ginger, minced*
                    ½ C. "Chekiang" vinegar*

Work the center bone of shoulder out without cutting meat. Rub salt all over shoulder including the inside as well as the outside. Place it in a covered pot and refrigerate 2 days.

Take out and wipe off some of the salt with a clean, damp cloth. Put back in pot and pour in water. Bring to a boil. Turn to medium heat and cook an hr. Remove from pot and squeeze into a large baking pan. Put flat cover on, then weigh down cover with a heavy stone to press into an oblong shape. Let stand several hrs. Then chill in refrigerator. Slice as much as needed for lunch and serve with ginger in Chekiang vinegar. This should last the average family of five for a few days.

     * "Chekiang" vinegar: 1 C. soy sauce
                                       ½ C. vinegar
                                       1 t. sugar

209. August 27—Tuesday

STEAK SANDWICH

4½ lb. sirloin steak   *1 T. ginger, minced*
8 T. soy sauce   *4 T. onion, chopped fine*
2 T. sugar   *¼ C. water*
1 clove garlic, minced   *6 round buns, slit open*
                    6 T. butter

Prick meat both sides. Score fat edges. Marinate in mixture of soy sauce, sugar, garlic, ginger, onion and water about 2 hrs., in refrigerator, if possible, to tenderize, turning the meat several times. Drain meat. Meanwhile start charcoal fire in grill. When coal becomes hot, grill steak 12 min. each side if you wish it rare, 14 min. each side if you wish it medium, and 16 min. on each side if you wish to have it well done. Remove steak. Slice very thin against the grain and serve on toasted, buttered buns. Serves 6.

210. August 28—Wednesday

ICE BOX TOMATOES *

6 garden ripened tomatoes
2 T. sugar

Pour boiling water over washed tomatoes. Peel skin. Cut into wedges. Sprinkle with sugar. Chill in refrigerator. Serves 6.

* Anyone who doesn't consider the above an adequate Chinese recipe may consider the one below.

210A.

EGGPLANT

2 lb. eggplant
¼ C. peanut oil
2-3 cloves garlic, mashed and minced

2 t. salt
½ C. vegetable stock or water

Peel eggplant. Halve lengthwise, then cut across into bite-sized chunks.

Heat oil. Try eggplant and garlic 2 min. stirring constantly. Add salt. Pour in stock or water. Cover. Cook gently for 15 min. Serves 6.

211. August 29—Thursday

PARTRIDGE

4 T. oil	2 C. celery, sliced diagonally
4 dressed partridges, boned and cut into slivers	2 C. stock
	2 T. cornstarch
2 C. water chestnuts, sliced	2 t. soy sauce
2 C. mushrooms, sliced	1 t. salt

¼ C. water

Heat 2 T. oil in pan. Fry partridges 4-5 min. Put in dish. Heat other 2 T. oil. Put in vegetables. Stir 2 min. Add ½ stock. Cover. Cook 15 min. Put back partridge meat. Mix well. Add rest of stock. Cover. Cook another 5 min. Blend together cornstarch, soy sauce, salt and water. Add to pan. Stir till juice thickens. Serves 6-8.

212. August 30—Friday

HOT WATER FISH

10 lb. very fresh cod	2 t. salt
1½ gal. boiling water	Parsley

SAUCE: 1 T. cornstarch   ½ t. sugar
       1 t. salt   1 C. vinegar
       2 C. sweet pickles, shredded

Clean fish but leave whole. In a large clean pan, pour boiling water over fish. Add salt. Cover. Do not take fish out till water cools to a lukewarm temperature.

Put fish on oval platter. Blend together cornstarch, salt, sugar, vinegar, and pickles. Pour over fish. Garnish with parsley. Serves 10.

213. August 31—Saturday

BEAN CURD OMELET

¼ C. oil	*1 pt. bean curd*
1 doz. eggs, beaten	*½ C. water*
1 T. salt	*Parsley*

Heat half the oil. Sauté bean curd 1 min. Add water. Cover. Cook 10 min.

In another pan heat remaining oil. Pour in eggs but keep turning with spatula. Just before the eggs set, add bean curd. Cook a min. more, then garnish with parsley. Serves 12.

214. September 1—Sunday

CHICKEN WITH ONION

2-3 lb. fryer, cut up	*1 C. stock*
¼ C. oil	*2 T. rice wine or sherry*
1 very large onion, chopped	*1 T. cornstarch*
¼ C. soy sauce	*½ C. water*

Heat oil. Put in onion and brown lightly. Add clean chicken and fry till golden brown on both sides. Add wine, stock and soy sauce. Cover and cook 25 min. Blend together cornstarch and water. Add to pan. Stir. When liquid turns translucent, turn off heat and serve on fresh-boiled rice. Serves 4-6.

215. Sept. 2—Monday: Labor Day (For the workers of the world let's celebrate with a recipe worthy of them)

"LIONS' HEADS"

1 lb. pork, minced	*2½ T. wine*
3 dried mushrooms, soaked,	*2 T. soy sauce*
or ¼ C. fresh mushrooms,	*1 t. salt*
chopped fine	*1½ t. sugar*
3 T. dried shrimplet, soaked,	*½ lb. hearts of celery cab-*
or ⅓ C. fresh shrimp,	*bage, quartered lengthwise*
chopped fine	*¼ C. oil*
1 scallion, chopped fine	*1 C. chicken broth, boiling*

Mix meat with mushrooms, scallion, shrimp and ginger. Add wine, soy sauce, salt and sugar. Form meat into 4 balls.

Heat oil. Put in celery cabbage and stir for a few min. Arrange balls on cabbage, then pour in broth. Bring to a boil. Cover. Turn to low heat, and simmer ¼ hr. Serves 4.

216. September 3—Tuesday

CELERY STEAK

¼ C. oil	*5 t. soy sauce*
1 lb. flank steak, sliced against	*2 t. wine*
the grain	*¾ t. salt*
1 lb. celery, sliced diagonally	*¾ t. sugar*

Mix together wine, sugar and 2½ T. soy sauce with meat. Heat 2 T. oil. Sauté celery 2 min. Take out.

Heat rest of oil. Put in meat mixture. Stir another 2 min. Return celery to pan with salt and remaining soy sauce. Mix well. Serves 4.

217. September 4—Wednesday

RAW CELERY CABBAGE

1 head celery cabbage,   *1 T. salad oil*
* shredded diagonally*   *3-4 drops sesame oil*
1 clove garlic, split   *2 t. vinegar*
1 scallion, minced   *½ t. salt*
¼ t. pepper

Rub garlic on salad bowl. Mince garlic and put into salad bowl. Put all other ingredients into the salad bowl. Toss gently. Serves 6.

218. September 5—Thursday

LAMB WITH CHINESE CABBAGE

3 T. oil   *1 bunch Chinese or celery*
1 lb. lamb   * cabbage (about 2 lb.) cut*
1 t. salt   * diagonally*
½ t. pepper   *½ C. stock*
1 clove garlic, mashed and   *1 T. cornstarch*
* minced*   *⅓ C. water*
1 t. soy sauce

Heat oil. Slice lamb paper-thin. Fry and add salt, pepper, and garlic. Stir constantly 5 min. Add cabbage. Pour in stock. Cover. Cook 10 min. Blend together cornstarch, soy sauce and water. Add to pan. Stir till juice thickens. Serves 4.

219. September 6—Friday

STUFFED PEPPERS

8 green peppers, hollowed and washed
1½ lb. halibut fillet, flaked
⅓ C. oil
1 t. salt
½ t. pepper

1 T. cornstarch
1 onion, minced
¼ C. oil
1 C. stock
2 T. cornstarch
2 t. soy sauce

½ C. water

In a large bowl mix fish, ⅓ C. oil, salt, pepper, cornstarch and onion. Stuff green peppers with mixture.

Heat remaining ¼ C. oil in a large skillet. Arrange peppers inside. Add stock. Cover. Cook 15-20 min. Take out and keep warm. Blend together cornstarch, soy sauce and water. When juice thickens, pour over peppers. Serves 8.

220. September 7—Saturday

CAULIFLOWER OMELET

1 head cauliflower
1 pt. water
1 t. salt
1 C. ground chicken meat

3-4 egg whites
½ t. celery salt
1 T. cornstarch
⅛ C. stock

⅛ C. oil

Break cauliflower into small florets. Put in pot with water and salt. Boil at high heat 10 min. Drain.

Combine ground chicken, egg whites, celery salt and stock. Beat with electric beater till whites form peaks.

Heat oil. Put in white mixture and stir about 2 min. Then add florets and fry another 2 min. If desired, garnish with ham chips. Serves 6.

221. September 8—Sunday: This the 15th Day of the 8th Moon, is the Harvest Moon Festival* equivalent to Thanksgiving

MOON CAKES

STUFFING: *1 lb. red lentils*   ½ *C. lard*
(may be purchased in   *1 t. salt*
Chinese stores)   ¼ *C. sugar*

Cook lentils in water 3 hrs. Wash. Strain and allow to dry. Mix with lard and sugar to form a paste.

UNBAKED PIE CRUST: 7½ *C. flour*
     1 T. salt
     2¼ *C. shortening*
     1 C. cold water

Sift flour and salt once. Cut in shortening. Add water to hold ingredients together. Form into balls. Roll out ¼ C. dough on floured board into round crust ⅛" thick. Fit into small individual pie tins. Fill with sweet bean paste. Roll out another ¼ C. dough, as before, to place on top of other crust. Cut slits in center to allow steam to escape. Press edges together. Bake in oven till crust is a golden brown. Yields 12 moon cakes.

* 4654 was Leap Year. There were *two* 8th Moons, thus we have *two* 15th Days of the 8th Moons. The next Harvest Moon Festival occurred October 8, 1957.

The Harvest Moon festival is a family holiday. Everyone goes home. Moon cakes are eaten to honor the moon. In the celebration, 108 gauze and wire-framed lanterns are set on rows of red lacquer square tables. The lanterns are exquisitely embroidered. Big red candles and joss sticks are placed at one end. Children are dressed up and playing with gift clay rabbits or firecrackers. Later comes the family feasting at round tables to signify togetherness. Then moon cakes are eaten by all.

The Harvest Moon Festival (September 8 and October 8 were Harvest Moon Festivals for the year 4654 because it was Chinese leap year.)

The Story of the Harvest Moon Festival

ONE DAY AS EMPEROR SHIA TRAVELED FORTH FROM HIS CASTLE in his yellow sedan chair, he spied a man with a bow and arrows along the highway. The red bow was a huge one—bigger than any seen before by the Emperor. He stopped to discourse with the man.

"Hou Ye, the Bowman, am I. This bow can send these long arrows through the world, from end to end. I can also ride on the winds."

The Emperor's eyes twinkled as he said, "I need an Imperial Archer, Bowman. Shoot an arrow through the top branch of that spruce tree on yon mountain peak and you shall fill that post."

With true aim, Hou Ye set his arrow. In no time the arrow struck through the top branch of the spruce tree. Immediately Hou Ye leaped upon a blowing wind and floated up to the far mountain tree to bring back the arrow to his Majesty.

The Emperor was wide-mouthed with astonishment, but he didn't forget to make Hou Ye Imperial Archer. Time and again he was to call upon Hou Ye to shoot some public enemy. Hou Ye performed his duty well. Then one year calamity struck in the form of a flood.

"Take your magic bow, O' Archer, and shoot Ho Po, the Water God who is causing so much mischief with his terrible floods," commanded the Emperor.

Hou Ye leaped on to the next passing wind. When he found Ho Po, his beautiful sister, Heng O, was standing beside him. Rather than wound her, Hou Ye aimed at her hair coiled on top of her head. Thus the arrow pierced Ho Po and wounded

188

him. After that Ho Po fled and never returned to cause more suffering. As for Heng O she was so grateful to Hou Ye for sparing her life that she later married him.

Shortly after this another crisis yet befell the earth. Ten suns appeared to send their relentless rays against earth. They scorched all plants till the Emperor begged Hou Ye to shoot the suns to spare men's lives.

With accurate aim he made short work of those suns. Just as he was to pull his bow back for the last time, a voice from the sky stopped him.

"Leave one sun in the heavens if you want to remain on earth, Archer!"

Hou Ye obeyed and that is why one sees one sun shining to this day.

His fame as Archer was made. Even the Goddess of Kun Lun wanted to bestow recognition by giving him a pill of everlasting life. However, she warned him to put it away till the time came to take it.

Hou Ye hid it under one tile of his roof. One day when he was away, his wife, Heng O, spied it. She swallowed the bright object and fled as she heard her husband's footsteps. In her escape, she was surprised to find herself flying.

When her husband discovered her theft, he took flight after her. She flew into the moon. The cold there made her sneeze and she coughed up the pill which straightaway changed her into a jade rabbit.

Goddess Kun Lun took pity on Hou Ye, so she gave him a magic cake. When he ate it he, too, had everlasting life and went to dwell in the Sun. In time he forgave his wife, Heng O. He built a magnificent palace for her in the moon, and visited her every 15th Day of the Moon (month). While he is visiting her every 15th Day, the moon is full and round. However, it is on the Harvest Moon Festival which comes the 15th Day of the 8th Moon that the Chinese say the moon is the brightest and roundest of the whole year.

222. September 9—Monday

FRAGRANT PORK

2 lb. boned fat pork, cut into big bars	½ C. soy sauce
	1 t. aniseed
⅔ C. sugar	3 sticks cinnamon
1½ C. wine	1 dried tangerine peel
1 scallion	8 cloves
1½" ginger	1 t. salt

Place all ingredients in a pot. Cook at high heat for several hrs. Keep pouring in a little water to keep from burning. When meat is tender take meat out and cut into 1½" squares. (Save sauce for future red-stewing dishes.) Serves 8.

223. September 10—Tuesday

PEPPER STEAK

¼ C. oil	1 clove garlic, minced
1 lb. round steak, cut into strips then sliced diagonally into slivers	3 large red and green peppers, cut up
	1 C. stock
1 t. salt	2 T. cornstarch
½ t. pepper	2 t. soy sauce
1 scallion, chopped	¼ C. water

Heat oil. Brown meat. Season with salt and pepper. Add scallion, garlic and red and green peppers. Pour in stock. Cover. Cook 10 min. Blend together cornstarch, soy sauce and water. Stir into pan. When liquid is translucent, stop stirring and turn off heat. Serves 4.

224. September 11—Wednesday

HONEY PEARS

4 pears, halved lengthwise, cored
½ C. honey
4 t. preserved ginger candy, minced
½ C. hot water

Wash pears. Arrange on baking pan. Pour honey over pears. Sprinkle with ginger candy. Add water. Bake in 350° oven ¾ hr. Serves 4.

225. September 12—Thursday

LAMBKINS

6 C. lamb stock   *1 t. salt*
2 C. lamb slivers   *½ t. pepper*
1 C. onions, shredded   *½ t. M.S.G.*
2 T. soy sauce   *Parsley or watercress*

Heat stock. Add all other ingredients. Bring soup to a boil. Turn to low heat and simmer 10 min. Garnish with parsley or watercress. Serves 6.

226. September 13—Friday

BARBECUED OYSTERS

2½ doz. oysters   *1 T. sesame oil*
Salad oil   *2 t. sugar*
1 C. red vinegar   *2 t. salt*

Wash oysters. Dry with paper towels. Dip in salad oil. String oysters through skewers and roast over charcoal fire in grill till done.

Blend together vinegar, sesame oil, sugar and salt. Use as a sauce for oysters. Serves 4-5.

Don't forget to serve a lettuce salad among other cook-out foods.

227. September 14—Saturday

EGG TOMATO SOUP

1 qt. stock
2 eggs, beaten

2 C. tomato wedges
Salt to taste

Heat stock. Add tomatoes and salt. Bring to a boil. Stir in eggs and keep stirring for 2 min. Serves 4-6.

228. September 15—Sunday

BARBECUED CHICKEN

2-2½ lb. broilers, quartered
Juice of 1 lemon
1 T. salt
1 t. pepper
3 T. sugar

1 t. paprika
1 t. soy sauce
3 T. melted chicken fat, (if not available use butter)

Wash chicken. Dry well. Mix salt, pepper, paprika and soy sauce. Rub into chicken. Brush half the chicken fat onto chicken. Sprinkle chicken with half the sugar. Place in broiler pan. Broil 10 min. Mix remaining sugar with remaining fat. Brush onto chicken pieces. Set pan 4″ from heat source. Broil 30 min. or till tender in 350° oven, basting with juice from time to time. Turn chicken to brown evenly. Serves 6.

229. September 16—Monday

CHINESE CABBAGE AND HAM SOUP

1 lb. Chinese cabbage, shredded diagonally
½ lb. cooked ham, diced
6 C. duck broth made from: bones of 1 duck cooked 2 hrs.
with 7 C. water which will boil down to 6 C.
Salt to taste

Put cabbage and ham in broth. Cook 10 min. Add salt to taste if necessary. Serves 6.

230. September 17—Tuesday: One last summer cook-out!

BEEF, BARBECUED

2 lb. porterhouse steak, sliced	*1 clove garlic, minced*
against the grain	*1 t. salt*
¼ C. soy sauce	*½ t. pepper*
	2 t. sugar

Mix together all ingredients. Marinate beef in liquid to tenderize for about 2 hrs. Build charcoal fire in grill. When hot, broil meat slices 5 min. each side. Goes well with French bread. Serves 4-6.

231. September 18—Wednesday

SWEET AND SOUR CELERY CABBAGE

1 head cabbage	*½ T. cornstarch*
2 T. vinegar	*2 T. water*
2 T. sugar	*1 T. vegetable oil*
½ T. soy sauce	*1 t. salt*

Wash cabbage. Cut in 3½" shreds. In bowl mix vinegar, sugar, soy sauce, cornstarch and water.

Heat oil. Sauté cabbage stirring for 3 min. Add salt and continue to stir till tender. Liquid will continue to come out of cabbage. Add diluted cornstarch mixture to form a thin sweet and sour sauce. As soon as sauce sticks to vegetable turn off heat. Serves 4.

232. September 19—Thursday

LAMB AND EGGPLANT

2 lb. lamb leg meat, cubed into 1" pieces	1 onion, sliced
1 T. oil	2 cloves garlic, sliced
⅓ T. vinegar	1 eggplant (about 2 lb.), peeled, quartered and sliced
2 t. salt	3 T. lamb fat
1 t. pepper	1 C. lamb stock
½ t. M.S.G.	2 T. soy sauce

Mix oil and vinegar. Rub garlic into lamb cubes. Put lamb in oil mixture. Season with salt, pepper and M.S.G. Add onion and garlic. Mix. Cover. Let lamb marinate in this mixture overnight. Drain.

Melt fat in skillet. Put in lamb and brown quickly. Add eggplant and stir about 2 min. Pick up the onion and garlic slices from the marinating juice and put in skillet. Then pour in stock and soy sauce. Reduce to low heat. Cover skillet and simmer 15 min. Serves 8.

233. September 20—Friday: This, the 27th Day of
the 8th Moon, was Confucius' (550 or 551-479
B.C.) birthday. Noodles, signifying long life,
are eaten at birthday celebrations. A series of
noodle recipes will follow.

CANTONESE CHOW MEIN

¾ lb. egg noodles, boiled 8
min., rinsed in cold water,
drained

3 T. oil

¼ lb. shrimp, sliced thin
(other fish or meat slices
may be substituted)

1 oz. bamboo shoots, sliced
thin

4 leaves Chinese cabbage, cut
thin diagonally

2 stalks celery, cut thin
diagonally

6 mushrooms, sliced

6 snowpeas, or 12 string
beans, julienned

1 clove garlic, minced

1 C. stock

1 T. cornstarch

1 t. soy sauce

1 t. salt

½ t. pepper

½ t. M.S.G.

½ C. water

1 scallion, cut into slivers

Brush some oil on noodles to separate.

Heat 2 T. oil very hot. Put noodles in skillet, making sure
noodles are separated by shaking loose with fork. Brown
evenly. If noodles become hard, sprinkle a little water on
them during the frying period.

Heat 1 T. oil. Put in garlic. When oil gets very hot, put in
shrimp and brown. Add vegetables and mix. Pour in stock.
Cover. Cook 3 min. Blend together cornstarch, soy sauce, salt,
pepper, M.S.G., and water. Add to pan. When juice thickens,
turn off heat and pour mixture over noodles. Garnish with
short scallion slivers. Serves 4.

234. September 21—Saturday

CHINATOWN "WOR MEIN"

5 oz. egg noodles, boiled 8   *½ C. onion, cut fine*
min., rinsed in cold water,   *½ C. mushrooms, cut fine*
drained, divided into four   *½ C. stock*
soup bowls   *1 T. cornstarch*
1 lb. pork, sliced thin   *1 t. soy sauce*
1 C. celery, cut fine   *¼ C. water*
                4 eggs, hard-boiled, halved

Heat oil. Put in pork. Brown. Add vegetables. Mix well.
Cover. Cook 10 min. Blend together cornstarch, soy sauce and
water. Add to pan. When juice thickens, turn off heat and
pour mixture over four bowls of noodles. Mix. Garnish with
egg halves. Serves 4.

235. September 22—Sunday *

"YAT KOI MEIN"
(INDIVIDUAL NOODLE SOUP)

¾ lb. egg noodles, boiled 8   *2 T. fat*
min., rinsed in cold water,   *1½ C. chicken, sliced*
drained   *Salt to taste*
½ t. pepper   *1½ C. mushrooms, sliced*
1 T. soy sauce   *1 C. water chestnuts, sliced*
1 t. oil   *1 T. cornstarch*
4 drops sesame oil   *½ C. water*
                1 qt. chicken stock

Divide cooked noodles into 6 bowls with oil, sesame oil, soy
sauce, and pepper.

* In Cantonese homes chicken is eaten for birthday celebrations too. When
I was a youngster, the birthday child always got the drumstick.

Melt fat in pan. Put in chicken with salt to taste. Brown. Add mushrooms and water chestnuts. Stir. Blend together cornstarch and water. Add to pan. Cover. Simmer 10 min. till vegetables are cooked and the juice begins to thicken.

Heat stock. When it boils, divide into bowls of seasoned noodles. Last, divide chicken mixture into bowls and serve. Serves 6.

236. September 23—Monday

CHINESE FRIED NOODLES

1 lb. egg noodles, boiled 8 min., rinsed in cold water, drained
2 T. oil
1 T. fat
½ lb. lean pork, sliced thin
¾ C. roast pork, shredded
1½ C. onion, shredded
1 egg, beaten, fried, shredded
½ T. lard (used to fry egg)
1 T. cornstarch
1 T. soy sauce
3 C. pork stock
1 t. salt
½ t. pepper

Loosen boiled noodles with fork. Heat oil in pan. Fry noodles to brown evenly. Put in deep dish.

Melt fat in skillet. Sauté onion. When slightly translucent, put in pork. Stir constantly till meat is brown. Blend together cornstarch, soy sauce, salt, pepper and cold stock. Add to skillet. When juice thickens, add roast pork and egg shreds. Mix well. Turn off heat and pour hot mixture over noodles. Serves 6.

237. September 24—Tuesday

CHINA SPAGHETTINA

1 lb. spaghetti, boiled 15 min. in 1 t. salted water, rinsed in cold water, or
1 lb. egg noodles, boiled 8 min. in 1 t. salted water, rinsed in cold water, drained
⅓ C. oil
2 lb. chuck, chopped fine

1 clove garlic, minced
1 onion, minced
2 t. salt
1 t. pepper
2 T. sugar
3-4 tomatoes, cut in wedges
1 pt. boiling beef stock
2 t. cornstarch
½ C. cold water
Parsley

Heat oil. Put in garlic and onion. Stir 1 min. Add chopped beef. Season with remaining t. salt and pepper. Brown beef lightly. Add sugar, tomatoes, and stock. Mix well. Bring mixture to a boil. Blend together cornstarch and water. Pour into pan and cook till juice thickens. Separate noodles with fork, put in deep dish and pour boiling meat mixture over them. Garnish with parsley. Serves 8.

238. September 25—Wednesday

NOODLE SOUP

½ lb. egg noodles, boiled 8 min., rinsed in cold water, drained
1½ qt. vegetable soup, or 1½ qt. water with 1 t. M.S.G.

2 t. soy sauce
1 t. salad oil
3-4 drops seasame oil
1 t. pepper

Mix noodles with soy sauce, salad oil, sesame oil and pepper. Divide noodles into 4-soup bowls. Heat vegetable soup or water with M.S.G. to a boiling point. Pour into soup bowls of noodles and fill. Serves 4.

239. September 26—Thursday *

"YANG CHOW MEIN"

2 lb. noodles, boiled 8 min.,   3 C. mushrooms, sliced
   rinsed in cold water,   ¾ C. water chestnuts, sliced
   drained   1 T. cornstarch
¼ C. oil   1 t. soy sauce
2 qt. stock   1 t. salt
1 C. lamb, shredded (chicken   ½ t. pepper
   may be used too)   ½ t. sugar
             ¼ C. water

With 2 T. oil, brown noodles evenly. Put in deep bowl.

Heat rest of oil. Brown lamb. Add mushrooms and water chestnuts. Mix well. Blend together cornstarch, soy sauce, salt, pepper, sugar and water. Add to pan. Stir for 10 min. till juice thickens.

In sauce pan bring stock to a boil. Put in noodles and meat sauce. Mix thoroughly. Serves 8.

* This concludes the noodle series.

240. September 27—Friday

SHRIMP WITH PEPPER

2 T. oil   ½ T. cornstarch
1 lb. cooked shrimp   ¼ C. water
1 green pepper, cut to size of   ½ t. wine
   shrimp   ½ t. salt
           3 T. tomato sauce

Heat oil. Put in pepper. Stir 2 min. Add shrimp and tomato sauce. Blend together cornstarch, water, wine and salt. Add to shrimp and pepper. When juice thickens, turn off heat. Serves 4.

241. September 28—Saturday

ONION CUSTARD

½ doz. medium onions,   1 T. cornstarch
   sliced   2 eggs
4 slices bacon   ½ C. water
⅓ C. powdered milk   ¼ t. nutmeg
              1½ t. salt

Fry bacon till crisp. Drain on absorbent paper. Put onions in bacon fat. Fry till soft and a little golden. Meanwhile mix powdered milk with cornstarch. Add eggs and beat till smooth. Stir in water, nutmeg and salt. Beat well.

Crush bacon and mix with onions. Put in greased casserole. Pour in egg batter. Bake casserole ¾ hr. in pan of hot water till custard is set. Serves 4.

242. September 29—Sunday

SWEET AND SOUR CHICKEN LIVER

2 T. oil   4 slices canned pineapple,
1 lb. chicken livers, quartered   cut up in chunks
½ t. salt   ⅓ C. stock
¼ t. pepper   3 T. cornstarch
3 green peppers, cut up in   2 t. soy sauce
   pieces   ½ C. sugar
             ⅔ C. water

Heat oil. Put in livers. Brown lightly. Place into warm dish.
Put peppers in frying pan. Stir several min. Add pineapple
and stock. Cover. Turn to low heat and simmer about 15 min.
Blend together cornstarch, soy sauce, vinegar, sugar, and water.
Add to pan. Stir till juice thickens. Pour boiling liquid over
livers. Serves 4-5.

243. September 30—Monday

SWEET AND SOUR PORK

1½ lb. pork meat, sliced into slivers	2 eggs, beaten
	2 T. flour
6 peppers, quartered	1 T. water (opt.)
4 rings canned pineapple, quartered	1 t. salt
	½ t. pepper

1 C. oil

SAUCE:	½ C. vinegar	2 T. soy sauce
	Juice of 1 lemon	½ t. M.S.G.
	1 T. cornstarch	1 C. cold water

Mix eggs, flour, salt, pepper and water. Soak pork in batter.
Heat oil. Slip coated pork into pan. Stir till brown. Pour off
oil. Add peppers and pineapple. Blend together vinegar, sugar,
lemon juice, cornstarch, soy sauce, M.S.G., and water to make
sauce. Add to meat and stir till juice thickens in about 5 min.
Serves 6.

244. October 1—Tuesday

CAULIFLOWER STEAK

¼ C. oil
1 lb. rump steak, sliced thin
  against the grain
1 t. salt
Dash of pepper
½ t. M.S.G.

2 T. scallion, or chives,*
  chopped
1 clove garlic, minced
1 head cauliflower (1½ lb.),
  diced
1 C. stock

SAUCE: 2 T. cornstarch   ¼ C. water
                   2 t. soy sauce

Heat oil. Put in beef. Add scallion and garlic. Brown evenly.
Put in cauliflower. Pour in stock. Cover. Simmer 10 min.
Blend together starch, soy sauce and water. Add to pan and
stir. When juice thickens, turn off heat. Serves 4.

* This is a good time to put some chives into a pot to cultivate on your
kitchen window. Chives come in very handy in the cold weather when scallions
are not readily available, or if you run out of onions. They are very good for
most soups and much more mild than onions or garlic. Parsley is another
handy spice to pot for winter consumption.

245. October 2—Wednesday

VEGETARIAN SOUP

1 qt. boiled water
2 T. soy sauce
1 scallion, chopped

4 drops sesame oil, or olive
  oil
1 t. salt
½ t. M.S.G.

Put all ingredients in a pot. Bring to a boil again. Serves 4.

246. October 3—Thursday

CHOP STEW

2 C. cooked lamb, cubed	4 onions, quartered
2 T. oil	1 C. carrots, sliced
3½ C. water, or lamb stock	1 C. peas
2 t. salt	1 T. cornstarch
1 t. soy sauce	2 T. water

1 qt. hot, cooked rice

Heat oil. Brown lamb in pan. Add water or stock, salt, and soy sauce. Bring to a boil, then simmer over low heat for 5 min. Add onions, carrots and peas. Cook 15-20 min. Pour off liquid into a sauce pan. Blend cornstarch with water. Add to liquid. Stir till juice thickens. Pour over lamb and vegetable mixture. Serve with hot, flaky rice. Serves 4.

247. October 4—Friday

FISH ROLL

6 eggs	1 C. roast pork, diced
1 lb. fillet of halibut	1 T. ham, diced
1 C. peanuts, crushed	2 t. salt

1 T. oil

SAUCE: 1 T. cornstarch   ½ C. water
1 t. soy sauce

Break eggs. Add 1 t. salt and 1 t. oil. Beat well.

Heat 1 t. oil. Put in a ladle-ful of egg. Tip pan to let egg run all over surface. A thin egg-layer will form.

Grind fillet fine in chopper several times. Add remaining salt and oil.

Add diced pork and ham to remaining egg. Stir in fish and peanuts. Mix thoroughly.

Place mixture onto egg layer. Roll egg layer into 1″ diameter. Steam fish roll 45 min. Cut into dainty lengths.

Blend cornstarch, soy sauce and water. Heat till sauce thickens. Pour over fish roll. Serves 6.

248. October 5—Saturday

CHICKEN OMELET

1 doz. extra-large eggs
1 t. oil
1 t. salt
1½ lb. chicken meat,
shredded
2 onions, shredded

2 C. bamboo shoots,
shredded
2 C. water chestnuts,
shredded
2 C. mushrooms, shredded
Oil for deep frying

SAUCE: *2 T. cornstarch*   *1 C. water*
                    2 t. soy sauce

Break eggs. Add oil and salt. Beat well. Put in all other ingredients except oil for deep frying and mix thoroughly.

Bring oil to boil in a pan. Ladle in ½ C. egg batter. Fry to a golden brown. Take out and drain. Stack each omelet on a platter. Blend together cornstarch, water and soy sauce. Heat sauce and stir till liquid is translucent. Pour over platter of omelets. Serves a dozen.

249. October 6—Sunday

SUCCULENT DUCKLING

3 lb. duckling, dressed
1 scallion, cut in 1" sections
20 cloves
3-4 slices ginger
3 sticks cinnamon

1 t. aniseed
3 T. wine
⅓ C. soy sauce
2 t. salt
Oil for deep frying

DIPPING SALT MIX: *2 T. salt*
                        2 T. pepper

Slit duck down back. Put duck in mixture of scallion, cloves, ginger, cinnamon, aniseed, wine, soy sauce and salt. Marinate in this mixture several hrs. Put duck in large pan inside a big steamer with water inside. Steam 2½ hrs. till duck is soft.

Heat oil till very hot. Deep fry duck to a golden brown. Drain. Cool a little, then chop in strips and finally into small bars. Serve along with dipping-salt mixture. Serves 4.

250. October 7—Monday

SWEET AND SOUR PIGS' FEET

4 lb. pigs' feet (about 6 feet)	2 t. salt
⅓ C. soy sauce	Dash of pepper
3 slices ginger root	3 T. vinegar
2 T. wine	3 T. sugar

Put clean feet in large pot. (Here's where it's absolutely necessary to have clean feet.) Cover with cold water. Bring to a boil. Stew over low heat 2 hrs. Add wine, ginger, soy sauce, salt and pepper. Simmer 2 more hrs. Last add vinegar and sugar. Simmer another hr. Serves 6.

251. October —Tuesday: This is the 15th Day of the 8th Moon again the Harvest Moon Festival.

DE LUXE MOON CAKES

STUFFING: *1 C. lard*
     1½ C. sugar
     ¾ C. coconut, shredded
     ⅛ C. sesame seeds, toasted
     ⅛ C. watermelon seeds, shelled
     ½ C. ham, chopped fine

24 unbaked 4" pie crusts

Heat lard very hot. Add all other ingredients. Mix well. When cool, pour into unbaked crusts in small pie tins. Cover with top crusts. Slit centers and bake in oven till crusts are a golden brown. yields 1 doz. moon cakes.

Taro pudding is also eaten during the Harvest Moon Festival.

251A.

TARO PUDDING

2 lb. taro (may be purchased in Chinese stores, called "Wu Tao")	1 C. shrimp, chopped coarsely
1 lb. rice flour	1 C. onion, chopped
1 C. cooked pork, chopped coarsely	1 C. olives, pitted and chopped
1 C. Chinese sausages, chopped coarsely	3 C. cold water
	Salt to taste

Pare taro roots. Grate. Mix all ingredients thoroughly. Pour into pan. Steam in a steamer 1 hr. Cut into bars.

252. October 9—Wednesday

BAKED ONIONS

8 onions, 2" in diameter, peeled	2 T. oil
Boiling water to cover	½ C. water
¾ t. salt	¼ t. M.S.G.
⅛ t. pepper	1½ t. cornstarch
	2 T. water
Parsley	

Put onions in pot of boiling water. Add salt and cover.
Bring to a boil. Cook 5 min. Drain and place in a qt.-size
casserole. Brush with vegetable oil. Season with pepper and
M.S.G. Pour in ½ C. water. Bake in 375° oven for about 55
min. Mix cornstarch with 2 T. water. Blend with onion liquid.
Bake 5 min. more till sauce thickens a bit. Garnish with parsley. Serves 4.

253. October 10—Thursday: Double Ten Tea Celebration *

STEAMED STUFFED DUMPLINGS
(PORK OR LAMB STUFFING)

DOUGH: *3 C. flour*
4 t. baking powder
1 C. water

FILLING MIX: *1 lb. lamb, minced*
1 T. wine
3 T. soy
1 t. sugar
½ t. salt
2 T. sesame oil
1 t. cornstarch

Sift flour and baking powder. Add water and knead well.
Cover with a wet cloth and weight with a plate. Let rise 2 hrs.

---

* 46 years ago today the Republic of China came into being. It threw off
the yoke of Manchu rule, and resumed Chinese control. I remember my
father's telling us how happy he and his friends were to cut off the humiliat-
ing queues, a hateful badge of a conquered people, imposed upon them by the
arrogant, barbaric Manchus.

When I was a child this date was a very important one to the Chinese.
We children not only got a holiday from school lessons, but the Chinese
school also held a special assembly on the history of the Chinese revolution
leading up to the birth of the Republic. Afterwards the school invited all the
pupils to a Chinese tea party held at various Chinese restaurants. Here are
listed a few popular recipes for a tea party. Hot black tea is served throughout
while waiters sail past with endless trays giving off tantalizing aromas.

at room temperature. Divide dough in half. Knead and place on floured board. Roll each half into 2″ rolls. Cut in 1½″ pieces. Flatten each piece into 3″ circles. Place 1 T. filling in center of each circle. Hold dumpling in one hand and hand pinch-gather with the other. Put piece of cheese cloth on rack of steamer with water. Steam dumplings 20 min. Yields 30.

254. October 11—Friday

FRIED "WON TON"
(CLOUD SWALLOWS)

1 qt. oil for deep frying

STUFFING: *1 lb. shrimp, ground fine*
　　　　　　1 egg, beaten
　　　　　　1 scallion, chopped fine
　　　　　　3 t. soy sauce
　　　　　　½ t. salt
　　　　　　¼ t. pepper

Mix all ingredients thoroughly.

DOUGH *: *1 lb. or 2 C. flour, sifted*
　　　　　1 t. salt
　　　　　1 egg, beaten slightly
　　　　　⅓ C. water

Sift flour again with salt in large bowl. Blend in egg. Add water gradually. Form into dough. Knead well on flour dusted board. Cover and let set for half an hr. Roll into paper-thin sheets. Cut sheets into 3″ boxes.

Place 1 t. shrimp stuffing in center of dough. Fold dough into triangles, pressing together edges with fork tines. Leave hole in peak for air to escape.

* Dough, called "skin" in Chinese, may be purchased in Chinese noodle factories.

Heat oil till hot. Slip in stuffed dough and turn to low heat. Fry each side to a golden brown. (Cooking time is 15 min.). Fish out with a slit spoon and drain on absorbent paper towels. Serve hot. Serves 5-6.

255. October 12—Saturday

STEAMED SPONGE CAKE

10 eggs, beaten	*2½ C. flour, sifted*
1 lb. or 2 C. sugar	*4 drops lemon extract*

Mix eggs with sugar in bowl. Beat well, or beat with electric mixer for 20 min. Blend in flour, then lemon extract smoothly. Put into pan and steam in steamer for 45 min. Cut into diamond shapes.

256. October 13—Sunday

ROAST DUCK BUNS

1 duck, dressed	*1 T. salt*
4 C. flour	*¼ C. baking powder*
½ C. lard	*½-⅔ C. water*

Roast duck. Tear off meat. Cut into small pieces.

Sift flour with salt and baking powder in mixing bowl. Cream with lard. Gradually add water to form dough. Roll dough flat. Cut into bun-size pieces. Flatten buns. Put about half the bulk of roast duck as dough on buns and roll into balls. Arrange stuffed buns in double boiler and let stand 10 min. before turning on the heat. Steam 45 min. Save duck carcass to make Duck Broth. If any roast duck is left, serve with Plum Sauce.

257. October 14—Monday

DOT HEARTS

1 qt. oil for deep frying

STUFFING: *1 lb. pork, ground fine*
    1 egg, beaten
    1 onion, minced
    1 T. soy sauce
    ½ t. salt
    ½ t. pepper

Mix all ingredients thoroughly.

DOUGH OR "SKIN": *1 C. flour, sifted*
      ½ t. salt
      1 egg yolk
      3 T. water
      1 egg white

Sift flour once more with salt. Blend in yolk. Add water slowly. Form into workable mass. Knead dough until smooth on lightly floured board. Cover with towel for ⅓ hr. Roll out as thin as possible. Cut into 1" x 3" rectangles.

Form meat mixture with spices into ping-pong sized ball. Flatten top and bottom. Wrap thin dough around meat leaving top and bottom uncovered. Use egg white to glue sides together.

Heat oil hot. Slip in meat balls gently. Fry 10-15 min. Take out with slit ladle. Drain on absorbent paper towel. Serves 6-8.

258. October 15—Tuesday

SALTY BUNS

STUFFING: *2 C. roast beef, chopped coarsely*
2 C. sausage meat, chopped coarsely, or 4 C. roast beef
3 T. Chinese "Southern Cheese," or any soft cheese, melted
Salt to taste

Mix all ingredients thoroughly.

DOUGH: *6 C. flour, sifted*
1 yeast cake
2 scant t. salt
1 T. sugar
3 potatoes
1 T. lard

Peel potatoes. Wash. Put in pan. Cover with cold water. Boil 20-30 min. till tender. Mash when boiled. Let stand till mashed potatoes are lukewarm. Add salt and sugar to mashed potatoes, then yeast cake and lard. Let them dissolve in this mixture.

Sift flour two or more times into big mixing bowl. Make a hole in center of bowl and slowly pour in potato mixture. Mix well.

Dust-clean hands lightly with flour. Remove dough and knead on floured board 10 min. Put dough in covered pan. Let stand overnight. Next day divide dough into 2 equal parts. Knead each lump of dough separately, then let stand until double in size. Cut into the size of buns and flatten. Place stuffing in center (equaling ½ size of dough) and enclose in balls.

Let buns stand 10 min. in steamer on stove before turning on heat. Steam ¾ hr.

259. October 16—Wednesday

BEAN BALLS

Oil for deep frying

STUFFING: ½ *lb. red lentils*
½ *t. salt*
2 *T. sugar*

Boil lentils 3 hrs. Mash. Strain. Let dry. Cream in lard and sugar to form a bean paste.

DOUGH: ½ *C. brown sugar*
⅔ *C. boiling water*
1 *C. glutinous rice flour*
½ *C. sesame seeds*

Dissolve brown sugar in water and boil again. Remove from heat. Blend in rice flour to form dough. Pinch off round lumps of dough and flatten. Spoon in 1 t. bean paste. Reroll into balls. Sprinkle with sesame seeds.

Heat oil. Fry balls to a golden brown. Scoop up with a slit ladle. Drain on absorbent paper. Serve warm.

260. October 17—Thursday *

STEAMED "CHIAO-TZU"
(WITH LAMB STUFFING)

STUFFING: 1 *lb. lean lamb, ground*
1 *lb. cabbage, ground*
1 *lb. carrots, ground*
1 *onion, ground*
¼ *C. soy sauce*
1 *T. ginger, minced*
1½ *T. vegetable oil*

* This concludes our tea party.

Grind meat through medium cutter. Take vegetables and do the same but drain well. Add soy sauce, ginger and vegetable oil. Mix all ingredients thoroughly.

DOUGH: *2 lb. or 4 C. flour*
       1 pt. hot water

Add water to flour slowly. Knead into smooth dough. Divide into forty 8″ lengths. Cut into uniform pieces. Roll out into tiny pie crusts (about 3″ in diameter). If desired, use rim of cup to cut out perfect circles. Place about 2 t. stuffing on center of crusts. Fold into half moons. Pinch edges to enclose.

Put stuffed dough in steamer and steam till dough is shiny and a little translucent.

Serve warm with tiny saucers of soy sauce and vinegar. Dip "Chiao-Tzu" into these saucers for added flavor before eating.

261. October 18—Friday

SOY SAUCE SHRIMP

2 doz. fresh shrimp, shelled   4 T. rice wine, or sauterne
   and washed   4 T. olive oil
4 T. soy sauce   1 T. ginger, ground
              1 clove garlic, minced

Dry shrimp on absorbent paper towel.

Marinate shrimp for 1 hr. in mixture of soy sauce, wine, oil, ginger and garlic.

Heat skillet. Put shrimp and a bit of the mixture in skillet. Cook several min. till shrimp turn pink. Serves 4.

262. October 19—Saturday

RED STEWED EGGS

6 extra large eggs, hard-　　¼ C. soy sauce
　boiled　　　　　　　　　2 slices ginger
1 pt. stock　　　　　　　　1 onion, cut into 6 wedges
　　　　　2 T. rice wine, or sherry

Shell eggs. Put in pot with stock, soy sauce, ginger, onion, and wine. Bring to a boil and simmer 1½ hrs. Serves 6 with hot rice.

263. October 20—Sunday

CHESTNUT CHICKEN

½ lb. chicken, sliced　　　1 lb. mushrooms, quartered
1 lb. chestnut meat, chopped　1 t. salt
　coarsely　　　　　　　　1 T. soy sauce
1 can water chestnuts,　　　Oil for deep frying
　chopped coarsely　　　　1 C. stock
　　　　　　　Parsley

Rub salt and soy sauce on chicken. Bring oil to a boil. Put in chicken. Fry to a golden brown. Take out. Drain. Put in a pot. Add stock. Boil chicken till nearly tender. Add chestnuts, water chestnuts and mushrooms. Cook till everything is tender. Garnish with parsley. Serves 4-6.

264. October 21—Monday

STEAMED SPARERIBS

2½-3 lb. spareribs, chopped　1 T. soy sauce
　into 1½" pieces　　　　　1 t. salt
2 t. brown bean sauce, or　　Dried tangerine peel,
　substitute Bovril　　　　　crumbled

Put ribs in bowl. Spread bean sauce or Bovril on spareribs. Add soy sauce and salt. Sprinkle with tangerine peel. Put a trivet in a large pot—add water. Place bowl of spareribs on top of trivet. Cover pot. Steam ¾ hr. Serves 4-5.

265. October 22—Tuesday

POTATO STEAK

¼ C. oil
1 lb. flank steak, cut into strips and sliced into thin slivers against the grain
1 t. salt
½ t. pepper
1 onion, chopped
1 clove garlic, minced
2 C. potatoes, diced
¾ C. stock
1 C. celery leaves, cut up
2 T. cornstarch
2 t. soy sauce
¼ C. water

Heat oil in pan. Put in beef, salt, pepper, onion and garlic. Brown evenly. Add potatoes. Pour in stock. Cover. Cook over medium heat 10 min. Add celery leaves. Stir just till leaves are tender (no more than 5 min.). Blend together cornstarch, soy sauce and water. Add to pan. Stir till juice thickens. Serves 4.

266. October 23—Wednesday

SAUTÉED CELERY CABBAGE

2 lb. celery cabbage, cut diagonally in ½" strips
3 T. vegetable oil
½ t. salt
¼ C. water

Heat oil. Sauté cabbage 1 min. Pour in water and salt. Cover. Cook 4 min. Serves 8.

267. October 24—Thursday

LAMB KIDNEY STEW

2 T. oil	*1 t. salt*
1 lb. lamb kidney (discard	*Dash of pepper*
white membrane and cube	*1 ½ pt. stock*
into red dices)	*2 T. cornstarch*
2 onions, sliced	*2 t. soy sauce*
1 t. dry mustard	*¼ C. water*

Put lamb kidney in cold salted water. Let stand 1 hr. Drain. Parboil. Drain.

Heat oil. Brown kidney evenly. Pour in stock. Bring to a boil. Skim. Add onion, mustard, salt and pepper. Simmer ½ hr. till kidney is tender. Blend together cornstarch, soy sauce and water. Pour into pan. Stir till juice thickens. Serve with hot, steaming rice. Serves 4.

268. October 25—Friday

FRIED FISH

6 lb. pike	*Salt*
1 C. water	*Oil for deep frying*
8 T. vinegar	*1 T. cornstarch*
2 t. flour	*1 t. soy sauce*
¼ C. water	

Clean fish. Salt all over. Let stand 15 min. Wipe off some salt. Fry in deep oil until brown. Mix water, vinegar and flour. Add. Cover. Cook over moderate heat 10 min. Blend together cornstarch, soy sauce and water. Add to fish in pan. When juice thickens, turn off heat. Serves 6.

269. October 26—Saturday

VEGETABLE FLOWER SOUP

3 eggs, beaten	1/3 C. mushrooms, sliced
2 qt. stock	1/3 C. pimentos, sliced
1/3 C. bean sprouts	1/3 C. onions, shredded
1/3 C. water chestnuts, sliced	2 T. soy sauce
1/3 C. bamboo shoots, sliced	Dash of pepper

Bring stock to a boil. Add all other vegetables. Cook 5-10 min. Turn to high heat. Pour in beaten eggs and continue to stir soup another 5 min. Season with soy sauce and dash of pepper. Serves 8.

270. October 27—Sunday

DUCK DICES

5-6 lb. duck	2 C. bamboo shoots, sliced
2 T. oil	2 C. small mushrooms, sliced
	3½ C. duck broth

SAUCE:	1 t. cornstarch	1 t. salt
	1/4 C. water	1/2 t. pepper
	1 t. soy sauce	1/2 t. sugar

Stew duck for 2 hrs. Save broth. Dice duck.

Heat oil. Put in shoots and mushrooms. Add ½ C. broth. Cover. Cook 20 min. Mix with duck dices. Pour in rest of broth. Bring to a boil. Blend together cornstarch, water, soy sauce, salt, pepper, and sugar. Then add to duck mixture. Mix thoroughly. Serves 6.

271. October 28—Monday

"WON TON" SOUP
("RAVIOLI" OR "KREPLACH" IN CHICKEN SOUP)

STUFFING: *½ lb. pork, ground*
             ½ t. salt
             ¼ t. pepper
             1 onion, minced

Mix all ingredients thoroughly.

"SKIN": *1½ C. flour, sifted*   *1 egg, beaten lightly*
          1 t. salt   *⅛ C. water*

Sift flour with salt into mixing bowl. Blend in egg and water. Turn onto flour dusted board and knead into smooth dough. Cover with clean towel. Leave alone for ¼ hr. Roll dough out on dusted board very thin. Cut into 3" squares.

Place 1 t. stuffing in center of each square. Fold into triangle. Pinch edges together.

Boil qt. of salted water. Put in "Won Ton." Boil ¼ hr. Drain.

SOUP: *1 qt. chicken stock*
       ½ C. celery, chopped
       ½ C. roast pork, shredded
       1 C. celery leaves, cut up

Heat stock to a boil. Put in celery, pork shreds and celery leaves. Slip in "Won Ton." Cook 1 min. If desired, garnish with one hard-boiled egg, quartered. Serves 4.

272. October 29—Tuesday

RICH OXTAIL STEW

*3 lb. oxtail, chopped into
small pieces
½ C. dried black beans *
(opt.)*

*3 slices ginger root
2 qt. water
1 T. salt*

Parboil oxtail. Drain. Add clean water. Bring to a boil. Add black beans, ginger and salt. Simmer 5 hrs. Serves 6.

* Dried black beans are sold in Chinese stores, called "Hark Doe."

273. October 30—Wednesday

SWEET AND SOUR CABBAGE

*1 head cabbage, cut up in
triangles
⅛ C. vegetable oil
1½ t. salt*

*½ C. hot water
1 T. cornstarch
1½ C. cold water
3 T. sugar*

3 T. vinegar

Heat oil. Put in clean cabbage. Fry 1 min. Season with salt. Pour in hot water. Stir several min. more. Blend together cornstarch, water, sugar and vinegar. Add to pan. Stir till liquid is translucent. Serves 4-6.

274. October 31—Thursday: Double Ninth *

BARBECUED LAMB

5 lb. leg of lamb, sliced   *1 T. salt*
    against the grain   *2 T. sugar*
½ C. soy sauce   *Italian garlic bread, sliced*
1 clove garlic, minced   *thick*
1 t. onion salt

At home, mix soy sauce, garlic, salt, onion salt, and sugar together. Marinate lamb slices in this liquid to tenderize. Put lamb in marinating liquid in picnic basket. At the picnic grounds, start a hot charcoal fire. Place dripping slices of lamb on flat, tinfoil-lined grate for about 2 min. Turn and cook the other side another 2 min. Serve on garlic bread, sliced very thick. Serves 6 hearty, lively humans.

* Today is the 9th Day of the 9th Moon. This day was reserved for family gatherings at the cemetery to tidy up grave mounds. At the conclusion there was usually a picnic on the hills.

275. November 1—Friday

STOVE PARTY

A STOVE PARTY IS A COOL WEATHER SHINDIG THAT TAKES PLACE from November 1-March 1 in Chinese homes. Place an electric plate on the center of the dining room table. Put on it a huge chafing pot filled with 2 qt. boiling chicken broth. Cut into slivers 6 lb. raw meat, fish, or poultry. Put out 2 pr. chopsticks, or 2 forks, for each person is responsible for cooking and eating his own food. Have as many bowls as there are persons present. In each bowl mix a beaten egg with 1 T. soy sauce, ½ t. salad oil and 4 drops sesame oil. (This is for dipping the self-cooked meat in.) Keep everyone moving. Here's suggestion for one.

2 qt. chicken broth   1½ T. soy sauce
1 onion, minced   4 drops sesame oil
                1 C. spinach, cut up

On separate plates place:

1 lb. fish fillet, shredded   1 lb. shrimp, cleaned and
1 lb. white duckling meat,   sliced horizontally
shredded   1 lb. lean pork, sliced into
1 lb. rump steak, sliced into   slivers
thin slivers against the grain   1 lb. lobster meat, sliced

Each guest may select whatever food he wishes to cook by picking up slivers with chopsticks or forks and immersing it in bubbling broth for about 2 min. Remove it from broth and dip it into his personal bowl with egg sauce. He eats it with the other pair of chopsticks or fork.

When everyone has cooked and eaten all he desires, the host or hostess will put the onion, soy sauce, sesame oil, and spinach into the broth to simmer several min. more before ladling soup into each guest's personal bowl. Serves 8.

276. November 2—Saturday

EGG FLOWER SOUP

1 egg, beaten   1 T. onion, chopped
1 qt. stock   1 C. watercress
½ C. celery, sliced
diagonally

In saucepan bring stock to a boil. Add celery and onion. When liquid boils again, stir in egg. It will form into a flowery pattern. Add watercress and stir at high heat another min. Serves 4.

277. November 3—Sunday

"MOCK PEKING DUCK"

4-5 lb. duckling, dressed
2 C. hot water
½ C. honey
¼ C. vinegar
1 T. molasses
½ C. soy sauce
2 T. gin
2 T. flour

1 T. salt
½ C. oil
Thin biscuits, if not available,
    substitute thin-sliced sand-
    wich bread
Scallions, cut into 1½" lengths
Mustard
Plum Sauce

Celery salt

Wash duck. Parboil in hot water ¾ hr. Drain. Rinse in running water. Dry with paper towels. Blend together honey, vinegar, molasses, soy sauce and gin. Baste duck with mixture. When dry, baste again. Sprinkle duck with flour and salt, then heat oil very hot, and fry duck.

Duck will brown in few min. Take duck out and drain. Cut off skin and serve first. Enclose crisp skin in a thin biscuit, or use thin-sliced bread with scallions, mustard, plum sauce and celery salt. Next slice duck and serve likewise. By the time nearly all the meat is sliced off, take away the duck frame to make Chinese cabbage soup, or make stock for Steamed Egg Custard. Serves 4.

278. November 4—Monday

STEAMED PORK STEAK

1 lb. lean pork, ground
1 C. mushrooms, diced
½ C. water chestnuts, diced
½ C. onion, minced
½ t. M.S.G.

1 T. salad oil
1 T. cornstarch
4 T. water
1 T. soy sauce
1 t. salt

½ t. pepper

Mix all ingredients thoroughly. Form into flat pie on a round plate. (Make sure plate is at least 1″ bigger in diameter than pie.) Pour 1″-2″ hot water into pot. Place meat plate on trivet in big covered pot. Steam ½-¾ hr. Serves 4.

279. November 5—Tuesday

BEEF NOODLES

¾ lb. egg noodles, boiled 8 min., rinsed in cold water, drained
⅓ C. oil
1 lb. chuck, ground
1 t. salt
½ t. pepper
1 clove garlic, minced

1 onion, minced
2 C. mushrooms, sliced
1 C. stock
1 C. celery, diced
2 green peppers, diced
2 T. cornstarch
¼ C. water
2 t. soy sauce

Heat oil. Put beef in and season with salt, pepper, garlic and onion. Brown. Stir 5 min. Pour in stock. Add celery, mushrooms and green peppers. Cover. Cook 5 min. Blend together cornstarch, soy sauce and water. Add to pan. When juice thickens turn off heat and pour over noodles. Serves 4.

280. November 6—Wednesday

CANTON FRUIT CUP

1 can chunk-style pineapple
2 oranges, peeled and skinned, cut up

2 bananas, peeled, cut in rings
1 piece preserved ginger candy, minced

Mix all ingredients. Chill. Divide into 4 sherbet cups. Serves 4.

281. November 7—Thursday

LAMB SWEETBREAD

2 pr. sweetbreads, halved   1 t. salt
    crosswise   1 C. flour
1 qt. cold water   1 t. garlic salt
1 qt. boiling water   ½ t. pepper
1 T. vinegar   2 T. oil
            1 C. stock

SAUCE: 2 T. cornstarch   ¼ C. water
             2 t. soy sauce

Cover sweetbreads with cold water. Let stand ½ hr. Drain. Pour in boiling water. Add vinegar and salt. Simmer 20 min. Drain. Rinse in cold water. Remove membrane.

Mix flour with garlic salt and pepper. Roll sweetbreads in flour.

Heat oil. Sauté sweetbreads. Brown evenly. Pour in stock. Simmer 20 min. Blend together cornstarch, water, and soy sauce. Add to pan. Stir till juice thickens. Serves 4.

282. November 8—Friday

GOLD AND SILVER SMELTS

1 lb. smelts, cleaned   ¼ t. pepper
¼ C. oil   ¾ C. soy sauce
½ t. salt   ⅛ C. scallion, chopped fine
           ⅛ C. water

Heat oil. Sauté fish till golden. Season with salt and pepper. Add soy sauce. Put in scallion and water. Cover. Cook another 2 or 3 min. Serves 4.

283. November 9—Saturday

CHOPPED OYSTER

2 T. oil
5 dried oysters
2 T. bamboo shoots, ground
10 water chestnuts, ground
2 T. salted peanuts, ground
¼ lb. pork, ground

¼ t. M.S.G.
½ t. gin
½ t. soy sauce
¼ C. water
1 small head lettuce, washed
    and drained

1 t. salt

Soak oysters for 6 hrs., or till soft. Grind.

Heat oil. Put in pork. Season with salt and M.S.G. Stir. Add oysters and stir another min. Mix in bamboo shoots, water chestnuts, peanuts, soy sauce, gin and water. Continue stirring till everything is cooked. Serve on lettuce-lined platter, or let each guest roll up a lettuce leaf and scoop in a spoonful of meat and eat with fingers. Serves 4.

284. November 10—Sunday

FRIED DUCK

½ C. oil
3½ lb. duckling, cleaned and
    quartered
½ C. flour
1 t. salt

½ t. pepper
¾ C. stock
1 T. cornstarch
¼ C. water
1 t. soy sauce

Dredge duckling with flour mixed with salt and pepper.

Heat oil. Put duck in frying pan (fat side up). Brown evenly for 20 min., turning occasionally. Pour off fat and pour in stock. Cover. Simmer 1½ hrs. Uncover last 10 min. to get skin crisp. Serve plain, or if desired, thicken liquid by blending together cornstarch, soy sauce and water, then add to pan and stir till juice thickens. Serves 4-6.

285. November 11—Monday

BAKED PORK CHOPS

6 lean pork chops	1 C. celery, chopped fine
2 cloves garlic	1 green pepper, chopped
1 t. salt	fine
½ t. pepper	1 can tomato soup
½ t. M.S.G.	1 can pork stock
1 onion, minced	1 C. rice, washed

Slit garlic open. Rub into chops well. Season with salt, pepper, and M.S.G. Arrange in a greased baking pan. Spread rice all over surface. Mix onions, celery and green pepper into rice. Pour can of tomato soup on top, then can of stock. Mix with rice and vegetables. Bake in slow oven (325°) till rice is fluffy and chops are very tender. Serves 6.

286. November 12—Tuesday

RED STEWED TONGUE

4 lb. tongue	¼ C. soy sauce
1 qt. water	2 t. salt
1 T. ginger, minced	

Put clean tongue in water. Bring to a boil. Peel skin. Add all other ingredients. Simmer 3-4 hrs., or till tender. There will be enough cold sandwich meat to last one for a week. If served hot, there will be enough to serve 6-8.

287. November 13—Wednesday

SWISS CHARD WITH CATSUP

2 lb. Swiss chard, sliced diagonally	1 t. salt
	½ C. water
3 T. vegetable oil	¼ C. catsup

Heat oil. Put in chard, white section first. Season with salt. Stir for a min. Add water. Cover. Cook 5 min. Add catsup. Stir several min. more. Serves 6-8.

288. November 14—Thursday

BEAN CURD, LAMB SLICED SOUP

1½ qt. lamb stock	1 C. mushrooms, sliced
1 pt. bean curd, diced	⅛ C. soy sauce
½ lb. lamb, sliced thin against the grain	½ t. salt
	½ t. M.S.G.
½ T. cornstarch	

Mix meat with cornstarch and half of soy sauce.

Heat stock. Put in mushrooms. Boil 1 min. Add bean curd. Boil another min. Add salt, M.S.G., and rest of soy sauce. Finally put in meat mixture. Boil 4 min. more. Serves 6.

289. November 15—Friday

DE LUXE STUFFED PEPPERS

1 lb. shrimp, shelled, cleaned and ground	1 onion, chopped fine
	1 t. salt
1 lb. haddock, chopped fine	½ t. pepper
1 t. M.S.G.	⅛ C. cornstarch
⅛ C. oil	¼ C. water
⅛ C. soy sauce	1½ C. stock
12 green peppers	

Mix together shrimp, haddock, onion, M.S.G., oil, soy sauce, cornstarch, salt, pepper, and water. Cut tops off peppers. Clean, then put fish mixture into hollow peppers.

Place stuffed peppers in large frying pan. Pour in stock. Cover pan. Cook 10-15 min. Serves 12.

290. November 16—Saturday

EGG AND CHICKEN SOUP

2 eggs, beaten	6 C. stock
½ lb. cooked chicken, diced	1 t. salt
2 tomatoes, peeled and cut up	¾ t. M.S.G.

Bring stock with chicken and tomatoes to a boil. When bubbling vigorously, stir in eggs. Season with salt and M.S.G. Serves 6.

290A.

OMELET IN SOUP

2 eggs, beaten	1 T. oil
1 t. salt	1 qt. stock
½ t. pepper	1 C. noodles, boiled 8 min.,
½ t. sugar	rinsed in cold water,
1 onion, minced	drained

Mix eggs, salt, pepper, sugar and onion together. Heat oil. Scramble batter. When eggs set, take out. Cut into cubes.

Bring stock to a boil. Add noodles and egg cubes. Stir and turn off heat. Serves 6.

291. November 17—Sunday

CHINESE ROAST CHICKEN

5-6 lb. capon, dressed and ½ *C. soy sauce*
 washed   2 *T. sugar*
½ *C. chicken fat*   *1 t. salt*
1 clove garlic, minced ½ *t. pepper*
1 dried tangerine peel, 4 *drops sesame oil*
 crushed   *1*½ *C. hot stock*

Mix all ingredients such as garlic, peel, soy sauce, salt, pepper, sugar, and sesame oil, with stock. Marinate capon in this mixture overnight if possible. Brush melted chicken fat liberally on capon. Roast in moderate 350° oven for 2-3 hrs. uncovered, basting often with liquid mixture. Use pan dripping as light gravy. Serves 6-8.

292. November 18—Monday

SPINACH SOUP

1 lb. spinach, cut up ½ *C. celery, diced*
½ *lb. lean pork, diced* *1*½ *qt. stock*
½ *C. onion, diced*   ½ *t. M.S.G.*
    Salt to taste

Heat stock in pot. Add all ingredients. Bring to a boil. Cook 10-15 min. Serves 6.

293. November 19—Tuesday

OYSTER SAUCE STEAK

2 lb. round steak, cut into   1 T. cornstarch
   thin slices against the grain   ⅛ C. water
⅛ C. soy sauce   1 large onion, chopped
1 T. wine   ⅛ C. oil
½ t. salt   ⅛ C. Oyster Sauce
¼ t. M.S.G.   1 t. sugar

Mix meat, soy sauce, wine, salt, M.S.G., cornstarch, and water.

Heat oil. Sauté onion and beef about 2 min. Turn to moderate heat. Stir 8 min. more. Turn off heat. Add Oyster Sauce and sugar. Mix thoroughly. Serves 8.

294. November 20—Wednesday

CREAMED CABBAGE

1 small head cabbage (about   1 t. salt
   1 lb.)   ½ t. pepper
¼ C. milk   3 T. cornstarch
2 T. butter, or margarine   ¼ C. water

Wash cabbage. Shred into 2″ strips. Cook cabbage in water for 5 min. Dissolve butter or margarine and cornstarch in milk. Stir over medium heat till thick. Combine with cooked cabbage. Stir over medium heat another min. or two. Serves 4.

295. November 21—Thursday

SEAWEED SOUP

3 oz. dried laver *   *1 T. fresh shrimp, shelled,*
1 T. lean lamb, beef, or pork,   *minced*
minced   *6 C. stock*
                             1 t. salt

Soak dried laver in warm water 30 min. Wash off sand.
Put all ingredients together in pot. Mix. Cook 10 min.
Serves 4-6.

  * Laver is an edible marine algae. It's sold in Chinese stores, called "Tzu Chia."

296. November 22—Friday

FISH SOUP

2-3 lb. fish fillet, flaked   *1 t. soy sauce*
2 qt. stock   *¼ C. water*
1 C. water chestnuts, diced   *1 t. salt*
1 C. bamboo shoots, diced   *½ t. pepper*
1 C. mushrooms, diced   *½ t. M.S.G.*
1 T. cornstarch   *1 scallion, chopped fine*

Pour stock and vegetables in pot. Cook together 20 min.
Add fish. Cook 15 min. more. Blend together cornstarch, soy
sauce, water, salt, pepper and M.S.G. Stir into soup. Mix well.
Garnish with scallion. Serves 8.

297. November 23—Saturday

FRIED COOKED EGGS

Oil for deep frying   *1 piece ginger root*
1 doz. eggs, hard-boiled and   *1 C. stock*
   shelled   *4 scallions, cut into 1½"*
2 C. mushrooms, shredded   *pieces and julienned*
      1½ lb. chicken, shredded

SAUCE: *1 T. cornstarch*   ¼ *C. water*
     1 t. soy sauce   *1 t. salt*
      Dash of pepper

Heat oil and put in eggs. Brown evenly. Take eggs out and drain on absorbent paper. Pour off oil, leaving only a couple of tablespoonfuls in pan. Put in chicken, mushrooms, and ginger. Stir 5 min. Pour in stock. Cover. Cook 10-15 min. Blend together cornstarch, soy sauce, salt, pepper and water. Add to pan. Stir till juice thickens. Garnish with scallions. Serves 8.

298. November 24—Sunday

BROILED DUCK

4 lb. duckling, dressed   *2 T. sugar*
1 t. salt   *1 T. soy sauce*
½ *t. pepper*   ⅓ *C. stock*

Split bird lengthwise. To keep duckling flat during broiling, snap drumsticks, thigh, and wing joints. Season by rubbing on soy sauce, then sprinkling with salt, pepper, and sugar. Remove rack of broiler pan and put duck, skin side down, flat on pan. Place broiler 7" below heat source. Broil gently for 1 hr. Turn bird every ¼ hr. and spoon off oil. If not served immediately, put duck in pan with stock. Cover and leave in warm oven. Serves 4-6.

299. November 25—Monday

RED STEWED PIGS' FEET

4 pigs' feet   *2 T. wine*
¼ C. soy sauce   *1 t. salt*
2-3 slices ginger   *2-3 C. water*

Put washed feet in big pot. Add water. Boil over high heat 1½ hrs. Add soy sauce, ginger, wine and salt. Turn down heat. Simmer another 3 hrs., or till skin is very tender. Serves 4.

300. November 26—Tuesday

BEEF AND CUCUMBER SOUP

2 lb. soup bones   *1 t. wine*
2 cucumbers, cut in large   *1 slice ginger*
*   cubes*   *¼ lb. rump steak, sliced thin*
¼ t. sugar   *   against the grain*
1 qt. water   *1 t. salt*
1 t. oil   *½ t. pepper*

Boil water in pot. Put in bones and cucumber. Bring to a boil, then simmer 1 hr. Add all other ingredients. Cook 15 min. more. Serves 4-6.

301. November 27—Wednesday

FRIED BEAN CURD

Oil for deep frying   *1 pt. bean curd, cubed*
                               1 t. salt

Heat oil very hot. Add bean curd and salt. Fry each cube to a golden puff. Serves 2-3.

302. November 28—Thursday: Thanksgiving Day

CHINESE ROAST TURKEY

8 lb. broiler turkey, dressed   4 drops sesame oil
2 t. allspice   2 t. salt
2 C. soy sauce   1 pt. hot water
Melted chicken fat, or butter

Put turkey in hot water for about 2 min. Add allspice, soy sauce, sesame oil and salt. Let turkey sit in this liquid for ¾ hr. turning several times. Remove and brush with fat. Stuff as desired.

Place in a pan. Cover loosely with tinfoil. Roast in 325° oven about 3½ hrs. Baste occasionally with soy sauce liquid. To crisp skin, remove tinfoil last half hr. Serves 8-10.

303. November 29—Friday

FRIED OYSTERS

⅓ C. oil   ½ t. pepper
1 pt. oysters   2 onions, chopped
1 egg, beaten   1 T. cornstarch
1 T. water   1 t. soy sauce
1 t. salt   ¾ C. water

Dilute beaten egg with a little water. Season with salt and pepper. Dip oysters in egg batter. Drain.

Heat oil. Brown oysters evenly. Pour off all oil except for 2 T. Put in onions to brown. Blend together cornstarch, soy sauce, and water. Pour into pan. Stir till juice thickens. Serves 4.

304. November 30—Saturday

WHITE CUT CHICKEN

6-7 lb. fowl, dressed
½ gal. water
Salt to taste

Oyster Sauce, put in small
individual saucers for
dipping

Place washed chicken in big pot. Pour in water. Season with salt. Bring to a boil. Simmer 2½ hrs. till tender. Save liquid for stock. Chill in refrigerator. Chop into bite-sized pieces. Serve with Oyster Sauce. Serves 8.

305. December 1—Sunday

TURKEY SOUP

BROTH: *Bones of 1 turkey*
        ½ gal. water
        Salt to taste

Put bones in pot. Add water and salt. Bring to a boil. Simmer 4 hrs. Discard all bones.

SOUP: *1 C. mushrooms, sliced*
       ½ C. celery, sliced diagonally
       ½ C. onion, shredded
       ½ C. cooked turkey meat, shredded

Put mushrooms, onions, celery and turkey shreds into broth. Bring to a boil. Cook 10 min. more. Serves 10.

306. December 2—Monday

FRIED SPARERIBS

1½ C. oil for deep frying	½ C. flour
3 lb. spareribs, chopped in 1½" pieces	2 eggs, beaten
	1 t. salt
2½ C. bread crumbs	½ t. pepper

½ t. M.S.G.

Blend together bread crumbs and flour. Stir in eggs seasoned with salt, pepper, and M.S.G. Coat spareribs with batter. Heat oil. Fry spareribs till golden brown. Drain. Serves 6.

307. December 3—Tuesday

RED STEWED BEEF

1 T. oil	½ t. pepper
2 lb. chuck, cubed	1 T. sugar
½ C. soy sauce	¾ C. wine
3 C. water	3 stalks celery, cut diagonally
3-4 slices ginger	
1 t. salt	4 white turnips, cubed

Heat oil in pot. Brown beef cubes. Mix soy sauce, water, ginger, salt, pepper, sugar and wine. Stir into beef. Cover. Bring to a boil. Simmer 1½ hrs. Add turnips and celery. Cook 20-30 min. more. Serves 8.

308. December 4—Wednesday

CELERY CABBAGE AND CHESTNUTS

1 celery cabbage, cut diagonally into shreds	3 T. vegetable oil
	⅛ C. soy sauce
15 chestnuts, boiled, shelled, skinned and halved	1 t. salt
	1 t. sugar

Heat oil very hot. Sauté cabbage, stirring 5 min. Add chestnuts, soy sauce, salt and sugar. Cover. Cook over moderate heat several min. Serves 4.

309. December 5—Thursday

ROLLED LAMB SHOULDER

4 lb. lamb shoulder, boned and rolled by butcher	*2 t. soy sauce*
	1 t. salt
2 T. cornstarch	*½ t. pepper*
1 C. lamb stock	*2 T. melted lamb fat*

Bake lamb in 300-325° oven 3 hrs. Blend together cornstarch, soy sauce, stock, salt, pepper and melted fat. Heat till liquid is translucent. Serve with lamb. Serves 8.

310. December 6—Friday

SESAME SEAFOOD

6 halibut fillets	*Dash of pepper*
1⅛ t. salt	*3 T. sesame seeds, toasted*
6 T. oil	*½ t. dried tangerine peel,*
1½ pt. soft bread crumbs	*crumbled*

Arrange fillets in well-greased roasting pan. Salt. Pour oil over fillets. Mix together crumbs, pepper, sesame seeds, and crumbled peel. Sprinkle fillets with this mixture. Bake ½ hr. in 350° oven. Serves 6.

311. December 7—Saturday

EGG BATTER RIBS

2 lb. spareribs, chopped in   2-3 C. dried bread crumbs
  1½" pieces   2 T. flour
2 eggs, well beaten   1 C. mixed sweet pickles
        1½ C. oil for deep frying

SWEET AND SOUR SAUCE: 1 pt. cold water
                       ½ t. M.S.G.
                       ½ C. vinegar
                       Juice of 1 lemon
                       ¾ C. sugar
                       ¼ C. soy sauce
                       2 T. cornstarch

Mix eggs with crumbs, flour and ribs.

Heat oil. Fry ribs till golden brown. Drain on absorbent paper.

Blend together water, M.S.G., vinegar, lemon juice, sugar, soy sauce, and cornstarch. Cook till juice thickens. Add sweet pickles and ribs. Mix thoroughly. Serves 6.

312. December 8—Sunday

CHICKEN VEGETABLE SOUP

6 C. chicken broth   ¼ C. onions, sliced
¼ C. bean sprouts   ¼ C. celery, sliced
¼ C. water chestnuts, sliced   3 eggs, beaten
¼ C. bamboo shoots, sliced   1 T. soy sauce
¼ C. mushrooms, sliced   1 t. salt
            ½ t. pepper

Heat stock. Add vegetables. Boil 5-10 min. Stir in eggs. Add soy sauce, salt and pepper. Serves 8.

313. December 9—Monday

PORK SOUP

1 lb. pork shoulder, cubed
1 qt. stock
1 large onion
1 t. salt

½ t. pepper
4 water chestnuts
1 C. celery cabbage, sliced diagonally

Put pork cubes in stock. Bring to a boil. Slip in onion wedges. Simmer 1½ hrs. Add water chestnuts and cabbage. Cook ½ hr. more. Serves 6.

314. December 10—Tuesday

OYSTER SAUCE BEEF RICE

1 lb. rice
1½ lb. round steak, cut into strips and sliced into thin shreds against the grain
½ t. M.S.G.
1 T. salad oil

1 C. mushrooms, sliced
1 T. cornstarch
2 T. soy sauce
1 t. salt
½ t. pepper
Oyster Sauce

Wash rice in several changes of water. Put rice in 3 qt. sauce pan. Add enough water to go 1″ above rice level. Cover. Bring to a boil for one min. Turn from medium to low heat. Mix all other ingredients except oyster sauce thoroughly and pour on top of rice. Cover sauce pan tightly and cook gently 20 min. Uncover and mix thoroughly beef and rice. Serve with saucers of Oyster Sauce for 6.

315. December 11—Wednesday

SWISS CHARD
(THIS WILL PROBABLY BE THE LAST OF OUR GARDEN SWISS CHARD)

1 T. vegetable oil
1 lb. Swiss chard, cut off tough white part, wash leafy part and slice diagonally

½ t. salt
¼ t. pepper
¼ M.S.G.
¼ C. water

Heat oil. Put in all other ingredients except water. Mix well for a min. Pour in liquid. Cover. Cook about 5 min. Uncover. Turn to high heat and stir constantly for a few min. more. Serves 4.

316. December 12—Thursday

STUFFED GREEN PEPPERS

3-4 lb. lamb breast, boned and ground
1 T. oil
2 t. salt
½ t. pepper
1 T. soy sauce
1 onion, minced

4 large green peppers, hollowed and cleaned
2 T. fat
½ C. lamb stock
1 T. cornstarch
½ t. garlic salt
½ t. M.S.G.

¼ C. water

Mix together lamb, oil, salt, pepper, soy sauce and onion. Stuff into green peppers.

Heat oil. Put stuffed peppers in pan. Pour in stock. Cover. Simmer 1 hr. Remove peppers to plate. Blend together cornstarch, garlic salt, M.S.G., and water. Add to pan. Stir till juice thickens. Pour over peppers. Serves 4.

317. December 13—Friday

FISH BALLS

3 lb. fish fillet (pike)   1 t. salt
1 ½ C. salted almonds   1 t. cornstarch
½ C. ham   1 C. water
1 bunch Chinese cabbage
  about 3 lb.

GRAVY: 2 T. cornstarch   2 t. soy sauce
         ½ C. water

Grind fish fine.

Chop almonds, ham and cabbage into small pieces. Put ground fish in bowl and mix with water and cornstarch. Mix in ham and almonds. Scrub hands thoroughly. Form fish mixture into small, nickel-sized balls. Slip balls into huge pot of boiling water. When balls float to surface, take out with slit ladle and place in bowl.

Cook cabbage for 20 min. Mix balls and vegetable together. Blend together cornstarch, soy sauce, and water. Heat to a boil. When juice thickens, stop stirring and pour over fish-ball dish. Serves 8.

318. December 14—Saturday

"HOT" FLOWER SOUP

4 eggs, beaten   ¼ C. white vinegar
1 qt. stock   2 T. cornstarch
2 t. salt   ½ C. cooked pork, sliced
1 t. pepper   thin diagonally
       2 T. soy sauce

Mix 1 C. stock from required qt. with soy sauce, cornstarch, salt and pepper. Add rest of stock. Bring to a boil. Turn to low heat. Pour in eggs while stirring constantly. Add vinegar and pork. Bring to a boil again. Serves 6.

319. December 15—Sunday

CHICKEN "CHOW MEIN"

1 lb. noodles

GRAVY

2 T. fat
1 lb. chicken meat, shredded
1 C. onion, shredded
1 beaten egg, fried and cut into shreds
1 lb. mushrooms, sliced

1 T. cornstarch
1 T. soy sauce
1 t. salt
½ t. pepper
3 C. stock
2 T. oil

Boil noodles 8 min. Rinse in cold water. Drain. Put oil on noodles to keep from sticking.

Melt fat. Sauté chicken and onion. Blend together stock, soy sauce, salt, pepper and cornstarch. Heat till juice thickens. Add mushrooms and egg. Cook 5 min. Pour chicken and gravy over noodles. Serves 4.

320. December 16—Monday

FRIED PORK LIVER

1 lb. pork liver, sliced into slivers
4 dried mushrooms, soaked or 8 mushrooms, sliced
2 scallions, cut into 1" sections

2 cloves garlic, crushed
½ lb. spinach leaves, cut into large pieces
6 slices ginger
½ C. oil

SAUCE: ¼ C. soy sauce
       2 T. wine
           2 T. water

2 t. sugar
1 T. cornstarch

Heat oil till it smokes. Add liver, mushrooms, scallions, garlic, spinach and ginger. Brown liver. Blend together soy sauce, wine, sugar, cornstarch, and water. Add to frying pan. When juice thickens turn off heat. Serves 4.

321. December 17—Tuesday

STEWED BEEF WITH CARROTS

3 lb. chuck, cubed	⅓ C. soy sauce
1 onion, quartered	6 slices ginger
1 bunch carrots, diced	1 t. salt
1 pt. water	½ t. pepper
2 T. wine	½ t. M.S.G.

Brown meat with onion. Put in pot. Cover with water. Bring to a boil. Add wine, soy sauce, ginger, salt, pepper, and M.S.G. Simmer 1½ hrs. Add carrots. Cook ½ hr. more. Serves 6.

322. December 18—Wednesday

CANDY PEEL *

Peels of 1 lemon	2 C. sugar
1 orange	1 C. water
1 grapefruit, or	Salt, pinch
peels of 3 grape-	Cold water
fruits	

Cut peels into thin strips. Cover with water. Add pinch of salt. Boil ½ hr. Drain. Cover with water and boil for another ½ hr. Drain. Mix sugar with 1 C. water. Boil to a syrup. Put in peels. Cook until tender and clear. Remove from pot. Spread out. Dry in sun. Excess syrup may be stored for future use.

* Candy peel is eaten during the New Year's holiday, but we make it for the Christmas season, too.

323. December 19—Thursday

LAMB CUSHION

4 lb square-cut lamb shoul-
   der, boned and 3 sides
   sewed by butcher
1½ C. cooked rice
⅛ C. green pepper, chopped
½ t. salt

¼ t. M.S.G.
⅛ C. oil
3 T. cornstarch
3 t. soy sauce
2 C. stock
¼ C. pan drippings

Mix together rice, pepper, salt, M.S.G. and oil. Fill in cavity of lamb cushion. Sew edges together. Place in baking pan, fat side up. Roast in 300-325° oven 2⅔ hrs. Blend together cornstarch, soy sauce, lamb stock and drippings. Heat till liquid thickens. Pour over lamb cushion. Serves 8.

324. December 20—Friday

SWEET AND SOUR SHRIMP

10 oz. frozen-breaded shrimp
6 T. oil
3 T. onion, minced
1 small green pepper,
   chopped
½ C. sugar
1 T. cornstarch

1 t. dry mustard
¼ t. M.S.G.
¼ t. salt
½ C. vinegar
⅓ C. water
3 slices canned pineapple, cut
   into 6 pieces each

Heat oil. Sauté shrimp for 5 min. till golden brown. Place on warm plate. Turn to low heat and sauté onion and pepper for another min.

Blend together cornstarch, mustard, M.S.G., salt, vinegar and water. Add to skillet. Put in pineapples last. Stir constantly till juice thickens. Put back shrimp. When thoroughly heated, serve with hot, boiled rice. Serves 4.

325. December 21—Saturday: Winter begins.

EGG ROLLS

4 T. oil

6 eggs

1 t. salt

¼ C. mushroms, cut in
slivers

⅛ C. bean sprouts

⅛ C. chicken, shredded

⅛ C. ham, shredded

¼ C. water

1 egg white, unbeaten

Break eggs into bowl. Add ½ t. salt and 2 T. oil and beat
well. Heat 6″ pan with little oil. Ladle in a big spoonful of egg.
Tip pan all over so that a very thin pancake will form. Stack
pancakes.

In a skillet, heat more oil; put in mushrooms, sprouts,
chicken, and ham. Season with ½ t. salt. Fry 5 min. Add
water, cover and stir another 5 min., or till water has almost
evaporated. Roll stuffing. Fold into oblong shape. Seal with
egg white. Serve with Plum Sauce. Serves 6.

326. December 22—Sunday

WINE VAPOR DUCK

4 lb. duckling, dressed

¾ C. wine

½ t. celery salt

Ham slivers

Parsley

Cut duck on back 4″. Wash and dry. Rub duck inside and
out with celery salt. Put duck, back up, in deep dish, then onto
a steamer with enough water for steaming. Last, place cup of
wine carefully into duck opening. Cover steamer. Steam 2½
hrs. till duck is tender. Remove wine cup with pot holders or
tongs.

327. December 23—Monday

PORK NOODLES

¾ lb. noodles, boiled 8 min.,   ½ t. pepper
   rinsed in cold water,   ½ C. stock
   drained   3 large onions, shredded
⅛ C. oil   2 T. cornstarch
1 lb. pork, cut into shreds   2 t. soy sauce
1 t. salt   ¼ C. water

Heat oil; put in pork. Brown. Pour in stock. Add onions.
Cover and simmer 10 min. Blend together cornstarch, soy
sauce and water. Add to pan. Stir until juice thickens. Pour
over noodles. Serves 4.

328. December 24—Tuesday: Christmas Eve *

MIXED VEGETABLE STEAK

2 T. oil   ½ C. celery, sliced diagonally
1 lb. flank steak, cut into   1 C. onions, chopped
   strips, sliced into thin slivers 4 scallions, chopped
   against the grain   3 C. stock
1 C. bamboo shoots, sliced   3 T. soy sauce
1 C. mushrooms, sliced   1 t. sugar
1 C. water chestnuts, sliced   1 t. M.S.G.

Heat oil very hot. Sauté onions and scallions. Add ⅓ each
of stock and soy sauce. Stir constantly 4 min. Add beef, vegetables, and rest of stock, soy sauce, and sugar. Cover and cook
10-15 min. Add M.S.G. and turn off heat. Mix well and serve
with steaming rice. Serves 4-6.

* When we think of Christmas Eve we think of the birth of a very special
baby, but a baby nonetheless. In Chinese homes the birth of an infant son
is celebrated by the passing out of red dyed, hard-boiled eggs and preserved
ginger.

329. December 25—Wednesday: Christmas Day

SOFT IMMORTAL FOOD (MEATLESS)

1 doz. pieces bean curd,   *¼ lb. Chinese vermicelli*
   quartered   *4 sticks dried bean curd*
2 lb. mushrooms   *4 T. oil*
     ¼ cake "Southern Cheese"

GRAVY: *2 T. cornstarch*   *2 t. soy sauce*
            ¼ C. water

Soak vermicelli and dried bean curd sticks 30 min. Cut vermicelli into 3" sections.

Put all ingredients in pot with cold water. Cook 1 hr. Blend together cornstarch, soy sauce and water. Stir into pot and mix well. When juice thickens turn off heat. Serves 8.

330. December 26—Thursday

LAMB LOIN

3 lb. loin, chine bone (backbone) loosened and ribs cut short
   by butcher
1 t. salt
½ t. pepper

SAUCE: *¼ C. drippings*   *1 t. soy sauce*
      3 T. cornstarch   *2 C. lamb stock*

Season lamb with salt and pepper. Roast in 300° oven 3¼ hrs. Blend together drippings, cornstarch, soy sauce and water. Cook till liquid thickens. Pour over lamb loin. Serves 6.

331. December 27—Friday

FRIED FISH FLAKES

¼ C. oil

2½ lb. fillet, washed, sliced
thin

1 C. mushrooms

3 slices ginger, minced

1 C. bamboo shoots, cut into
pieces

1 C. bean sprouts

1 C. stock

GRAVY: 1 T. cornstarch
¼ C. water
1 t. soy sauce
Parsley

Heat oil. Fry mushrooms, ginger, bamboo shoots, and bean sprouts, for 5 min. Add stock. Cover. Cook 15 min. Blend together cornstarch, soy sauce, and water. Pour into pan. Add fish flakes. When juice bubbles turn off heat. Garnish with parsley. Serves 6.

332. December 28—Saturday

ONION EGGS

6 eggs, hard-boiled
1½ T. pickled onion, minced

SALAD DRESSING: ½ C. salad oil
3 T. vinegar
1 t. sugar
¾ t. M.S.G.
2 drops sesame oil
¾ t. salt
½ t. pepper

1 scallion, minced

Cut eggs lengthwise. Take out yolks and mash. Moisten with onion, and salad dressing. Beat till fluffy. Stuff white cavities. Sprinkle with minced scallion. Serves 6.

333. December 29—Sunday

ROAST GOOSE

8 lb. goose, dressed	*1 C. soy sauce*
1 C. hot water	*4 drops sesame oil*
1 t. allspice	*1 t. salt*

Put goose in hot water for about 2 min. Add allspice, soy sauce, and salt. Let goose soak for ½ hr. turning several times. Save liquid. Stuff as desired.

Roast in 325° oven 3 hrs. Baste several times with liquid. Serves 8.

334. December 30—Monday

REPEAT PORK

4 lb. pork loin	*2 cloves garlic, sliced*
1½ qt. water	*2 scallions, chopped*
2 t. oil	*4 slices ginger*
¼ C. soy sauce	*2 t. sugar*
1 t. salt	*1 t. chili sauce*

Put loin in big pot. Add water. Bring to a boil. Simmer an hr. or two. Take out to remove bone. Store stock for future use. Slice meat diagonally.

Heat oil. Add garlic, then meat slivers. Fry a few min. Add scallions, soy sauce, salt, sugar, ginger and chili sauce. Stir a few more min. Serves a dozen people.

335. December 31—Tuesday: New Year's Eve

"LICHEE" COCKTAILS

10 oz. dry gin   *10 oz. "lichee" syrup from*
10 oz. vermouth   *can No. 2*
                    10 oz. rum

Mix all ingredients. Put in 1 canned "lichee" nut per cocktail. Serves 10.

336. January 1—Wednesday: New Year's Day

HARD IMMORTAL FOOD (MEATLESS)

¼ C. vegetable oil   *2 C. "ginkgo" nuts, shelled*
1 doz. pieces bean curd,   *and skinned and soaked ½*
quartered   *hr.*
East melon,* sliced (double   *1 pt. water*
volume of bean curd)   *¼ cake "Southern Cheese"*

Heat oil. Fry bean curd, melon slices and "ginkgo" nuts. Pour in enough water to cover. Put in cheese. Mix and cover. Cook 1 hr. Serves 8.

  * East melon may be purchased in Chinese stores. It's called "Doong Gwa."

337. January 2—Thursday

STUFFED CABBAGE

1 head cabbage (about 1-2   *1 t. salt*
lb.)   *Dash of pepper*
1 clove garlic, minced   *3 T. catsup*
1 onion, minced   *¼ t. soy sauce*
6 T. oil   *1 scallion, minced*
              1 lb. lamb shoulder meat, ground

Put whole washed cabbage into pot. Cover with salted water. Boil gently ½ hr. Drain and cool. Scoop out center with care. Heat oil. Brown garlic and onion. Add lamb. Season with salt, pepper, catsup and soy sauce. Stir 5 min.

Stuff cabbage with sautéed lamb. Put in greased oven casserole. Cover. Bake in 350° oven 30-35 min. Garnish with scallion. Serves 4.

338. January 3—Friday

FRIED SHRIMP BALLS

1½ C. oil	*1½ t. salt*
2 lb. shrimp, shelled	*½ t. pepper*
1 C. onions, diced	*1 t. M.S.G.*
3 eggs, beaten	*1 T. cornstarch*
3 T. flour	*2 T. soy sauce*
¾ C. water	

Mix eggs, flour, salt, pepper and M.S.G. in bowl; dip shrimp in batter.

Heat oil. Deep-fry shrimp to a golden ball. Place on plate. Pour away all but 1 T. oil. Sauté onions 1 min. Blend together cornstarch, soy sauce and water. Pour into onions. Stir till juice thickens. Pour over shrimp balls. Serves 6-8.

339. January 4—Saturday

GOLD AND SILVER EGGS

1 doz. eggs, separate whites and yolks	*1 T. ham, chopped fine*
Water	*Salt*
3 lb. fish fillet, ground	*2 T. oil*
	Parsley

Take two mixing bowls. In each one pour in as much water and egg.

Put fish in egg white bowl. Add salt to taste. Beat.

Put ham in egg yolk bowl. Add salt to taste. Beat.

Combine the two into one bowl without letting each mix, if possible. Steam 20 min. When done there will be a gold and silver dish.

Heat oil and splash over dish. Garnish with parsley. Serves 12.

340. January 5—Sunday

FRIED FRYERS

3 fryers, 2 lb. each, dressed	*Oil for deep frying*
1 C. soy sauce	*Celery salt*

Marinate fryers in soy sauce, turning occasionally. Heat oil very hot. Fry chickens till golden brown. Chop up and serve with celery salt. Serves 6.

341. January 6—Monday

CRISP PORK

3 lb. pork, cut into slivers	*1 egg*
1 star aniseed, crushed	*1 T. cornstarch*
2 T. gin	*Oil for deep frying*

Boil pork and aniseed in water for 10 min.

Put cornstarch and egg in mixing bowl. Beat. Stir in pork.

Fry coated pork till golden. Drain on absorbent paper. Put dried pork in bowl. Add gin. Steam for 2 hrs. Serves 6.

342. January 7—Tuesday

STUFFED FLANK STEAK

1 ½ lb. flank steak	1 bay leaf, crushed
⅓ C. vinegar	1 C. cooked rice
2 T. sugar	1 t. parsley, chopped
2 t. soy sauce	Salt to taste
½ t. pepper	2 T. salad oil
½ t. whole cloves	1 onion, sliced
¾ t. cinnamon	2 T. fat

Hot water

Put steak in large bowl.

Heat vinegar, sugar, soy sauce, pepper, cloves, cinnamon and bay leaf in sauce pan to boiling point. When cool, pour over steak. Cover. Let marinate in refrigerator overnight, turning 3 times. Drain beef.

Mix rice, parsley, salt and oil. Spread over steak. Roll up and tie tightly.

Melt fat. Put in onion and steak. Brown evenly. Pour in enough hot water to almost cover steak. Cover pan. Simmer 1½ hrs., or till meat is tender. Serves 4-6.

343. January 8—Wednesday

SAUTÉED STRING BEANS

1 T. vegetable oil	2 C. string beans, julienned
1 T. onion, minced	3 T. chili sauce

Heat oil. Sauté onion and string beans. Add chili sauce. Cover. Cook over medium heat 15 min. Add water whenever necessary. Serves 4.

344. January 9—Thursday

BROILED LAMB CUBES

2 lb. lamb shoulder, cut in   *1 clove garlic, minced*
  1" cubes   *½ t. soy sauce*
½ C. oil   *½ t. salt*
⅓ C. vinegar   *¼ t. pepper*
Dash of oregano

Mix together oil, vinegar, garlic, soy sauce, salt, pepper, and oregano. Marinate lamb cubes in liquid overnight. Drain. Place on broiler pan 3" below unit in oven. Broil ¼ hr. turning 3 times. Serves 4.

345. January 10—Friday

SHRIMP FRIED RICE

1 qt. cold cooked rice   *1 t. salt*
2 T. oil   *½ t. pepper*
2 C. cooked shrimp, chopped   *2 T. soy sauce*
1 egg, beaten   *1 onion, minced*

Heat oil. Add onion and shrimp. Sauté 1 min. stirring all the time. Add egg, salt, and pepper. Mix well with shrimp. Add rice and soy sauce. Stir constantly for 5 min. Serves 4.

346. January 11—Saturday: Today is "Kwan Yin" Day.*

ANGEL MEAT

2 lb. pork, boned and cubed   1 C. soy sauce
1 C. wine   ¾ C. sugar

In bowl mix all ingredients. Take large pot and fill with 2″ of hot water. Put rack in pot. Place bowl on top of it. Cover pot. Steam several hrs. Serves 6.

* "Kwan Yin" is the Goddess of Mercy. "La Pa Chou" porridge is eaten on "Kwan Yin" Day. It takes 20 ingredients mixed together to make up this porridge: 5 kinds of grains, beans, peanuts, chestnuts, walnuts, dates, lily and melon seeds, 4 different fruits, sugar and spices.

For the Legend of "Kwan Yin" see the next page.

Kwan Yin

KWAN YIN LEFT THE WORLD TO LIVE IN THE NUNNERY OF THE White Sparrow. Here is her legend.

Long ago Emperor Po Chia and his Empress ruled the land well, but they were childless. They went to the Western Mountain and prayed for children. Thereafter three girls were born but no sons. Po Chia decided that when his daughters married he would choose one of their husbands to succeed him. Miao Shan, the youngest, was their favorite daughter so they decided to make her husband Emperor. However, Miao Shan said, "I only want to sit alone and pray to become perfect. To care for the ill and help the poor are my only desires. I don't want to wed."

Her father became so angry he ordered Miao Shan to be cast out to perish in the cold from hunger. She did not die. Her family came and begged her to change her mind but she asked only to go to the Nunnery of the White Sparrow.

The Emperor allowed her to enter the Nunnery but ordered the mistress there to assign Miao Shan only the most menial tasks to discourage her from becoming a nun.

Miao Shan cheerfully carried out her hard chores. This report angered the Emperor more. He ordered the buildings of the Nunnery to be burned to the ground.

Heaven must have taken pity on Miao Shan for it began to rain and the fire was put out.

The Emperor wanted his troops to seize Miao Shan and behead her. However, the Empress intercepted. She begged the Emperor to win their daughter back to their way of life with music and feasting.

Miao Shan would not be tempted. On her execution day a miracle occurred. The ax shattered to smithereens as it touched her white neck. It was said that a spirit in the form of a tiger carried Miao Shan away to the underworld. She prayed there till the underworld became bright with light.

When she returned to earth, she sought a quiet place to pray for perfection.

On the island of Pu To she meditated for nine years. By thinking only pure thoughts, she became perfect.

The day came when Miao Shan was ready to enter the Kingdom of Heaven. As she was about to set foot inside she stopped to listen. Wails of all the poor, troubled people made her turn back to help them. Because of her great compassion, from that time on her name has been changed to Kwan Yin meaning she who hears prayers.

347. **January 12—Sunday: In China curry recipes are used only during the winter. Below will be listed a series of curry dishes.**

CURRIED CHICKEN

4 lb. broiler, chopped into pieces	6 T. curry powder
1½ t. salt	2 C. stock
½ t. pepper	1 T. cornstarch
½ C. oil	¼ C. water
	Parsley, chopped

Dry chicken with paper towel. Sprinkle with salt.

Heat oil in frying pan. Put chicken in to brown. Heat curry in sauce pan. When powder is extremely hot, add ⅛ C. oil gradually. Mix well. Stir constantly while slowly pouring in stock. Bring to a boil. Pour over chicken. Cover pan. Simmer an hr. Blend together cornstarch and water. Add to pan. Stir till liquid thickens. Garnish with parsley. Serves 4.

348. January 13—Monday

CURRIED PUNGENT PORK SAUSAGES

1 lb. baby pork sausages   *1 t. cornstarch*
8 pineapple rings, halved   *1 C. pineapple syrup*
½ t. curry powder   *Hot, boiled rice*

Put sausage links in covered pan. Simmer 5 min. in a little water. Drain. Cook at low heat turning to brown evenly.

Brown pineapple slices in 4 T. sausage fat. Drain on absorbent paper.

Blend together cornstarch, curry powder and pineapple syrup. Add to oil in pan and stir till liquid thickens.

Put rice on center of platter and on edge, place pineapple slices and sausages in a ring. Pour liquid over rice. Serves 4.

349. January 14—Tuesday

CURRIED BAKED BEEF

WHITE SAUCE: *3 T. butter*
                  3 T. flour
                  1½ C. milk
                  ¾ t. salt
                  Dash of pepper

Melt butter. Stir in flour. Slowly add milk. Cook over double boiler. Stir till thick. Season with salt and pepper. Cook 5 min.

1½ t. curry powder   *1½ C. carrots, diced*
1 T. soy sauce   *3 T. onion, minced*
1 lb. cooked beef, chopped   *2 C. hot, boiled rice*
1½ C. cooked peas   *1 egg, sliced*

Mix white sauce, curry and soy sauce. Add beef, peas, carrots and onion. Pour in baking dish. Mix in rice. Bake in 400° oven ⅓ hr. If desired, garnish with egg slices. Serves 4.

350. January 15—Wednesday

AROMATIC ONIONS AND PEAS

1½ lb. tiny white onions, peeled
1 C. boiling water
1½ t. salt

½ lb. peas, shelled, or frozen
3 T. vegetable oil
1 t. curry powder
⅛ t. pepper

Put onions in sauce pan with boiling water. Season with 1 t. salt. Boil 5 min. without cover. Cover and cook 10 min. Add peas and cook another 5 min. Drain.

Heat oil in pan. Blend in curry powder, ½ t. salt and pepper. Add onion and peas. Stir till hot and glazed. Serves 8.

351. January 16—Thursday

CURRIED LAMB

2 T. oil
1 lb. lamb shoulder, cubed
1 t. salt
¼ t. pepper
½ t. soy sauce
¼ t. M.S.G.
½ t. allspice
1 C. celery, diced

½ C. onion, sliced
1 clove garlic, sliced
½ C. stock
1 T. cornstarch
2 t. curry powder
¼ C. water
2 T. chutney (opt.)
2 C. hot boiled rice

Heat oil. Put lamb in pan to brown. Season with salt, pepper, soy sauce, M.S.G. and allspice. Add celery, onion, garlic and stock. Cover and simmer 1 hr. Blend together cornstarch, curry powder and water. Add to pan and stir 10 min. If desired, garnish with chutney. Serve with steaming rice. Serves 4.

352. January 17—Friday

CURRIED SHRIMP

4 T. oil
2 T. cornstarch
½ t. salt
Dash of pepper
½ t. soy sauce
1½ C. milk

3 T. catsup
4 T. wine
¾ lb. shrimp, shelled and
*   cleaned*
2 C. hot boiled rice
1 scallion, minced (opt.)

Blend together and heat oil and cornstarch with salt, pepper, curry powder, and soy sauce. Slowly stir in milk. Add catsup, wine and shrimp. Stir till shrimp turns pink. If desired, garnish with scallion. Serve with steaming rice. Serves 4.

353. January 18—Saturday

EGG CURRIED BROCCOLI

1 bunch broccoli (peel off
*   tough outer skin and wilted*
*   leaves)*
½ C. boiling water

1 t. salt
½ C. oil
2 hard-boiled eggs, chopped
½ t. curry powder
Dash of paprika

Boil broccoli in salted water 15 min. turning occasionally. Drain if necessary. Blend together and heat oil, curry powder, and chopped eggs. Pour over broccoli and sprinkle with paprika. Serves 6.

This ends our curry series.

354. January 19—Sunday

RICE WINE DUCK

5 lb. duckling, dressed	1 clove garlic, split
1 orange	½ T. ginger, minced
1 onion	1 t. salt
4 T. melted chicken fat, or butter	½-¾ C. rice wine, or if not available, use gin

Pierce orange and onion all over and place inside clean duck. Rub duck with garlic. Brush with melted fat. Roast in 325° oven 2½ hrs. At end of 2nd hr., drain off fat. Pour wine over duck. Sprinkle with ginger and salt. Continue roasting for another ½ hr. Serves 6.

355. January 20—Monday

EGG PORK BALLS

1 lb. lean pork, ground	1 egg, beaten lightly
1 C. water chestnuts, chopped coarsely	1 t. salt
	¼-½ C. cornstarch
4 T. crystallized ginger, minced, rinsed and dried	1-2 C. peanut oil for deep frying

Mix pork, water chestnuts, ginger, egg and salt. Form into small meatballs. Coat lightly with cornstarch.

Fry balls in hot oil till they float to surface. Drain on absorbent paper. Serves 4.

356. January 21—Tuesday

BEEF WITH OYSTER SAUCE

¾ lb. lean, tender beef, sliced   Dash of pepper
   in thin slivers against the   2 t. cornstarch
   grain   2 egg whites
1 t. baking soda   4 slices ginger, shredded
1 t. salt   2 scallions, cut into 1"
Dash of sugar   sections
1 t. oil   Oil for deep frying
½ t. wine   2 T. fat
     5 T. Oyster Sauce

Mix together soda, salt, sugar, oil, wine, pepper, cornstarch, and egg whites. Put meat in mixture and marinate an hr. or more. Heat oil for deep frying. Put in beef and let it brown for ⅓ min. Take meat out and drain. Melt fat in another pan. Put in scallions and ginger. Add beef and oyster sauce. Mix well. Serves 4.

357. January 22—Wednesday

BAKED GRAPEFRUIT

2 grapefruit, halved   4 T. margarine, melted
2 C. cornflakes, crushed   4 t. rice wine, or substitute
½ C. brown sugar   ½ t. cinnamon

Core grapefruit. Remove seeds and loosen sections. Place mixture of cornflakes, sugar, margarine, and wine, or cinnamon on grapefruit. Bake in 400° oven ¼ hr. Serves 4.

358. January 23—Thursday

"HOT" AND SOUR SOUP

1 C. cooked lamb, cut into   *½ C. soy sauce*
shreds against the grain   *½ t. M.S.G.*
6 C. lamb stock   *⅛ C. cornstarch*
1 t. salt   *3 T. vinegar*
½ t. pepper   *3 eggs, beaten*

Mix salt, pepper, soy sauce and M.S.G. with 1 C. cold stock.
Bring other 5 C. stock to a boil in pot and add this to seasoned
C. of stock. Turn to low heat. Add eggs while stirring con-
stantly. Add vinegar and lamb shreds. Cook 5 min. more.
Serves 6.

359. January 24—Friday

LOBSTER TAILS

4 raw lobster tails, shelled and   *4 water chestnuts, peeled and*
cut into ½" slices   *sliced*
4 T. soy sauce   *16 slices bacon, halved*
4 T. rice wine, or sauterne   *Colored toothpicks*

Mix soy sauce and wine. Marinate lobster in mixture. Drain.
Combine a slice of lobster with a slice of water chestnut. Wrap
in bacon. Fasten with toothpicks. Bake in 400° oven till bacon
is crisp. Serves 4.

360. January 25—Saturday

LAMBS' TAILS
(A CHINESE MUSLIM SWEET)

FILLING: *⅓ C. sugar*
         1 T. flour
         2 T. water

BATTER: *3 egg whites*
3 T. cornstarch
2½ T. water

Peanut oil for deep frying
2 T. sugar

Mix sugar, flour and water for filling. Form into 5 balls. Beat egg whites till stiff. Add cornstarch and water and mix well.

Heat oil till it bubbles. Meanwhile, hold filling with fork and using a spoon, coat it with batter. Slip each lamb's tail into oil and fry to a golden brown taking care not to let the oil get too hot. Put on plate and sprinkle with sugar. Serves 5.

361. January 26—Sunday: On this, the 23rd Day of the 12th Moon, the Kitchen God * Flies to Heaven for 7 Days' Holiday.

SYRUP COATED APPLES

2 doz. crab apples, washed *¾ C. water*
2 C. sugar *Red food-coloring liquid*
½ C. light corn syrup *Dash of cinnamon*
4 bamboo sticks

* Today is the Ceremony of the kitchen god. And one day to have some sticky syrup handy. Maybe we can borrow a bit of this syrup from those syrup coated apples. Why? Because on this night the master of the house takes down the old picture of the kitchen god. A sweet sticky syrup is smeared on the kitchen god's mouth so he will lick his lips and remember only good things to report to the Emperor of the Sky during his celestial vacation. (Not that he can report many bad things since most people remember to turn his picture over when they want to do something not strictly honorable, such as killing a chicken or stealing a kiss in the kitchen.)

This ceremony is carried out with a little sedan chair to receive the kitchen god's picture. Outside the courtyard a bonfire is built. There the picture, chair, and paper horse will be burnt. Cups of tea and wine will be poured on the flames so the god won't be thirsty. Firecrackers will sputter to ensure a favorable send-off. On New Year's Eve a new picture of the kitchen god will hang in the kitchen to symbolize his return.

Skewer 6 dry apples on each bamboo stick.

Mix sugar, syrup and water in top of double boiler, stirring till sugar is dissolved. Add enough coloring to get a deep red. Heat gently. When a small quantity becomes brittle in cold water, take away from stove. Mix in dash of cinnamon. Place over double boiler filled with boiling water. Dip apples skewered on sticks into syrup, twirling stick so as to coat all over. Place on wax paper to cool. For 4 kids.

362. January 27—Monday

CHINESE STUFFED MUSHROOMS

2 doz. large dried mushrooms	2 T. wine
¼ lb. lean pork, minced	1 t. ginger, minced
2 T. soy sauce	1 t. onion, minced
	2 T. lard

Soak mushrooms till soft, then squeeze dry gently. Mix pork, soy sauce, wine, ginger and onion together. Remove mushroom stems and stuff caps with pork mixture. Dot them with lard. Place on dish. Set dish on rack of steamer with boiling water on bottom of pot. Cover. Turn to high heat and steam 20-30 min. Serves 4.

363. January 28—Tuesday

BEAN BURGERS

¼ C. oil	1 onion, minced
1 lb. green beans, julienned	1 clove garlic, minced
1 lb. lean hamburger	1 C. stock
1 t. salt	4 small eggs, beaten
½ t. pepper	2 T. cornstarch
	¼ C. water

Heat oil in pan. Put in hamburger. Add onion, and garlic. Season with salt and pepper. Brown. Put in stock and beans. Mix well. Cover. Cook over medium heat 10 min. Turn to low heat and pour in eggs. When eggs begin to set, blend together cornstarch and water. Add to pan. Stir till juice thickens. Serves 4.

364. January 29—Wednesday

THREE-COLOR DESSERT

⅔ C. peas, cooked
unseasoned

⅔ C. potatoes, cooked
unseasoned

⅔ C. kidney beans, cooked
unseasoned

⅔ C. sugar

⅔ C. vegetable oil

Add about 4 scant T. sugar to each purée. If they appear dry, put in a little water to make creamy. Heat 4 scant T. oil till smoky and fry peas till sugar dissolves (about 5 min.). Empty into serving dish and add a little oil to give it a sheen. Do the same thing with the potatoes and kidney beans. Before serving, stir so the colors will run together. Serves 6.

365. January 30—Thursday

STUFFED BREAST OF LAMB

4 lb. lamb breast (2 pieces),
have butcher cut pocket in
wide end of lamb breasts

¼ C. oil
2 t. salt
½ t. pepper
1 C. water

RICE STUFFING: 1½ C. cooked rice
⅛ C. green pepper, chopped
⅛ C. onion, minced
¼ t. salt
¼ t. pepper
2 T. oil

SAUCE: *1 T. cornstarch*
      ½ C. water
      1 t. soy sauce

Clean lamb. Fill lamb cavities with rice stuffing consisting of mixture of rice, green pepper, onion, salt, pepper, and oil. Close openings.

Heat oil in very large pot. Put in lamb breasts. Season with salt and pepper. Brown evenly. Add water. Cover. Simmer 2 hrs., or till meat is well cooked. Blend together cornstarch, water and soy sauce. Add to pot. Stir till juice thickens. Serves 8.

366. January 31—Friday

FRIED FISH BALLS

3 lb. fish fillet, ground fine	*2 C. stock*
¾ C. salted nuts, chopped	*1 t. cornstarch*
¼ C. ham, chopped	*1 C. water*
1 egg, beaten	*1 t. salt*
1 bunch celery cabbage	*2 T. cornstarch*
(about 3 lb.), chopped	*2 t. soy sauce*
½ lb. mushrooms, chopped	*Oil for deep frying*

Put ground fillet into large mixing bowl. Blend in 1 t. cornstarch, salt, water and egg. Beat with electric beater 20 min. Add ham and nuts. Mix thoroughly.

Scrub hands well. Form fish batter into nickle-sized balls.

Heat oil till it bubbles. Slip in fish balls. Fry to a golden brown. Take out. Drain. Pour off all but 4 T. oil. Put in celery cabbage and mushrooms. Mix well. Pour in half the stock. Cover and simmer 10 min. Put drained fish balls back. Blend together 2 T. cornstarch, soy sauce and remaining stock. Add

to pan and stir constantly till liquid becomes translucent.
Serves 6.

367. February 1—Saturday: Chinese New Year's Eve For the Men's Vegetarian Dinner

ARHAN'S FAST *
(FOOD FOR THE BUDDHIST SAINTS)

½ C. peanut oil

1 pt. bean curd

2 C. "ginkgo" nuts

2 C. "ears of wood" (black
fungus)

2 C. dried bean curd stick

2 C. bamboo shoots

2 C. dried mushrooms

2 C. green beans

2 C. chestnuts

2 C. carrots

1 C. Chinese vermicelli

Salt to taste

1 T. M.S.G.

GRAVY: 1 t. cornstarch

1 C. water

½ t. soy sauce

Dash of salt

Pinch of sugar

4 drops sesame oil

Cut bean curd into 48 pieces. Deep fry in oil until golden.
Rinse in cold water till no more oil floats to the surface.
Remove hard shells of "ginkgo" and chestnuts. Soak nuts in
bowl of boiling water then peel off inner skin. Soak the "ears
of wood," and dried bean curd sticks for 30 min. Slice the
bamboo shoots. Heat some peanut or vegetable oil in a big

* This dish is also known as "vegetarians' ten varieties." If some of the
ingredients are difficult to get, make up your own ten varieties, with such
vegetables as:
1. Chestnuts, shelled & skinned.
2. Peas, shelled.
3. String beans, strung and cut into 1½" pieces.
4. Carrots, diced.
5. Wax beans, cut into 1½" pieces.
6. Potatoes, diced.
7. Celery, diced.
8. Cabbage, shredded.
9. Onions, diced.
10. Fresh mushrooms, diced.

pot. Add all ingredients and cover with about 1½ gal. water. Sprinkle salt and M.S.G. to taste. Cover pot and cook for 1 hr. Make the gravy by blending cornstarch in water with soy sauce, salt, sugar and sesame oil. Then add gravy to pot of saints' food. Keep stirring this mixture until soup boils and thickens a bit. Serves 24.

Chinese New Year's Eve

THOUGH THE 1ST DAY OF THE 1ST MOON WAS THOUGHT TO BE the very best day for luck of the whole year, New Year's Eve is the merriest of all holidays on the Chinese calendar. This is the day when many, many new things appear. For example, new pictures of the kitchen god and gate guardians must be hung. Here's the story of the gate guardians.

Once upon a time there lived in China an Emperor named Shih Meng. One time he became ill. In the evenings he always became delirious, imagining all kinds of spirits. One morning his condition became grave. Physicians went into long consultations. Still they knew not what to do.

Then one of the Emperor's generals named Chin Shu-pao appeared. He suggested to the Emperor that he and his companion, Hu Ching-te, stand guard at the Emperor's gate to keep tormenting spirits from His Majesty. They posted themselves outside the palace gates. No more bad dreams in the form of evil spirits came to trouble the Emperor that night. He received his much needed rest. From then on the Emperor's health began to improve. Every evening Chin Shu-pao and Hu Ching-te stood watch until the Emperor had fully recovered.

The Emperor was grateful to the weary generals. He ordered the court artists to paint life sized portraits of Generals Chin Shu-pao and Hu Ching-te in full regalia.

When completed these fierce portraits were pasted on the palace gates. The evil spirits were fooled, for none reappeared that night to disturb the Emperor.

The Chinese continue to mount pictures of kitchen god

and guardians over their hearth and gates every New Year's Eve. They know that the only spirits present are those creations of the mind. The guardians and kitchen god remind each and everyone to think only kind, guarded thoughts. These pure thoughts will ward off a guilty conscience and vanquish the evil in the world.

PART IV

Varying Your Menu

Sunday—Chicken

CHICKEN CHOW MEIN

1 T. peanut oil
1 fryer, boned and sliced
1 clove garlic, minced
6 mushrooms, sliced
2 stalks celery, sliced diagonally
½ C. bean sprouts
¼ C. canned bamboo shoots,
sliced

1 C. stock
1 t. salt
2 T. cornstarch
½ C. water
1 t. soy sauce
8 oz. noodles
3 qt. boiling water
1 T. salt

Heat oil in pan. Brown chicken and garlic. Add mushrooms, celery, bean sprouts, bamboo shoots, stock and salt.
Cook over medium heat several min.

Blend cornstarch, water and soy sauce till smooth. Add
to chicken mixture and stir until sauce is translucent. Pour
contents over cooked noodles. Serves 4.

(To cook noodles, put dried noodles in boiling water with
salt. When noodles are tender, drain in collander.)

Sunday—Chicken

CHICKEN IN SOY SAUCE

1¼ C. soy sauce	1 T. cornstarch
1½ C. rice wine or sherry	¼ C. water
1 onion, chopped	1 cucumber, peeled and sliced
3 slices ginger root, minced	in discs
¼ C. sugar	Parsley
5-6 lb. roaster, dressed	

Combine soy sauce, wine, onion, ginger and sugar in large pot or Dutch oven. Place over high heat and bring mixture to a boil. Put in whole chicken and bring liquid to a boil again. Reduce to low heat. Cover and simmer for 1 hr. Turn chicken often for even cooking. Place chicken on platter. Save 1 C. soy liquid in bowl. Put chicken and liquid into refrigerator.

Carve chicken before serving. Empty soy liquid into saucepan and bring liquid to a boil.

Blend cornstarch with water till smooth. Stir into liquid and cook until liquid thickens. Brush a bit of the sauce on skin of chicken. Garnish chicken platter with cucumber discs and parsley. At table, pass remaining sauce for dipping chicken pieces. Serves 6.

Sunday—Chicken

CHICKEN WITH MUSHROOM SAUCE

8 Chinese black mushrooms	½ t. garlic salt
½ C. water	3 T. peanut oil
1 t. sugar	1 T. vinegar
8 chicken breasts, boned	1 T. soy sauce
1 t. salt	1¼ C. stock
½ t. pepper	8 water chestnuts, chopped
2 T. cornstarch	1 scallion, chopped
2 t. paprika	1 T. sesame seeds, toasted

Place dried mushrooms in bowl with water and sugar. Let soak ½ hr., turning mushrooms occasionally. Meanwhile season chicken with salt and pepper. Enclose seasoning in chicken by rolling meat. Fasten roll with wooden picks.

Mix cornstarch, paprika and garlic salt. Rub into chicken rolls.

Heat oil in pan. Brown chicken evenly. Add vinegar, soy sauce and stock to chicken. Bring to a boil. Cover and cook over low heat for 20 min. Uncover. Add mushrooms and liquid and cook ¼ hr. Put in water chestnuts and cook a little longer. Sprinkle with scallion and sesame seeds. Pour over hot flaky rice. Serves 4.

Sunday—Chicken

DRUMSTICK BARBECUE

18 drumsticks	2 T. soy sauce
¼ C. wine and vinegar	2 T. honey
2 T. olive oil	1 T. lemon juice
1 t. salt	2 slices ginger, minced
½ t. pepper	½ C. bottled barbecue sauce
½ C. orange juice	

Mix vinegar, oil, salt, pepper, orange juice, soy sauce, honey, lemon juice and ginger in long baking pan. Place chicken pieces in pan and marinate overnight, turning occasionally. Take out chicken, brush each leg with sauce and place skin side down on rack 7″ from charcoal heat. Cook for approx. ½ hr. each side. Serves 6-8.

Sunday—Chicken

HOT AND SOUR CHICKEN SOUP

1 qt. chicken stock

4 or 5 dried Chinese fungi (cloud's ears)

4 dried Chinese black mush-rooms

⅓-½ C. chicken shreds

8 dried tiger lily buds (Fresh, unopened day lily buds may be used)

⅓ C. bamboo shoots, shredded

½ cake fresh bean curd, cubed

1 t. soy sauce

½ t. sugar

1 t. salt

¼ t. pepper

2 T. vinegar

¼ t. M.S.G.

2 T. cornstarch

3 T. water

1 egg, beaten

1 t. sesame oil

Pour stock into a pot and bring to a boil. Put fungi, mush-rooms, chicken, lily buds, bamboo shoots and bean curd into liquid. Bring to a boil again. Turn to low heat and simmer ¼ hr.

Add soy sauce, sugar, salt, pepper, vinegar and M.S.G. Blend together cornstarch and water and add to soup. Turn off heat. Pour in egg and stir. Add sesame oil. Serves 6-8.

Sunday—Chicken

ORIENTAL POULTRY CASSEROLE

6 C. toasted bread cubes

2 cans bean sprouts, drained

2 cans water chestnuts

1 C. mushrooms, sliced

2 t. salt

4 C. cooked poultry, shredded (chicken, duck, or turkey)

½ C. toasted almonds

SAUCE: ½ C. sugar

¼ C. cornstarch

½ C. soy sauce

1½ C. pineapple juice

¼ C. vinegar

Mix bread cubes, bean sprouts, water chestnuts, mushrooms, salt and poultry shreds.

Blend sugar, cornstarch, soy sauce and pineapple juice in saucepan. Bring to a slow boil over medium heat. Stir constantly until sauce thickens. Remove from heat before adding vinegar. Place chicken mixture into casserole dish. Pour sauce over chicken and top with toasted almonds. Bake in 350° oven for ½ hr. Serves 4-6.

Sunday—Chicken

PINEAPPLE CHICKEN

2 T. oil	2 T. cornstarch
2 chicken breasts	1 T. oil
1 can pineapple chunks	1 t. wine
2 slices ginger, slivered	1 t. M.S.G.
½ C. pineapple juice from can	½ t. sugar
	1 t. salt

Heat oil till very hot. Add chicken and stir until meat is done. Add pineapple, ginger and juice. Cover and bring to a boil. Turn to low heat.

Blend cornstarch, oil, wine, M.S.G., sugar, salt and water. Add to chicken mixture. Stir until juice thickens. Serves 4.

Sunday—Chicken

ROAST CHICKEN

5-6 lb. roaster	2 t. sugar
2 t. brown bean sauce (Mien Sea)	1 t. salt
1 clove garlic, crushed	½ t. pepper
1 slice ginger	1 scallion, chopped
½ t. M.S.G.	1 t. Hoisin sauce
2 t. soy sauce	Oil

Combine all the seasoning and rub the mixture inside the chicken cavity. Rub the chicken skin with 1 t. salt. Let chicken stand for 1 hr. Rub oil on skin. Turn oven to 400°. Roast chicken for ½ hr. Turn chicken once. Lower heat to 350° and continue roasting chicken for ¾ hr. Serves 6-8.

Monday—Pork

HASH ORIENTALE

2 T. *peanut oil*	3 T. *soy sauce*
1 *clove garlic, minced*	2 *eggs, well beaten*
1½ C. *cooked pork, cubed*	2 C. *lettuce, shredded*
2 C. *leftover cooked rice*	

Heat oil in skillet. Add garlic and pork. Brown meat. Add cooked rice and soy sauce. Stir for 10 min. Pour in eggs. Stir for another min. Remove skillet from heat, add lettuce, and toss well. Serves 6.

Monday—Pork

PIGS' KNUCKLES

½ C. *soy sauce*	¼ C. *sugar*
½ C. *rice wine or sherry*	6 *pigs' knuckles*
2 *slices ginger, minced*	6 *hard-boiled eggs (optional)*
1½ C. *water*	

Mix soy sauce, wine, ginger, water and ½ sugar in Dutch oven. Bring liquid to a slow boil. Add knuckles and cover. Simmer for 2 hr. Baste occasionally. Then add remaining sugar and cook ½ hr. more. Shell eggs and halve lengthwise. Add them to knuckles. Continue to cook for ½ hr. more, basting occasionally.

Place knuckles on platter surrounded by egg halves.

Skim excess fat from surface of gravy and pour over platter of knuckles and eggs. Serve with hot flaky rice. Serves 6.

Monday—Pork

PINEAPPLE-PEPPER PORK

½ C. flour
½ t. M.S.G.
½ t. salt
1 lb. pork, cubed
1 egg, well beaten
2 C. peanut oil
½ C. sugar
½ C. vinegar
⅓ C. pineapple juice

¼ C. catsup
1 t. soy sauce
2 T. cornstarch
2 T. water
1 C. pineapple chunks, drained
1 green pepper, cut in ½" slivers

Combine flour, M.S.G. and salt. Dip pork in egg batter, then into flour mixture. Coat evenly. Heat oil. Fry pork for about 10 min. until done. Drain pork on absorbent toweling and keep warm.

Combine sugar, vinegar, juice, catsup and soy sauce in saucepan. Bring to a boil. Blend cornstarch with water. Stir into sauce. Stir constantly until juice thickens. Put in pork, pineapple chunks, and green pepper. Stir for 5 min. more. Serve with rice. Serves 4.

Monday—Pork

PORK CHOPS DE LUXE

6 center pork chops
⅓ C. bread crumbs, seasoned
3 T. peanut oil
1 clove garlic, chopped
1 C. stock
6 small onions, quartered

6 T. rice wine or sherry
¼ C. soy sauce
1 T. sugar
1 T. cornstarch
3 T. water

Coat chops with crumbs 2 hrs. before serving.

Heat oil in big frying pan. Put in garlic and chops. Brown both sides of chops. Discard garlic and oil. Pour in stock. Bring to a boil. Turn to low heat. Add onions, wine, soy sauce, and sugar. Cover. Simmer 1 hr. Uncover. Place chops on warm platter.

Mix cornstarch with water till smooth. Add to liquid in pan. Stir till sauce thickens. Pour over chops. Serve with hot rice. Serves 4.

Monday—Pork

PORK LOIN

4-5 lb. loin, cracked	4 sprigs of parsley, chopped
1 t. salt	2 C. stock
½ t. pepper	1 bunch watercress, chopped
1 T. peanut oil	3 T. cornstarch
1 clove garlic, minced	¼ C. water

Sprinkle pork with salt and pepper. Heat oil in Dutch oven. Brown loin. Add garlic, parsley and stock. Cover. Simmer 2½ hrs., basting frequently. Take loin out of oven and keep warm. Skim off fat from liquid. Add watercress and continue cooking.

Mix cornstarch with water till smooth. Stir into liquid till sauce thickens. Pour over loin. Serves 6-8.

Monday—Pork

PORK SOUP

2-3 lb. pork soup bones	2 t. salt
2 stalks scallion, cut into 1" strips	¼ lb. fresh pork, cut into 1" strips
9 C. pork stock	¼ lb. snow peas, or frozen peas
1 slice ginger root	
3-4 Chinese black mushrooms	8 slivers lemon peel

Place bones in pot and pour in stock. Add scallion, ginger and mushrooms. Bring to a boil. Turn to low heat and simmer 1½ hrs. Add salt and M.S.G. Simmer 25 min. Add peas and simmer 5 min. Ladle into individual bowls, placing a sliver of lemon peel into each bowl first. Serves 8.

Tuesday—Beef

BARBECUED SPARERIBS

6 lb. spareribs	1 t. salt
4 T. sugar	½ t. pepper
6 T. honey	4 T. soy sauce
2 C. chicken stock	

Have butcher chop spareribs into 1½" pieces. Mix all ingredients. Marinate ribs overnight.

Remove ribs to rack of roasting pan. Pour a little water in pan. Roast in 350° oven for 1½ hr., turning occasionally. Serves 8-10.

Tuesday—Beef

BEEF AND PEPPER

1 T. peanut oil	½ t. pepper
1 lb. tenderloin, cubed	2 slices ginger root, minced
2 green peppers, cut into strips	½ t. M.S.G.
1 onion, chopped	1 t. soy sauce
1 clove garlic, minced	1 C. stock
1 t. salt	2 T. cornstarch
	3 T. water

Heat oil in pan. Brown meat. Add green peppers, onion, garlic, salt, pepper, ginger and M.S.G. Add soy sauce and stock.

Mix cornstarch and water till smooth. Add to mixture and stir till sauce is translucent. Serves 4.

Tuesday—Beef

BEEF "CHOP SUEY"

1 T. peanut oil
½ lb. top round steak, ground
1 can (4 oz.) mushrooms, sliced (save liquid)
1 C. celery, sliced diagonally
1 onion, sliced

3 T. cornstarch
1 C. stock
1 lb. bean sprouts
1 T. soy sauce
1 t. Worcestershire sauce

Heat oil in large frying pan. Brown beef. Add mushrooms, celery and onion. Mix cornstarch with mushroom liquid. Add stock and pour into meat mixture. Add bean sprouts, soy sauce and Worcestershire sauce. Simmer ¼ hr., stirring occasionally. Serve over hot fluffy rice. Serves 4.

Tuesday—Beef

BEEF DISH

2 T. peanut oil
1 lb. round steak, thinly sliced against the grain
1½ C. mushrooms, sliced
1½ C. celery, sliced diagonally

1 green pepper, sliced in slivers
1 can (10 oz.) onion soup
2 T. soy sauce
2 T. cornstarch
½ C. cold water

Heat oil in skillet. Brown beef. Add vegetables, soup and soy sauce. Cover. Cook over low heat for 20-30 min. until meat is tender. Stir occasionally. Blend cornstarch with water. Add to sauce. Stir until sauce thickens. Serve with steamed rice. Serves 4.

Tuesday—Beef

BRAISED BEEF WITH GINGER

1 T. peanut oil
1 lb. round of beef, sliced against grain
1 onion, thinly sliced
2 cloves garlic, minced
2 pieces crystallized ginger, thinly sliced
1 T. soy sauce
⅔ C. water
2 stalks celery, cut diagonally
1 t. salt

Heat oil in skillet. Sauté beef, onion and garlic until brown. Add ginger, soy sauce and water. Cover. Simmer 25 min. Add celery to beef. Cover. Simmer 5 min. more. Sprinkle with salt. Pour over hot steamed rice. Serves 4.

Tuesday—Beef

CHUNGKING HOT BEEF SHREDS

2 lb. flank steak, sliced against the grain
6 T. soy sauce
2 T. rice wine or sherry
1½ C. peanut oil
2 slices ginger, minced
2 T. crushed red pepper
1 C. carrots, shredded
2 C. celery, sliced diagonally
2 t. salt
½ t. M.S.G.

Mix beef, soy sauce and wine.
Pour 1 C. oil into hot skillet. Heat oil. Add meat mixture,

stirring constantly over high heat for 10 min. Remove beef. Save gravy to put over cooked rice later.

Add remaining ½ C. oil to skillet. Put in ginger, pepper and carrot. Stir for 1 min. Add celery and stir together for another min. Also add cooked beef, salt and M.S.G. Pour the whole mixture over rice. Serves 8.

Tuesday—Beef

COCKTAIL MEATBALLS

2 C. soft bread crumbs	½ t. Tabasco sauce
½ C. milk	½ t. salt
1 lb. top round steak, ground	1 can (5 oz.) water chestnuts,
1 onion, minced	drained and minced
1½ T. soy sauce	2 T. peanut oil

Soak bread in milk. Combine ground beef, onion, soy sauce, Tabasco sauce, salt and water chestnuts. Shape into 1″ balls.

Heat oil. Brown a few meatballs at a time. Serve hot. Serve with colored toothpicks. Yields 50 balls.

Tuesday—Beef

OYSTER SAUCE BEEF

2-3 lb. flank steak, thinly sliced	½ t. sugar
1 C. peanut oil	2 onions, chopped
¼ C. soy sauce	3 lb. asparagus
1 T. rice wine or sherry	½ lb. mushrooms, sliced
2 T. cornstarch	2½ t. salt
2 slices ginger, minced	2 T. Oyster Sauce

Mix 1 T. oil, soy sauce, wine, cornstarch, ginger, sugar and onion with meat slices. Marinate one hour.

Discard white part of asparagus. Slice green, tender part diagonally.

Heat 6 T. oil in large frying pan. When oil is hot add asparagus, mushrooms and salt. Stir 10 min. Put on plate and keep warm.

Heat 9 t. oil in clean frying pan. Add meat mixture. Sauté 10 min. Stir in oyster sauce.

Place meat on platter surrounded by asparagus and mushrooms. Serve with hot steamed rice. Serves 6.

Tuesday—Beef

SINGAPORE SPARERIBS

5 lb. spareribs, chopped into 2" pieces
1 onion, peeled
1 T. salt
Water to cover ribs
3 T. brown sugar
1/3 C. concentrated orange juice
1/4 C. vinegar
4 T. honey
1/2 t. hot mustard
3 T. soy sauce
1/2 t. salt
1/2 t. pepper
1/4 C. rice wine or sherry

The night before serving, place ribs in pot with onion, salt and water. Bring to a boil. Cover. Simmer 3/4 hr. Place ribs in refrigerator.

Preheat broiler.

Combine sugar, orange juice, vinegar, honey, mustard, soy sauce, salt, pepper and wine in bowl. Place ribs in rows in long roasting pan. Brush sauce on both sides. Broil 7" from heat till ribs are brown. Serve immediately. Serves 8.

Tuesday—Beef

STEAK CABBAGE

2 lb. flank steak, sliced against the grain
4 T. soy sauce
2 T. rice wine, or sherry
6 T. cornstarch
2 t. sugar
½ clove garlic, minced
2 slices ginger root, minced
½ C. peanut oil
½ t. salt
2 lb. Chinese cabbage, sliced diagonally (celery cabbage may be used)
1 small can water chestnuts, chopped (optional)
1 small can bamboo shoots, chopped (optional)
½ t. M.S.G. (optional)

Several hours before cooking, mix beef with soy sauce, wine, cornstarch, sugar, garlic and ginger. Add 2 T. oil to the mixture ½ hr. before cooking.

Heat 4 T. oil, add salt, then cabbage and canned vegetables. Stir constantly over high heat until vegetables turn a garden green color, approximately 5 min. Transfer vegetables to a warm platter. Heat 2 T. oil in a clean skillet, then add meat mixture. When the meat browns, quickly add the vegetables. Stir together for a few min. and serve with hot boiled rice. Serves 8.

Wednesday—Vegetarian Day

BROCCOLI AND MUSHROOMS

1 bunch broccoli
½ lb. mushrooms
6 T. peanut oil
1½ t. salt

Peel off tough parts of broccoli stems. Cut into 1½" pieces. Wash and drain.

Clean mushrooms and quarter.

Heat oil till very hot in large frying pan. Add vegetables, then salt. Sauté evenly. Cover. Cook 2 min. Uncover. Continue to cook 5 min. more, stirring often. Serves 4.

Wednesday—Vegetarian Day

CABBAGE

1 T. oil	1 slice ginger, minced
1 t. salt	½ C. water
½ t. pepper	
1 head curly cabbage, shred-ded	

Heat oil. Sprinkle with salt and pepper. Add cabbage. Sauté 10 min. Add ginger. Pour in water. Stir well and cover. Cook another 10 min. (or till done). Serves 6.

Wednesday—Vegetarian Day

COLD TOMATOES

8 ripe tomatoes
Boiling water
3 T. sugar
2 t. Worcestershire sauce
Crushed ice

Wash tomatoes. Pour boiling water over them to loosen the skin. Peel off skin. Quarter tomatoes. Put into bowl and add Worcestershire sauce and sugar. Mix well. Place bowl over crushed ice to chill. Serves 6.

Wednesday—Vegetarian Day

CHINESE SUMMER SQUASH

4 *lb. summer squash*
4 *T. peanut oil or vegetable oil*
2 *T. soy sauce*
2 *t. salt*
½ *t. pepper*

Cut squash into paper-thin slices.

Heat oil in pan. Sauté squash, turning constantly for 2 min. Add soy sauce, salt and pepper. Stir 5 min. more. Serves 6-8.

Wednesday—Vegetarian Day

FLOWER SALAD

2 *C. bean sprouts, washed*
½ *C. sesame oil*
2 *T. rice wine or sherry*
¾ *C. olive oil*
2 *T. soy sauce*
2 *T. lemon juice*
1 *t. pepper*
2 *C. celery cabbage, shredded*

1 *head lettuce, washed and separated into leaves*
1 *can (12 oz.) bamboo shoots, cut in slivers*
14 *nasturtium leaves, cut in strips*
4 *nasturtium flowers*

Mix bean sprouts with sesame oil and wine. Put aside. Combine olive oil, soy sauce, lemon juice and pepper. Pour ½ mixture over celery cabbage and toss. Line platter generously with lettuce leaves. Place bean sprouts on one side of plate and celery cabbage on the other side. Border plate with bamboo shoots and decorate with nasturtium leaves and flowers. Spoon leftover olive oil mixture over bamboo shoots. Serves 4.

Wednesday—Vegetarian Day

GREEN BEANS

2 T. *peanut oil*
1 *lb. green beans, strung and broken into* 1½" *pieces*
1 t. *salt*
½ t. *pepper*
½ C. *water*

Heat oil till very hot in pan. Put in beans. Sprinkle with salt and pepper. Stir well. Pour in water. Cover. Bring to a boil. Turn to low heat and simmer 20 min., stirring occasionally so that beans cook evenly. Serves 8.

Wednesday—Vegetarian Day

GREEN BEANS AND MUSHROOMS

4 T. *butter*   1 *lb. bean sprouts*
1 *onion, chopped*   1 *can* (3 *oz.*) *mushrooms,*
1 *lb. green beans, washed,*   *drained and chopped*
  strung and cooked   3 T. *soy sauce*

Heat butter in pan. Brown onion. Add cooked green beans, bean sprouts, mushrooms and soy sauce. Stir. Simmer uncovered for ¼ hr., stirring occasionally. Serve with more soy sauce. Serves 6.

Wednesday—Vegetarian Day

MARINATED CUCUMBER

2 *cucumbers, thinly sliced*
1 t. *salt*
½ C. *vinegar*
3 T. *sugar*
¼ C. *water*

Salt cucumbers. Let stand ½ hr.

Heat vinegar in saucepan. Add sugar and water. Bring to a boil. Boil 2 min. Remove from heat and cool.

Add cucumbers. Let stand several hr. Serves 4.

Thursday—Lamb

DIPPING DUMPLINGS

1 C. flour	2 slices ginger, minced
2 C. water	2 scallions, minced
1 lb. lean lamb, ground	2 T. rice wine or sherry
½ C. water chestnuts, minced	4 T. soy sauce
	2 T. sesame oil
1 doz. Chinese mushrooms, soaked and minced	2 t. sugar
	1 t. salt

Wrapping: Pour water slowly into flour, kneading constantly. Let stand wrapped in damp cloth 20 min. Divide dough into a long thick rope that measures 1" in diameter. Cut into 60 equal lumps. Flatten lumps of dough and roll into circles 3" in diameter.

Filling: Mix remaining ingredients. Place small spoonful of meat mixture in center of crust. Fold over and form a semicircle. Pinch edges together. Place each dumpling separately in a large steamer of boiling water. Steam ¼ hr. Repeat process till all dumplings are steamed.

Dipping: Mix equal parts of soy sauce and vinegar with a bit of minced garlic. Dip each dumpling before eating.

Yield: 60 dumplings. Serves 4-6.

Thursday—Lamb

LAMB BARBECUE

1 envelope dried onion soup mix
½ C. wine
½ C. soy sauce
2 T. brown sugar
2 lb. boneless leg of lamb, cubed

Combine onion soup mix, wine, soy sauce and sugar. Thread meat on skewers and marinate several hours in soup mixture. Broil quickly, turning once and basting with remaining marinade. Serves 6-8.

Thursday—Lamb

LAMB "CHOP SUEY"

2 lb. lamb, cubed (beef or pork may be used instead)
2 T. peanut oil
2 onions, chopped
1 clove garlic, minced
2 cans condensed cream of celery soup
2 small cans mushrooms with the juice
1 C. water
4 t. Worcestershire sauce
6 C. hot boiled rice

Brown lamb in hot oil. Add onion and garlic. Pour in soup, mushrooms, juice, water and Worcestershire sauce. Mix well. Simmer ½ hr. Uncover and cook ¼ hr. more. Pour mixture over hot boiled rice. Serves 6-8.

Thursday—Lamb

LAMB "CHOW MEIN"

1 T. peanut oil
2 lb. lamb, ground (high grade hamburger may be used instead)
1 large onion, chopped
1 clove garlic, minced

2 C. celery, chopped
2 C. cooked rice
2 cans mushroom soup
2 cans cream of chicken soup
¼ C. soy sauce
2 cans chow mein noodles

Heat oil. Sauté lamb, onion and garlic. Add remaining ingredients. Use one can of noodles to line a large casserole. Add lamb mixture and top with second can of noodles. Bake in 350° oven for 1 hr. Serves 8-10.

Thursday—Lamb

LAMB DISH

½ C. peanut oil
3 lb. boned leg of lamb, cubed
2 onions, finely chopped
3 cloves garlic, minced
2 t. salt
1 t. pepper
½ t. allspice

1 t. tumeric powder
3 tomatoes, cut up
1 C. white raisins, soaked in rice wine
½ C. almonds, toasted
4 sprigs Chinese parsley, chopped

Heat oil in skillet. Brown lamb. Add onion and garlic. Sauté lightly. Sprinkle in salt, pepper, allspice, tumeric, tomatoes and raisins. Bring liquid to a boil. Cover. Add small amount of water, if needed. Simmer 1½ hr., or place uncovered in 350° oven for 1½ hr., basting occasionally. Garnish with almonds and parsley. Serves 8.

Thursday—Lamb

MUSHROOM FLOATS

24 *large mushrooms*	½ *t. tumeric powder*
½ *lb. lean lamb, ground*	1 *T. flour*
5 *water chestnuts, minced*	½ *C. stock*
2 *t. chutney, minced*	2 *T. soy sauce*
2 *slices ginger, minced*	

Remove mushroom stems. Wash caps and drain. Combine lamb, water chestnuts, chutney, ginger, tumeric powder and flour. Form into 1″ balls. Stick a ball on each dried mushroom cap. Place mushroom floats in a greased pyrex dish. Pour in stock mixed with soy sauce. Bake in 350° oven for 20 min. Remove from liquid and serve hot. Serves 4.

Thursday—Lamb

OUTDOOR ROAST LAMB

½ *lamb*	1 *ginger root, peeled and*
Salt	*halved*
Pepper	Oil
1 *bulb garlic, peeled cloves*	

Build big fire in morning. Let fire die down. Then spread and sprinkle with charcoal.

Place lamb carcass on long spit. Fix spit so lamb can be turned for even cooking. Season with salt and pepper. Rub on garlic, ginger and oil.

Cook gently, turning slowly from noon to 6 P.M.

Allow ¼ lb. lamb per serving.

Thursday—Lamb

ROAST LEG OF LAMB

½ C. prepared mustard   2 slices ginger, minced
2 T. soy sauce   2 T. oil
1 clove garlic, minced 6 lb. leg of lamb
1 t. thyme

Mix mustard, soy sauce, garlic, thyme, ginger and oil till creamy.

Brush mixture onto lamb with rubber spatula. Let stand in roasting pan all morning. Roast in 350° oven 1½ hr. Serves 24.

Friday—Seafood

BATTER-FRIED SHRIMP

30 shrimp, peeled and deveined except for tail
2 egg yolks, beaten lightly
1 C. cold water
1 C. flour
1 C. peanut oil

Rinse and dry shrimp. Score each underside in 3 places. Set aside.

To the beaten egg yolks gradually add water, then flour. Keep stirring mixture till batter is fairly smooth, but still lumpy.

Heat oil in frying pan till very hot. Dip each shrimp in batter and deep fry quickly. Drain on absorbent toweling. Serve with a mixture of equal parts of soy sauce and vinegar. Serves 4.

Friday—Seafood

CRAB MEAT SALAD

1½ C. lettuce
1 C. crab meat, cooked or
canned
¼ C. water chestnuts, peeled
and thinly sliced

¼ C. bean sprouts, washed
½ C. celery cabbage,
shredded
4 sprigs watercress

Arrange lettuce in individual salad bowl. Add crab meat, water chestnuts, sprouts and cabbage.

SOY SAUCE VINAIGRETTE:

1 t. soy sauce
¼ t. paprika
1 T. tarragon vinegar
2 T. cider vinegar
6 T. olive oil

1 T. green pepper, chopped
1 T. cucumber pickle,
chopped
1 t. parsley, minced
1 t. chives, minced

Combine all ingredients and mix well.
Dress the salad with the soy sauce vinaigrette. Garnish with watercress. Serves 1 person.

Friday—Seafood

EGG DIPPED OYSTERS

24-32 raw oysters, shelled
6-8 slices bacon, cut in 1½"
pieces
1 egg, beaten with 1 T. water
6 T. oil

4 scallions, chopped
1 T. cornstarch
¾ C. stock
1 t. soy sauce
½ t. M.S.G.

Clean oysters. Combine each oyster with a piece of bacon. Coat oyster and bacon piece with egg mixture. Place dripping pieces on plate.

Heat oil in frying pan. Put in oyster and bacon pieces and brown on both sides. Return oysters to plate. Pour off several T. oil. Put scallion in pan and cook quickly.

Blend cornstarch, stock, soy sauce and M.S.G. Add to scallions. When sauce thickens pour over oysters. Serves 4.

Friday—Seafood

FRIED SHRIMP

2 *lb. shrimp, shelled except for tail*
1½ *C. flour*
1 *T. baking powder*
1½ *t. salt*
½ *t. M.S.G.*

1½ *C. water*
Peanut oil for deep frying
SAUCE: 4 *t. Hoisin sauce*
            4 *T. Chili sauce*
            ½ *C. catsup*

Wash and dry shrimp.

Combine flour, baking powder, salt and M.S.G. Blend in water and stir into a smooth batter.

Heat oil to 375°.

Holding shrimp by the tail, dip in batter. Drop into the hot oil a few at a time. Cook for several min. until pink. Combine Hoisin sauce, Chili sauce and catsup. Drain shrimp on paper towel and serve with sauce for dipping. Serves 8.

Friday—Seafood

LOBSTER AND VEGETABLES

Boiling water
1 *lb. peas, shelled*
1 *C. carrots, diced*
3 *T. oil*
½ *lb. raw lobster meat, cut up*
½ *t. salt*
¼ *t. pepper*

1 *small onion, chopped*
1 *clove garlic, minced*
½ *C. green pepper, chopped*
½ *C. celery, chopped*
1 *C. stock*
2 *T. cornstarch*
¼ *C. water*
2 *t. soy sauce*

Cook peas and carrots in boiling water for 5 min.

Heat oil in pan.

Put in all other vegetables, lobster, salt and pepper. Stir for 5 min. Add peas and carrots. Blend together cornstarch, water and soy sauce until smooth. Add to lobster and vegetables. Stir 4 min. more till sauce thickens. Serve with rice. Serves 4.

Friday—Seafood

SAUTÉED SHRIMP

6 T. oil

6 jumbo shrimp, shelled

½ T. soy sauce

½ T. rice wine or sherry

1 slice ginger, minced

1 scallion, chopped

1 clove garlic, minced

½ t. dried red pepper

5 T. catsup

1 T. sugar

1½ T. salt

1 T. wine

½ t. M.S.G.

Heat oil in frying pan. Add shrimp and sauté. Add soy sauce and wine. Stir. After shrimp turn pink put on warm plate. Add ginger, scallion, garlic, and red pepper to frying pan and stir. To these spices add catsup, sugar, salt, wine and M.S.G. Mix well and heat thoroughly. Pour mixture over shrimp. Serves 4.

Friday—Seafood

SHRIMP WITH EGG

¼ C. oil.

2 C. pork, sliced against the grain (optional)

1 clove garlic, minced

1 can water chestnuts, chopped

2-2½ lb. raw shrimp, cleaned (if pork is not used add more shrimp)

2 T. soy sauce

2 T. cornstarch

1 C. water

2 eggs, beaten

4 T. onions, chopped

1 t. salt

Heat oil. Sauté pork, garlic and water chestnuts until brown. Add shrimp. Stir for 5 min. Mix soy sauce, cornstarch and water. Add to mixture and stir until sauce thickens. Simmer 2 more min. Pour in eggs and onions. Cook gently until eggs begin to thicken and hold form. Sprinkle with salt. Serve with hot flaky rice. Serves 6-8.

Friday—Seafood

SEAFOOD IN GREEN PEPPERS

½ lb. filet of haddock, ground

¼ lb. fresh shrimp, shelled and ground

3 T. peanut oil

½ t. salt

¼ t. pepper

2 t. cornstarch

1 T. scallion, chopped

4 green peppers, hollowed

2 T. oil

½ C. stock

1 T. cornstarch

¼ C. water

1 t. soy sauce

Combine haddock and shrimp, peanut oil, salt, pepper, cornstarch and scallion. Stuff peppers with this mixture.

Heat oil in heavy frying pan.

Place stuffed peppers in pan. Add stock. Cover. Simmer ¼ hr. Place peppers on a warm dish.

Blend together cornstarch, water and soy sauce. Add to stock in pan. Cook for 4 min. and pour over stuffed peppers. Serve with flaky rice. Serves 4.

Friday—Seafood

SNOW PEAS AND SHRIMP

2 T. *peanut oil*	½ t. M.S.G.
1 lb. *shrimp, shelled and deveined*	1 t. *cornstarch*
	½ t. *salt*
1 lb. *snow peas, stringed*	½ t. *sugar*
2 T. *scallion, slivered*	1 t. *soy sauce*
2 slices *ginger, slivered*	2 t. *cold water*
1 clove *garlic, minced*	

Heat oil in skillet. Add shrimp and cook until pink. Put in snow peas, scallion, ginger, garlic and M.S.G. Stir for 1 min. Blend cornstarch with salt, sugar, soy sauce and water. Make into a smooth sauce. Pour over shrimp. Toss and cook until juice thickens. Serves 4.

Friday—Seafood

SWEET AND SOUR SHRIMP

3 qt. boiling water	1 T. cornstarch
8 oz. dried noodles	½ C. carrots, shredded
1 T. salt	½ C. green pepper, chopped
1 C. peanut oil	½ C. pineapple, diced
1 egg, slightly beaten	1 piece candied ginger, cut in
¼ C. water	slivers
⅓ C. flour	⅓ C. sugar
1 lb. shrimp, shelled and	¼ C. vinegar
deveined	1 t. soy sauce
2 C. water	½ t. M.S.G.

Boil water in kettle. Put in noodles and add salt. Stir occasionally. When noodles are tender drain in colander.

Heat oil till hot. Meanwhile, mix egg, water and flour in a bowl. Dip shrimp in batter. Deep fry shrimp. Drain on absorbent toweling.

Heat 1¾ C. water in sauce pan. Add carrots, green peppers, pineapple, ginger, sugar, vinegar, soy sauce, salt and M.S.G.

Blend cornstarch and ¼ C. water till smooth before adding to mixture. Bring to a boil, then add shrimp and cook ½ min. longer. Pour hot mixture over noodles. Serves 4.

Saturday—Eggs

EGG IN SOUP

1 qt. stock	¼ C. ham, shredded
½ C. peas, frozen	1 egg, beaten
4 mushrooms, sliced	Salt to taste

Pour stock in a pot and bring to a boil. Add peas, mushrooms and ham. Bring to a boil again. Pour in beaten egg and stir. Salt to taste. Serves 4.

Saturday—Eggs

"FU YONG PUFF"

3 large eggs, separated   ½ t. salt
⅛ t. cream of tartar   1 t. butter
3 T. milk

Beat egg whites with cream of tartar until stiff. Add milk and salt to egg yolks and beat. Fold yolks into whites. Melt butter in pan. Pour in egg mixture. Cook over medium heat several min. until bottom of mixture sets. Place in 350° oven and bake for 10 min. until omelet is golden. Put on hot plate and fold in half.

MUSHROOM SAUCE:

6 dried Chinese mushrooms
½ C. warm water
1 t. sugar
¼ C. scallions, chopped
2 T. butter
1 large tomato, skinned and chopped
1 clove garlic, minced
1 t. cornstarch
2 t. water

Place mushrooms in bowl. Add water and sugar. Let mushrooms soak for 30 min. Cut mushrooms into strips. Cook scallions in butter. Add mushrooms, liquid of mushrooms, tomato and salt. Simmer until vegetables are done (about 10 min.). Blend cornstarch with cold water and add to sauce. Cook until juice thickens. Pour over omelet. Serves 2.

Saturday—Eggs

FRIED RICE WITH EGGS

3 T. oil
1 t. salt
½ t. pepper
2 eggs, beaten then fried
    and shredded
1 onion, minced

1 C. cooked ham, shredded
    (optional)
4 C. leftover rice
2 T. soy sauce
½ t. sugar

Heat oil in frying pan. Season with salt and pepper. Add shredded eggs, onion, ham and rice. Stir mixture constantly for 5 min. Dissolve sugar in soy sauce and add to rice mixture. Stir constantly until heated thoroughly. Serves 4.

Saturday—Eggs

QUICK "EGG FU YONG"

1 pkg. Egg Fu Yong mix
1 7½ oz. can shrimp, drained
1 large onion, minced

¼ C. mushrooms, sliced
4 eggs
2 T. oil

Combine vegetables, shrimp, onion and mushrooms in a large bowl. Sprinkle in seasoning included in mix. Add eggs, blending in gently without beating them.

Heat oil in pan. Ladle out ½ C. egg mixture into hot pan and fry both sides of omelet over medium heat for several min. Make a hot sauce with the ingredients provided in the mix package. Serves 4.

Saturday—Eggs

SOUFFLÉ

5 eggs, separated ·   1 T. parsley, chopped
3 C. potatoes, grated   ½ t. salt
½ C. onion, grated   ¼ t. pepper
2 T. peanut oil   1 t. soy sauce

Beat egg whites till stiff. Set aside. Beat egg yolks to a thick consistency. Add potatoes, onion, oil, parsley, salt and pepper. Fold mixture into stiffened egg whites. Pour into greased pyrex bowl. Bake in 350° oven for approximately 40 min. Season with soy sauce. Serves 4-6.

Saturday—Eggs

STEAMED EGGS

6 eggs, beaten   1 scallion, minced
1½ C. stock   ½ C. Chinese dried shrimps
1 t. salt   (optional)
½ t. pepper   2 T. peanut oil
1½ t. soy sauce

Mix all ingredients except oil in a deep bowl. Pour 2″ water into a wide pot. Place trivet inside pot. Then place bowl of mixture on top of trivet. Cover pot tightly. Steam 20 min.

Heat oil till very hot in a frying pan. Uncover pot and pour hot oil over custard. Cover again. Steam custard 5 min. more. Serves 6.

Abbreviations Used in This Book

C. — cup(s)
° — Degree (Fahrenheit)
doz. — dozen(s)
in. — inch(es)
gal. — gallon(s)
hr. — hour
hrs. — hours
lb. — pound(s)
min. — minute(s)
M.S.G. — monosodium
  glutamate

No. — number(s)
opt. — optional
oz. — ounce(s)
p. — page
pkg. — package(s)
pr. — pair(s)
pt. — pint(s)
qt. — quart(s)
sq. — square(s)
T. — tablespoon(s)
t. — teaspoon(s)

Measurements

Dash = Scant ⅛ t.
3 t. = 1 T.
2 T. = ⅛ C.
4 T. = ¼ C.
5 T. + 1 t. = ⅓ C.
8 T. = ½ C.

10 T. + 2 t. = ⅔ C.
12 T. = ¾ C.
16 T. = 1 C.
2 C. = 1 pt.
4 C., or 2 pt. = 1 qt.
4 qt. = 1 gal.

Index